BITTERSWEET FLIGHT
By Anne L Harvey

FOREWORD

FLIGHT (*noun*)

    1) The act of fleeing or running away as from danger

    2) The basic tactical unit of a military air force

Source: Collins English Dictionary

With grateful thanks again to my beta readers, Judith Lowe and Lynn Lilliman, whose input has been invaluable.

Thanks are again due to the multi-talented Berni Stevens, who has designed such an evocative cover. Check out more of her designs on www.bernistevens.com

In memory of my email friend, Bob Sutherland, whose memories and fund of stories provided much of the background RAF material for this book.

And, lastly, I've done my best to show RAF life as it would have been at the time but if I've portrayed it incorrectly, I apologise.

You can find out more about me on my blog, Passionate About The Past, at www.annelharvey.co.uk

CHAPTER 1

Today should have been her wedding day.

A sense of desolation swept over Sally Simcox, causing her to falter as she stepped off the train on to the platform of Blackpool Central station. She stood for a moment, gathering courage, aware that her solitude marked her out from her fellow passengers, who were either in family groups or gangs of lads and lasses. Conscious that several of the lads were eyeing her up, she automatically straightened her spine, hoping someone would offer to give her a hand. When no-one did, she shrugged her shoulders and leaned to the side to compensate for the weight of her suitcase.

She staggered onto the main concourse of the station, amid all the hustle of a normal Saturday, mostly day trippers at this time of year, come for the famous Illuminations. Fighting clear of the crowds, she made her way to the exit and on to the street beyond where she stopped to take in this first sight of her beloved Blackpool. She put her case on the ground the better to absorb the sights, the sounds, the smells.

The Tower soared up, gigantic at such close quarters. To her left was the grey choppy expanse of the sea. Its sharp saltiness, the sweetness of candyfloss from a nearby rock stall filled her nostrils as she breathed in. For the first time in several days, she felt the stirrings of anticipation and excitement. She was in Blackpool and at the beginning of a new life without her family.

1

Being here was either a gamble or, as her brother, Jud, had said, 'a bloody stupid idea.' Gently, she put both hands on her belly in a protective gesture. 'This is it, kid. It's you and me against the world'.

From behind, someone barged into her and she landed with a thump on the pavement, where she lay winded. She glanced up in time to see a group of blue-uniformed RAF boys, laughing and jostling each other, eager to be at the delights of the busy seaside town. 'You clumsy clots!' she yelled after them, uselessly as it turned out for they were oblivious to anyone but themselves.

Then she felt a hand under her elbow and a voice said in her right ear. 'Are you all right? Do you think you might have broken owt?' The familiar Lancashire accent was reassuring.

'No, I don't think so,' she said as, with help from her rescuer, she rose to her feet. Her suitcase had burst open and to her horror, her far-from-white underwear lay exposed to the world. 'Oh, no!' she said, inwardly cursing her mother's laziness at not separating the whites from everything else when doing the washing, no matter how many times Sally reminded her. She gathered her belongings up, shoved them out of sight and snapped the case shut again.

'You look a bit pale,' the young man said. 'Are you OK?'

She looked at him for the first time and saw that he, too, was an RAF serviceman, of medium height, good-looking in a quiet, restrained sort of way. Under his cap, his eyes were a grey-blue colour and he was fair-skinned. Troublingly, something about him was vaguely familiar. Aware that she was staring, she said, 'I do feel a bit wobbly.'

'Do you fancy a cup of tea? There's a café not far from here. It's a bit basic, but at least it's clean.'

She shouldn't; she didn't know him. On the other hand, she did feel shaky and there was the baby to think of. 'Thanks. But what about your mates?' She nodded in the direction the other RAF servicemen had gone.

He laughed. 'They're not my mates. They were probably erks – National Servicemen – on their first pass after being on an

2

armament course at Kirkham.' He picked up her suitcase with ease and indicated that they should turn right. 'I'm based at Kirkham too, only I'm a regular.' The lift of his muscular shoulders showed his obvious pride.

He led the way down Central Drive until they came to a brightly lit café. From a juke box came the sounds of Elvis Presley's 'Don't Be Cruel.' Leaving her sitting at one of the Formica-topped tables, the young serviceman went up to the counter where he chatted to the proprietor. He'd taken his cap off as they'd arrived, revealing fair hair ridged where the cap had rested. His manner seemed affable and easy-going, though he would never stand out from the crowd in the way Nick had done. A sharp pang of pain shot through her as she thought of Nick, lost to her now. Occasionally, she doubted the wisdom of passing up the chance of marrying him but the decision had been hers alone and she must live with the consequences. And she could never go back because she'd told her family – and Nick – that she'd had a miscarriage.

'Are you feeling dizzy? Faint?'

She looked up, saw the concern in his eyes and pulled her thoughts to the present. 'No, I'm OK thanks.'

He indicated the two thick white cups he'd placed on the table. 'Sorry about the mugs but it's a good cup of tea.'

'I'm more used to these than china cups and saucers.'

He raised his own mug to touch hers. 'I'm Phil, by the way, Phil Roberts.'

As he said that, the vague familiarity that had been troubling her since he'd first helped her to her feet, clarified in her mind and a sick feeling spread to her stomach. Improbable though it might seem, this personable young man was Nick's younger brother.

* * *

3

The sudden contorting of the girl's face told Phil of an unknown anguish and his heart went out to her. The bleached hair, the bright blue eye shadow, the tight-fitting sweater and skirt, might give the outward appearance of someone who knew her way around but he'd seen the tears spring to her eyes. 'What's wrong, love? Have I said summat to offend you?'

The girl pushed upwards with her hands on the table and said, her voice trembling, 'I must go. I can't stay here.'

He put out a hand to stop her. 'Don't go. At least drink your tea. You need it after the shock.'

Ignoring him, she struggled out from the confined space between chair and table and looked around for her suitcase. It was at the side of Phil's chair and she made a lunge for it. He forestalled her action by grabbing the handle himself and looking up at her. 'You're running away from home, aren't you?'

'Not exactly,' she said, her voice thick with emotion.

'But you are running away. From something? Or someone?'

Deflated, she sat down again and began to cry, her distress reaching deep into his soul. He passed her his regulation-issue blue handkerchief and she took it blindly, mopping her eyes. After a minute or so, the sobs subsided a little and she managed to croak, 'I had to get away. I couldn't stay.'

'What are your plans now you're here?'

'I were hoping I might get a job in a boarding house while the Illuminations are on. After that, I don't have any plans.' With her mascara smudged and her eyes red, she looked incredibly vulnerable.

'But the Illuminations finish tomorrow,' he said gently, not wanting to make her cry again.

Clutching the now badly stained handkerchief, she stared at him aghast. 'I didn't realise,' she said. 'I thought they went on longer. I can't go back home now, not after all that's happened.'

'Do you want to talk about it? Would it help?' She shook her head, biting her lip to emphasise her determination.

Thinking to soothe her, he offered her a cigarette.

'No, thanks, I don't smoke since ...' her voice tailed off and he wondered what she'd been about to say.

4

He lit a cigarette for himself, inhaling deeply. 'What's your name, by the way?'

She seemed to hesitate before replying, 'S...Sally. Sally Smith.'

'And where are you from, Sally Smith? I know you're a Lancashire lass.'

Again, there was a slight hesitation. 'Bolton.'

He started in surprise. Bolton was only a bus ride from where he lived. 'Really? I'm from Horwich myself.'

She gave him a weak smile. 'Small world, isn't it?'

He nodded in the direction of the man who'd served him. 'Let me have a word with Bob. He might know of summat.'

'Why are you doing this for me?' she asked.

He smiled. 'Rescuing damsels in distress is my speciality.'

At the counter, Bob was wiping down the already spotless counter.

'Can I have a word, Bob?'

Bob gave Phil his full attention. 'What can I do for you, lad?'

'Do you know of any jobs what might suit the lass over there?' Phil nodded in the direction of Sally, who was trying to clean her smudged make-up, with the aid of a hand mirror she'd taken from her handbag. On his handkerchief, he noted ruefully. He'd have to wash that one himself. 'She's run away from home and has nowhere else to go.'

Bob inspected the girl over his spectacles. 'Not in trouble with the police, is she?'

'I don't think so. I reckon as she's running from summat emotional.'

Bob chewed his lip. 'Let me nip next door to see the wife. She was only saying yesterday she could do with another pair of hands. What the ...?'

'What's up, Bob?'

'Looks like our help's not needed. Yon lass has just grabbed her case and run out the door.'

Phil strode to the door but there was no sign of her outside. She must have cut through to one of the side streets. 'Well, of all the ungrateful …!' He turned back to the counter. 'Sorry about that, Bob.'

'S'all right, lad. Not your fault,' Bob said, picking up a tea towel. 'Shame though, the wife could have done with a bit of help with being booked up till after Christmas.'

Phil sat down again and stared into his now cold mug of tea. It was then he saw his mascara-smeared handkerchief folded by the side of Sally's mug. He sighed and pocketed it. Ah well, he'd done what he could. No use brooding on her reasons for dashing off. He needed to pull himself together and go and meet his girlfriend.

* * *

Sally seized her opportunity while Phil Roberts was talking to the proprietor of the café. She had to get away from him as fast as she could and hope she never saw him again. Grabbing her suitcase, she dashed for the door and fled down the first street she came to. The town, although not as crowded as it could be in the summer, was still busy and she knew she could lose herself amid the throng of people. From there, she doubled back on herself and made her way to the Promenade. With the Illuminations finishing this weekend, she thought she'd stand more chance of getting a job in one of the larger hotels. Stopping to change hands, she found she was standing outside a handsome terra-cotta hotel, the Moncrieff. Drawing a deep breath, she decided she might as well try her luck here. Her suitcase was getting heavier by the minute and her feet ached after her sprint to get away from Phil Roberts.

At the reception desk, she plonked her suitcase down. 'Excuse me, but do you have any vacancies?' she asked the elegantly dressed receptionist.

The girl gave her a haughty look. 'I'm not sure but I can ask the housekeeper.'

After a brief telephone conversation, the receptionist said, 'Mrs Cummings is on her way to see you. You can wait there.' She indicated a hard-backed chair adjacent to the reception desk.

Some minutes later, a high-bosomed middle-aged woman with greying hair bustled into the reception area and came over to Sally. 'I understand you're enquiring about a job.'

Sally stood. 'Yes, that's right.'

'Well, we do have a vacancy for a chamber-maid. Do you have any experience?'

'No, but I'm willing to learn.'

Mrs Cummings gave a deep sigh. 'Well, we are a bit short-staffed at the moment. You'd better come through to my office and we'll have a chat about it.'

Within half an hour, Sally had a job. It wasn't really what she'd wanted. She'd have preferred to have more contact with the guests but it was a start and, at this time of year, she knew she was lucky to get a job at all. Better still, board and lodging were thrown in. How long she could keep it without her pregnancy becoming obvious was a worry but not one she was prepared to face now.

From then on, she was hurled into the confusion that was the working part of the hotel, with endless corridors and doors that led to goodness knew where. She was introduced to Sandra, a tall slim girl, with dark hair and green eyes, who reminded Sally of Kathy Armstrong. Sandra was the girl she'd be sharing a room with and who would show her the duties. In the gloomy canteen at tea-time, she was introduced to Ruth and Barbara, her two friends. Ruth was a little on the plump side but very pretty with ash-blonde hair and blue eyes, while Barbara was a small, slight girl with dark bubble-cut hair.

The following morning, she woke with a start, wondering where she was. With the street lights filtering through the window, she looked round, familiarising herself. Ah yes, she was in the little room high under the eaves of the Moncrieff. The room was strictly functional, with two iron beds, a chest of drawers, a wardrobe and a washbasin. Along the corridor was the toilet. To Sally, used to an outside lavvy and newspaper squares on a string to wipe your bottom, this was luxury indeed. And she'd got a bed to herself. Back in Horwich, she'd had to share a bed with her younger sister Eileen while another sister Mary had slept on a truckle bed. Separated from the sisters by an old blanket slung over a washing line, her brother Jud slept in a single bed.

Deliberately, she turned her thoughts away from her home and reflected on the day past. She'd been too tired last night to do so. It had been a momentous day in more ways than one. So much had happened. Hard to believe that only yesterday, she had been waking in her home in Horwich.

An alarm clock shrilled and from the adjacent bed, an arm reached out to quieten its din. 'You awake, Sally?'

'Yes. I have been for some time.'

Sandra yawned. 'I can't believe it's morning already. Don't feel as if I've been in bed that long. Did you sleep well?'

'Not bad, all things considered.'

'We'd better get a move on if we're going to have time for breakfast.'

After a hurried breakfast of tea and toast, it was straight into her duties, stripping beds of those patrons who'd checked out; making beds of others; changing towels where necessary; emptying waste-paper bins; cleaning. At the dinner table, she was glad to rest her aching feet and let the talk of the other girls wash over her, taking little notice until Sandra nudged her with her elbow. 'What about you, Sally? Are you up for it?'

'Sorry. Up for what?'

'I asked if you'd like to come with us to the Halloween Dance at RAF Kirkham next Saturday.'

'I don't think so, I've nowt to wear.'

'You'll have your first week's wages by then. You could buy a new dress.'

The thought was tempting. It would be the first time she'd be able to keep her wages to herself. At home, she'd always had to tip her wages up to her Mam, keeping only a little for pocket money. 'What's it in aid of anyway?'

'From time to time, they hold dances in the NAAFI and bus girls in from Blackpool and the surrounding villages,' Sandra explained. 'It's usually a good do and there's always those lovely RAF lads.'

With mention of the RAF, she was reminded of the incident on Central Station and the meeting with Nick's brother. She wavered, wondering what would be the chance of running into him again. Surely there must be hundreds of RAF lads stationed at Kirkham and the thought of dancing was tempting. And, with being three-and-a-half months pregnant, she might not be able to go dancing for much longer. 'Why not? I'll give it a go.'

CHAPTER 2

Thirty or so miles away, in the small Lancashire mill town of Horwich, a tall, slim young woman scuffled her way through the leaves piled up on the pavement in Lever Park Avenue. Joyce Roberts had desperately needed to get away from her often chaotic family home for a while to reflect on all the happenings of the past month or so.

Beyond the last of the houses, the countryside began, deepening into wooded areas lining the road. Did she want to go any further? Unsure, she sat down on an ancient bench, swinging her feet among the leaves, her hands on the edge, and thought back the beginning of it all. In the late spring and summer, she'd been enjoying a secret relationship with Dave Yates, the best mate of her older brother, Nick. Then, a few weeks ago, they'd been seen together, here in Rivington. Now they were forbidden to see each other, Dave by his devoutly Catholic mother and Joyce by her parents because, at sixteen, they thought she was too young for such a relationship. She missed him with a fierce ache in her heart and was saddened that people didn't seem to think it was possible to love someone at so young an age.

Ahead, she could see some boys collecting wood in a go-cart for Bonfire Night and an unexpected lump came into her throat. Her younger brother, Brian, wouldn't be doing that this year. In early September, he'd been knocked down by a bus and had died soon after. His going had left a hole in their lives. Mam, in particular, missed Brian's demands for a jam butty and regretted every slap, every harsh word, she had ever given him. Her usually boisterous Dad now seemed quieter though that might have something to do with the fact that, only months ago, he'd come out of prison after serving a sentence for GBH.

'Hey, kid, why so blue?' said a voice at her side. The pseudo American accent didn't fool her; she would have known his voice anywhere.

'Dave!' He sat down at her side. Not as close as he might once have done so that if anyone saw them, it would appear as if they'd met by accident. Which indeed they had. She couldn't have planned it better.

'What are you doing here?' she asked, drinking in his appearance, the blond Tony-Curtis style hair, the burgundy Teddy boy suit encasing long, lean limbs. She longed for him to put his arms around her. He wouldn't risk it, of course. 'Wandering aimlessly. Didn't know what else to do of a Saturday afternoon so thought I'd take a walk up Rivi.'

'None of your mates with you?' She didn't need to look around to know he was alone.

'I'm a bit of a Billy-no-mates these days. Saw your Nick a couple of weeks ago though.'

Nick hadn't been best pleased by what he saw as his friend's betrayal. 'Oh? How did that go?'

He made a see-saw movement with his hands. 'We sort of patched things up.'

'Did you know he's starting work full-time at Mac's garage in a couple of weeks?'

'That's good news. He'll be made up about that.'

'And he's now going out with Kathy Armstrong.'

'No surprise there, then.'

'I'll say. Though they're taking it steady, he says. I think she's still a bit wary after the Sally fiasco.' Joyce was silent for a moment, then said, 'Odd to think that today should have been his and Sally's wedding day.' She and Sally had worked next to each other on adjoining looms and had become good friends in the past few months. Joyce suspected that, despite her selfless decision to call off the wedding, Sally was devastated. She'd been in love with Nick for years.

'Aye, it can't have been easy for her losing the baby like that.'

'And now she's left the mill and gone to work in Blackpool despite not having a job to go to or a place to live.'

Surprise flitted across Dave's face. 'Bloody hell! That were brave of her.'

'Apparently, her decision caused a bit of a problem at home and Jud tried to forbid her to go.'

'Now why doesn't that surprise me?' Sally's brother, Jud, was a Teddy boy like Nick and Dave but he had mean side and wasn't well-liked in Horwich.

Up to now they could simply have been two people who knew each other exchanging pleasantries. Now Dave's voice changed, taking on the gentler note she was so familiar with, making her heart leap. 'But how are you doing, love?'

She struggled to put her feelings into words. 'I try to keep up appearances but I miss you like crazy.'

'You and me both, sweetheart. Right now, I want to put my arms round you, even here on this cold bench.' The softness of his voice spoke of his love for her.

'I know we can't. But I do feel better for having seen you. I've been wandering round Horwich for the past couple of weeks hoping to see you.'

'You must have missed me then, because I've been doing the same. I feel as if I know every nook and cranny of this damned place. It's like living in a goldfish bowl.'

He sounded so aggrieved, she had to laugh. 'When you think about it, how did we get away with seeing each other for so long without anybody knowing?'

'We were a bit naïve, weren't we?'

She sighed. 'It were good while it lasted though.'

'And it will be again. Don't forget I turned twenty last week.'

'I'm sorry I missed your birthday but there weren't owt I could do about it. I'd bought your present weeks ago too.'

'You did?'

'And a card.'

'Save them until I'm twenty-one, only next year now.'

'But I'll still only be seventeen and a half then,' she pointed out. 'I can't see how that will change owt.'

'We both know that, but we need to convince other people.'

She sighed. 'You're right, of course, but it's hard not seeing you at all.'

'We could always accidentally bump into each other again next Saturday,' he suggested, a mischievous glint in his eyes.

'Oh, Dave, dare we?'

'I don't see why not. We'll not meet in Horwich though, it'd be too obvious. How about if I were to go to Bolton, say to buy a record in Bullough's?'

She laughed aloud, suddenly happy again, even if it was a week away. They could both be browsing through the record selection, even huddle together in one of the listening booths. 'Why not? What time?'

He looked at his watch. 'It's half past three now. Shall we say three o'clock next week outside Bulloughs?'

'You're on. Now I'd better go in case someone does come.'

'I'll walk on a bit, as if I'm carrying on to Rivington. And Joyce?'

She stood and, feeling the brisk wind whipping at her legs, pulled her coat closer around her, hunching it up around the collar. 'Yes?'

'Remember forever together.'

* * *

'Do you fancy the pictures tonight, Phil?' The question came from Fred, a tall, good-looking Welshman, as he, Phil and Chipper enjoyed a leisurely cigarette in the NAAFI.

'Sorry, no can do. I'm on guard duty, the graveyard shift no less,' Phil said. The four to six am shift was the worst of the lot because you still had to go to work the following morning. Now he was a corporal, he was responsible for checking that the National Servicemen were indeed carrying out their duties, patrolling the station in twos, checking doors and the perimeter in all weathers. It was a thankless task because, being of a similar age, they resented his authority over them.

'Rather you than me,' Fred commiserated. 'What about you, Chipper?'

'No, you're on your own mate. I'm on duty in the Mess,' the stocky Londoner said, his round face wearing a mournful expression.

Fred gave an exaggerated sigh. 'Another poor sod! What is it this time?'

'Nothing special, just a routine night. Do we know who's Duty Officer tonight?'

Phil grimaced. 'Wilko.' Flight Sergeant Wilkinson was famous for being self-important and over-zealous. He had a voice like a foghorn and it was said that when he was square-bashing, you could hear him on Blackpool Promenade. Oh, well, he'd have to do his best to stay out of Wilko's way.

Chipper looked at his watch. 'It's all right for some but I've got to start work in about ten minutes.'

Phil laughed. 'Could be worse, Chipper. While you're tucked up in bed, warm and cosy, I'll be trudging round the camp making sure the sprogs are doing their job properly.'

After Chipper had left them, Phil and Fred stayed in the NAAFI playing cards and chatting about the Suez situation. They had been following the crisis with mounting interest, not least because of the possibility they might be involved. The stand-off had occurred when the Egyptians had taken over the Suez Canal in July and were refusing to relinquish it. Despite efforts by all concerned, diplomatic negotiations had failed.

'This uprising in Hungary looks a bit dodgy too, poor buggers,' said Phil, 'with the Soviet tanks going in the other day.'

'Aye, the Soviets were true to form, not tolerating any uprising.'

Phil sighed. 'You'd have thought the world would have had enough of wars after the last two. Instead, there's been the Korean War, this trouble in the Middle East, not to mention the Cold War.'

'You don't think a nuclear war could ever happen, do you?'

'Who knows?' Phil replied. 'There's talk of building nuclear shelters for the top nobs of the government.'

Chipper dashed back into the NAAFI, red in the face and with his eyes alight with excitement. 'Can't stay,' he gasped. 'Just come to tell you the latest buzz, the Israelis have invaded the Sinai Peninsula.'

'It's started at last then,' Phil said, catching some of Chipper's excitement. 'The Brits and the Frogs will be going into Egypt any time now.'

'It was odd they stood us down at the last minute, wasn't it?' Fred said. 'Not sure if that was a good thing or not.' Their flight had been on stand-by earlier in the year but nothing had come of it.

'Must have decided we were too valuable to let go,' quipped Chipper. 'After all, the base would grind to a halt without us three Corporals. Better go before I'm missed.'

After discussing the crisis a while longer, the talk turned to the Halloween Dance this coming Saturday. 'Are you bringing Pam?' Fred asked.

'Yes, I expect so.'

'What? Haven't you asked her yet?' Fred seemed surprised. Phil shook his head. 'You'd better do it now then. You know how girls like to plan ahead.'

He checked his watch to make sure Pam would be home from her job as a shorthand-typist with a firm of architects. 'I'll go and ring her now.' He went over to where the public telephone kiosk was, checking he had some coppers in change. Once inside the claustrophobic booth, which always smelled of sweat and stale cigarettes, he asked the operator for the number.

'Gregory's Builders,' came the gruff voice when the connection was made. Having a telephone was still rare but Pam's family had one for business reasons.

'Can I speak to Pam, please?'

'Who's this?'

'It's Phil Roberts, Mr Gregory.'

'Hold on a minute, lad. I'll give her a shout.'

Minutes later, Pam's voice came over the phone. 'Phil! This is a nice surprise.'

'I'm ringing to see if you want to come to the Halloween dance at the camp on Saturday night.'

'I'd begun to wonder if you'd ask me.' Pam sounded wistful.

'Sorry it's last minute, love, but I wasn't sure if I'd be on duty or not.'

'I thought you knew some time in advance when you've got to work.'

'Usually, I do, but I owed one of the lads a favour from a while back,' he explained. 'I found out today that he doesn't want to go, had a bit of bust up with the girlfriend.'

'So his loss is my gain, is it?' This time was an edge to her voice.

'If you want to put it like that,' Phil said. 'Are you coming or not?'

'Sorry. Of course I want to come.'

Phil rang off a couple of minutes later feeling irritated. For some reason, she seemed to think that they were courting. They'd been going out together for six months now and, although he liked Pam a lot, he knew he wasn't ready for that yet. He gave a deep sigh and went to join Fred in the Mess.

CHAPTER 3

Sally found a full-skirted deep rose pink dress in taffeta with a scalloped neckline and tiny sleeves in C & A Modes for the forthcoming dance. The style was different to what she usually wore but she could hardly wear her trademark pencil skirt and figure-hugging jumper. If it had been the Fling, a shabby dance club in Horwich, it wouldn't have mattered. As it was, she'd had to get a larger size to accommodate her growing bump and expanding bust but looking at herself in the mirror, she was quietly pleased with her choice.

In the end, only three of them, Sally, Sandra and Ruth, walked to where the coach taking them to RAF Kirkham waited. Barbara had a streaming cold and had opted to stay behind. Excitement and anticipation had them all giggling when they joined the crowd of girls jostling to get on the coach. Once aboard, their attention was caught by a girl from half-way down the bus calling out to them. 'Sandra, Ruth, here.'

'Oh, it's Pam,' Sandra said. 'Might as well go and sit with her.'

As they neared the girl, Sally could see that she had a pretty heart-shaped face and curly auburn hair. 'This is Pam, a girl we've palled up with before at the dances. Pam, this is Sally,' Sandra said.

The girl gave Sally a smile that lit up her face and said, 'Hiya Sally. Haven't seen you before.' She indicated that Sally should sit beside her while Sandra and Ruth took the seat behind.

'This is my first time,' Sally said.

'Oh, the dances are great fun. I met my boyfriend there.'

Ruth leaned forward. 'Still seeing him then?'

'Yes, I like to think it's getting serious.'

It didn't take long to reach the small town of Kirkham and within minutes they were at the entrance to the camp. The guards on the gate, trying not to be too obvious about ogling the girls, waved them through the barrier. Seeing the accumulation of huts scattered about the site, Sally asked where the dance was being held.

'In the NAAFI – No Ambition And Eff All,' said Sandra setting them off giggling again.

They had, it seemed, arrived early. With so few people, the room, decorated for the occasion in orange and white balloons, appeared empty and the sounds coming from the group of musicians set up an echo. There were some RAF lads dressed in their best blues grouped in clusters round the room, most of them looking self-conscious. A few of them were more boisterous than others and Sally wondered if they were National Servicemen, let off from the harsh regime for the evening.

'Is your boyfriend here yet?' Sandra asked Pam.

She shook her head. 'I can't see him at the moment.'

Sandra indicated a vacant table. 'While you're waiting, shall we sit down?'

They'd been sitting there for about ten minutes, watching the few couples dancing on the floor, when a male voice behind Sally said, 'Hello, Pam.'

Pam's face glowed as she looked up at whoever was behind Sally. 'Hello, love. You made it then.'

'Sorry I were bit late getting here. Had to finish a job and that delayed me.'

'You know Sandra and Ruth, don't you?' Pam said. 'And this is Sally. It's her first time.'

20

Sally half-turned in her seat to look up at the young man and felt the colour drain from her face. Pam's boyfriend was Phil Roberts, the last person she wanted to see. As shock chased over his own face, he said, 'We've met before, actually.'

Pam's head jerked upwards in surprise. 'Oh, where?'

'Sally was sent flying by a bunch of erks a couple of weeks ago on Central Station and I helped her up.'

Sally hoped he wasn't going to say anything about running away from home. To her workmates, she'd been deliberately vague about her reasons for coming to Blackpool. Thankfully, he didn't. Instead, he said, 'I came over to see if you all wanted to join us. Me and the lads are at a table over there.' With a sinking heart, she heard her companions agree. Still reeling from her dismay at finding that Phil was Pam's boyfriend, the names of the other lads on their table didn't register. Fortunately, the dance itself was beginning to take off and conversation was proving difficult. They were the only girls to about six lads and, with couples coming and going on to the dance floor all the time, it was difficult to discern who was dancing with who. As time went on, she began to relax and enjoy herself in the mixed company.

It was when Pam rose to dance with one of the other lads that Phil asked her to dance. She couldn't think of an excuse not to do so and followed him on to the dance floor for a waltz. As he held out his arm to her and she took his hand, he said, 'So, Sally whatever your name is, I never thought to see you again.'

Although he wasn't as tall as Nick, she still had to look up at him. 'I could say the same about you.'

'Why'd you run off like that? You knew I were asking Bob Parrott about the possibility of a job for you.'

'I panicked.'

'But why? Surely you didn't see me as a threat?'

She couldn't explain the real reason to him. 'I suppose it all caught up with me … leaving home … the uncertainty…' her voice tailed off.

'You made me look a bit of a fool.'

'Sorry.'

'Bob were keen to get someone to help his wife out, at least till Christmas.' He looked down at her with clear grey eyes and she saw only sympathy there. 'Where did you end up anyway?'

'I managed to get a job as a chamber-maid at the Moncrieff. That's where I met Sandra and Ruth.'

He whistled. 'Makes the Shangri-La the poor relation then.'

'The Shangri-La?'

'The boarding house Bob and his wife Betty run. Do you like it there?'

'It's hard work but it pays a wage. I'd have preferred to have more contact with the guests.'

'You'd have been OK at the Shangri-La. Lots of the guests return there because they like the friendly atmosphere. It's the same in the café.'

'Do you go there a lot then?'

'Usually, whenever we go into Blackpool. Bob's a great bloke and always makes us welcome.'

'Us?'

'Me and my two mates, Chipper and Fred.' Sally remembered being introduced to them.

'I like Pam. She seems a nice girl,' she said now. 'Have you been going out with her long?'

Was she imagining it, or did he seem to tense when she mentioned Pam's name. 'About six months, I think.'

'She seems to think it's serious.'

'It's early days yet and, in the RAF, you never know when you're going to be posted somewhere different,' he said, as the music finished. He seemed reluctant to release her but when he did finally drop his arm from her waist and let go of her hand, she felt oddly bereft. They didn't dance again; instead, he stayed at Pam's side.

Not that it mattered. Being a new face on the scene, she was proving popular and actually had to decline to dance a few times to draw breath and cool down. Afterwards, she could not remember having had such a fun and laughter-filled evening. It was, she reflected, a long way from her claustrophobic life in

22

Horwich and her problems there seemed to recede into the dimmer regions of her mind.

***

Phil lay in bed, hands behind his head while around him in the billet, the National Servicemen he was nominally in charge of snored or farted in varying degrees of loudness or vileness. He smiled ruefully to himself. It was something he'd had to become used to though it had been difficult at first. Nowadays, he could sleep through anything. Normally. Tonight it was proving impossible and he lay sleepless into the early hours reflecting on the events of the evening.

He'd been shocked to see Sally there. Yet he shouldn't have been. For those who lived there or at least close by, Blackpool still had a small town atmosphere and it was easy to bump into people you knew. Although he'd ostensibly been with Pam, he couldn't help noticing that Sally had looked stunning in her pink dress. Her blonde hair curled naturally to just below her ears and onto her neck. Once, when she returned to the table after a particularly energetic bop with Chipper, he had a strange urge to touch the damp tendrils of hair at the back of her neck. Her make-up was more subtle, with none of the top-heavy eye shadow or the bright red lipstick of that first day. She had turned out to be good company too, laughing and joking with the rest of the lads. With the girls, she seemed equally at ease, as if she'd known them all her life. She was a good dancer, too, with a feline grace which enabled her to follow anyone's lead.

There had been one incident which gave him some unease. It was Chipper who had started it. He had been larking about with the girl called Sandra and had happened to mention that Fred had a car on the camp.

'I don't believe you,' she'd laughed.

23

'I'll show you then, take you for a spin about the camp in it,' Chipper had responded. 'Can I borrow the car keys, Fred? I promise not to go off camp.' One of the advantages of being a regular was that, providing they stuck to the rules, they had the run of the camp.

Fred, deep in conversation about football with one of the other lads, took the keys from his trouser pocket and carelessly tossed them in Chipper's direction. Unfortunately, Sally had half risen as if to go to the cloakroom and the keys slipped down the slightly-gaping bodice of her dress. Before she could retrieve them herself, Chipper rose and with a brief, 'Excuse me, Sally,' plunged his hand down the front of her dress and pulled the keys out. He held them up, dangling them a little, and said, 'Can't beat the RAF. You ready for that spin, Sandra?'

To the sound of laughter, Sally had fled then to the cloakroom, and Phil guessed she'd been near to tears. Sensing her embarrassment, he'd left the group and gone to wait for her outside the cloakroom. When she came out, she'd refreshed her make-up but her eyes were still a little damp and he guessed she had been crying. When she saw him there, she said, 'Are you waiting for me?'

'Yes. I guessed you'd be upset but don't worry. These things happen, especially in the RAF. It'll be forgotten about by now.'

She gave him a tremulous smile. 'Thanks, Phil, it were thoughtful of you to wait for me.' And by the time they got back to their table, she had recovered her previous good spirits.

What was disturbing his rest now was the fact that he'd been physically aroused by her nearness when they were dancing and he'd had to be careful their bodies didn't get too close or she'd have noticed. He didn't know what to make of it all. Apart from a brief relationship with a girl when he was 17, he hadn't had many girlfriends. That had changed when he joined the RAF. The striking blue uniform acted like a magnet to the girls, local and holiday makers, of Blackpool and, like everyone else, he'd made the most of the attention. For that reason, he and the other lads tended to wear their uniforms on trips into Blackpool. And of course there was Pam. He liked her. She did rouse feelings in

24

him but not like he'd experienced tonight while dancing with Sally.

He must have fallen asleep at some point because towards morning, he was wakened by two of the lads coming into the billet, having been on guard duty. They were trying very hard to be quiet but it was the muffled, 'Oh, shit!' as one of them stubbed his toe on Phil's bed, that roused him.

'Be quiet, you two. You'll wake the others,' Phil hissed.

'Sorry, Corp,' whispered one of them.

He sat up in bed. 'Everything ok out there?' He knew these two had been on gate duty.

'No problems, Corp, apart from …,' one of the voices came at him from the darkness.

'Apart from what?' he queried.

'Someone …,' one started to say.

'…not us!' hissed the other.

'…had taken the flag down and hoisted a girl's bra instead.'

'You sure it wasn't you?'

'Honest, Corp. It were already up there when we went on duty.'

'Didn't the Duty Officer notice anything when he did his rounds?'

'Most people don't bother to look up, do they?'

'You know you'll be questioned about it, tomorrow?'

'I swear it weren't us, Corp,' the voice of one of them rose emphatically.

'Will you lot bloody well shut up,' shouted someone from the middle of the billet. 'It'll be reveille soon enough!' There were groans from one or two of the others by now.

'Get to your beds, you two, and be quick about it. And quiet.'

After the billet had settled down to sleep again, Phil turned over and smiled to himself. A girl's bra up the flagpole wasn't new; it happened at least once a year. He wondered idly which girl it had belonged to. Hopefully, she would have willingly participated in the prank and treated it all as a bit of a laugh.

CHAPTER 4

Joyce was feeling a bit down because she hadn't seen Dave since that first pre-arranged meeting. They'd agreed to meet each Saturday but he hadn't turned up last time and she couldn't help worrying. So, when her best friend, Sheila, suggested they go for a walk to Rivington, she was relieved. Going 'up Rivi,' the local name for Leverhulme Park, was the thing to do on a fine Sunday, whatever the season. It was a way of boys and girls eyeing each other up, while taking in the abundant natural beauty of the area.

As the two friends strolled arm in arm down the country lane towards Rivington, Joyce couldn't help hoping she might accidentally meet Dave and be able to grab a few minutes with him.

'Are you deaf or what, Joyce?' Sheila said.

'Sorry, love, I weren't concentrating. Did you say summat?'

Sheila scuffed at some leaves with the toe of her shoe, sending them scattering. 'I asked if you'd heard from that mate of yours from work, Sally What's-her-name? The one your Nick got in the family way.'

'I have. She seems to have landed on her feet, got herself a live-in job, at one of the big hotels in Blackpool.'

'That were a funny do, weren't it? First she were pregnant and they were getting wed. Then she had a miscarriage and they weren't.'

'It's not as if they'd been courting proper,' Joyce pointed out. 'Apparently, it were a one-off fling so happen it's as well she weren't having a baby.'

'Changing the subject, have your Mam and Dad had any more of their spectacular rows?'

Joyce giggled. She had previously recounted to Sheila how, after her father had come home drunk one Friday night, her mother had tipped his congealed but fortunately only lukewarm tea over his head. 'They argue a bit, usually over Dad's love of the gee-gees, but nowt like they used to.'

By that time, they had reached Rivington Great House Barn. 'Shall we go and have a pop, see who's about?'

'Good idea, though I think I'll have a cup of tea instead of pop.' She shivered as the fitful sun went in and the temperature dropped. 'I need summat to warm me up.'

The café was busy for a Sunday afternoon in November but nothing like as much as it would be in the summer, when the area attracted folk in their thousands. Today, there were couples, some with babies in prams; older people, serious walkers for the most part, their sturdy boots making no impact on the flagged floors, and numerous groups of young people. The two girls carried their cups of tea over to one of the tables under the 14th century beams. It was always chilly in the historic building and Joyce was glad to put two hands round her cup. 'Blooming perishing in here, isn't it?' Sheila commented, huddling herself deeper into her coat. There was an odd paraffin heater dotted here and there but, in such a spacious area, they weren't much use.

'Where did you say Brenda and Maureen had gone?' Joyce asked now, mentioning the other two girls who usually made up their foursome.

'A Christening, one of Brenda's sister's kids. Being a family 'do,' she weren't keen so she's taken Maureen along for company.' Sheila took a sip of her own tea and said in a conspiratorial whisper, 'Have you seen owt of Dave recently?'

Joyce pulled a face and shook her head. 'We managed to grab a cuppa in Bolton a couple of weeks ago but I haven't seen or heard from him since.' Loyal friend that she was, Sheila had known of her secret relationship with Dave almost from the beginning, providing alibis where she could.

'Speak of the devil! Look who's just walked in,' Sheila exclaimed, nodding her head in the direction of the door.

Joyce swivelled her head so fast in the direction of Sheila's nod that she cricked her neck. Dave had just entered and, being so tall, had to duck his head to avoid one of the beams supporting the roof. By his side, was a tall, slim girl with blonde hair. Joyce felt the hot thrust of anger. How dare he walk in here with another girl? Her face reddened and Sheila, as if sensing some kind of explosion from Joyce, put a hand on her arm. 'Steady on, love. It might not be what you think.'

'Come on, Sheila, we're getting out of here.' She rose, endeavouring to pull Sheila with her.

Sheila resisted and said, 'We can't, Joyce. They're coming across here.'

Unbelievably, they were but now Dave had his arm draped casually over the girl's shoulder. 'The bare-faced bloody cheek of him!' muttered Joyce through gritted teeth.

'Joyce! What a lovely surprise!'

'I'll bet!'

He looked at her with quizzical blue eyes, as if surprised by the tone of her voice. 'You don't think …? You do, don't you?' He laughed. 'You couldn't be more wrong. This is Susie, my cousin from America.'

The girl put out her hand. 'Hi there, Joyce, Dave's just been telling me about you.' The American accent convinced her as nothing else could have done. Now that she looked properly, there was a family resemblance, from the blue eyes to the blonde hair, except hers was curly.

Oh, hell! I'm sorry, both of you, I thought …,' she spluttered.

'Look, why don't you two guys have a chat while I get to know your friend here? From what I hear, you don't have too many opportunities to meet these days.'

Sheila, taking her cue from the American girl, moved to one side to give her room to sit down, and said, 'Hello, I'm Sheila, Joyce's friend.'

While Susie sat down with Sheila, Dave sat on the seat at the side of Joyce and took her hand. 'I'm sorry for not showing up the other Saturday. My Granddad died and I had no way of letting you know. Susie and her family have come over for the funeral.'

'Oh, I'm sorry about that. When is it?'

'It were last Wednesday. Susie's Mam and my Mam are sisters. We left the pair of them reminiscing about the old days.'

'Won't summat be said about us seeing each other this afternoon?'

He shook his head. 'No, Susie doesn't tell her mother owt if she can get away with it. She seems to have a lot more independence than we have. She thinks it's 'kinda cute' that you still have to be in by a certain time. She's never had such restrictions. Hell, she even drives a car!'

'Like in the films, then.'

'Never mind all that. I suggested this walk this afternoon in the hope I might see you.'

'Well, now you have.'

He squeezed her hand. 'I've missed you so much. It seems ages since our last meeting,' he said, lowering his voice. 'I know we said we'd be patient, but it's so bloody hard. I think about you all the time, want to be with you.'

She thrilled to his words and squeezed his hand. 'I know,' she whispered. 'I feel exactly the same.'

He looked over to where Sheila and Susie were sitting but they seemed to be engrossed in their conversation. 'I've been talking to Susie about it. Apparently in America, you can nip over the state border and get married straight away there. I wish we could do the same.'

There was something deliciously forbidden in talking like this even though she knew there was no possibility of such a thing happening here. 'No one would be able to stop us then, would they?'

He leaned closer to whisper in her ear. 'I've thought about running away together. Not permanently but long enough for us to fulfil the residential requirement in Scotland and get married.'

She looked at him, unable to comprehend what he was suggesting. 'Then come home to face the music?'

'Summat like that.'

'You're crazy, Dave Yates!' she said, laughing, more to lighten the situation than anything. Then, seeing his serious face, she said, 'You've been giving this some serious thought, haven't you?'

'Yes,' he said, leaning forward again. 'And I want you to think about it. I'm twenty now and you'll be seventeen in March. I were thinking of sometime in the summer.'

'When you two have finished whispering sweet nothings, Susie has suggested we all go up to Rivington Hall Barn,' Sheila interrupted.

Joyce shook her head slightly to clear her thoughts, so overwhelmed was she by what Dave had come up with. It was romantic, certainly, but would it be practical? Her heart was racing at the mere thought of it. She saw that Dave too was having difficulty pulling his thoughts back to the present.

Perhaps sensing something of her cousin's confusion, Susie spoke, 'Yeah, I've heard you have great dances there.'

'No dances on a Sunday afternoon,' Dave pointed out.

'Maybe not, but it would be great to have a look-see.' She waved an expansive arm around the cavernous barn causing Sheila had to duck a little. 'I just love seeing these old buildings. They're so …cute.'

'Ok, then why don't we all do that? Go up to the Hall Barn, then on to Rivington itself. What about you, Joyce? Want to tag along?' he said, looking from her to Sheila.

Did she ever! Especially as it meant being in Dave's company legitimately for much longer on this unexpected afternoon. She turned to Sheila. 'What do you think, Sheila? Do you want to?'

'I'm game if you are, lass.'

She turned to Dave. 'Let's go then.'

* * *

In the short time Sally had been working at the Moncrieff, she'd become used to walking almost every day. It was better than being cooped up all day in the hotel, spacious though it was. Sometimes she went up the Promenade to the North Shore, other times she went towards the Pleasure Beach and the South Shore, depending on her whim. Occasionally, she strolled along one of the three piers. She had long since discarded high heels. Instead she had bought a pair of ballet-style shoes. They were much more comfortable, not only for walking but for working in. More sensible with the baby too.

The town was quieter now, with fewer people about. Normally, only hardier folk ventured out, dog-walkers, elderly couples out for a constitutional stroll, young mums pushing prams or holding toddlers by the hand. Today was Saturday and more families were about, children, oblivious to the cold, being swung between indulgent parents or skipping alongside. It was cold too, with a brisk wind skittering around the ankles.

Her face and fingers stinging, she was scurrying along the pavement, anxious to reach the Moncrieff when a voice, long familiar, always feared, called out to her. 'Sal! Hey, Sal, wait for me.'

She shivered, feeling exposed. Had her brother been following her for some time? When she'd written to her family, telling them where she was working, why had she not realised Jud would come looking for her? Would he notice she was still pregnant? Before she turned to confront him, she took a deep breath and pulled her belly in as much as she could. 'What are you doing here?'

He galloped up to her, slightly out of breath. 'Come to see you, of course.'

'Why?'

'You're my sister and I've been worried about you.' His supposed concern did not mask the ever-present undercurrent to his words.

'There were no need. As you can see, I'm fine.'

'You look well, I must say.' He looked at her critically, his head to one side. 'Have you put weight on?'

'A bit,' she said. 'They feed us well at the hotel.'

He was walking alongside her now. What was she to do about him? She knew he would not leave her alone, would not be satisfied until she had talked to him. He had been like this since … she deliberately shut her mind to that earlier time … wanting to know where she was, who she was with.

'You're very quiet, Sal. Have you nowt to say to me?' His voice had an abrasive edge to it.

With an effort, she answered him. 'How's Mam? And the girls?'

'They're fine but Mam's moaning about not having enough money.'

'She always does,' she said. When Sally had announced her intention to come to Blackpool, she'd known Mam's tears were for the loss of money Sally had handed over every week from her pay packet at the mill.

'Let's have a cup of tea, Sal.' Deep in her thoughts, she hadn't noticed that they had drawn close to one of the few places still open for the winter. Reluctantly, she followed him into the café. Although she didn't feel like talking to Jud, she was grateful for the warmth of the place.

She watched Jud as he placed an order for tea and sticky buns. Her brother wasn't very tall, but his lack of height belied a wiry strength that she didn't underestimate. He had the same curly blond hair as she, his cut into a Tony Curtis quiff and a DA. The ubiquitous Teddy boy suit of dark green gabardine fitted his body well, accentuating the strong shoulders and arms. As he walked towards her balancing the two cups of tea and a plate of two sticky buns, she noticed that his face, still pock-marked from the acne he had suffered from for years, was going through one of its periods of remission.

'This is a cosy place, Sally. Do you use it a lot?' he said as he placed the cups and plate on the table, slopping the tea over the sides of the cups.

She grabbed the plate of sticky buns from him before they slid off the plate and onto the now messy table. 'I've been in a couple of times, that's all. It's handy for the hotel.'

'Are you happy working there?'

Wriggling on her seat, she said, 'Yes, I enjoy the work, get on well with my work mates.'

There was something in the way he was looking at her that she didn't like or trust. He put his hand on her arm and she flinched at the tightness of his grip. 'Come home, Sal. We miss you,' he wheedled.

She prised his fingers off her arm and picked up her cup, holding it in both shaking hands. 'Sorry, Jud. I can't.'

'You mean you don't want to.'

She shrugged. 'No, I don't. I'm having too good a time. I like my job and I've made some good friends.'

He was silent for a moment, contemplating her over the rim of his cup. Then he said, 'I suppose you want to know about Nick.' He had a smirk on his face and she knew he was taking delight in tormenting her. He always did.

'Not particularly.'

'Well, I'll tell you anyway. He's going out with Kathy Armstrong now.'

'That were always going to happen once I were out of the way.'

'He's left the building site. Got a job now working with that Scottish bloke who has the garage near the Crown.'

She hadn't known about that, even indeed that he'd been offered a job with Mac, the garage owner, but she wasn't surprised. Nick had always been keen on tinkering with cars. 'What Nick does now is of no concern to me,' she said.

'Are you sure about that? Not still hankering after him? I could have a quiet word with him, if it would help.'

The last time he'd had 'quiet words' had been when he and his two mates had beaten Nick up for getting Sally pregnant.

She looked at her watch and rose. 'I must go, Jud. I'm back on duty any time now.'

He, too, stood and blocked her exit to the door. 'Come home with me now, Sally.' His emphasis on the word 'now' made his statement an implied threat. 'I can wait while you pack your things.'

'No, Jud. I'm staying here.'

'I could tell people what happened, you know.'

Swallowing the fear that rose in her throat, she said, 'You wouldn't do that. You've too much to lose yourself.'

Jud glared at her over the table but she didn't back down. In the end, he moved aside to let her pass. 'I'll let you go for now but I'll be back.'

Walking on shaking legs back to the hotel, glad to be within its safe walls, she knew he would too. With a sinking heart, she realised she would have to move on. It had been a mistake to let her family know where she was, she wouldn't make the same mistake again. At least she didn't have to leave right away; he wouldn't come to Blackpool again for a while. She could do things properly, give her notice in. Where she would go, what excuse she could give to Sandra and the other girls, she didn't know, but she'd think of something.

CHAPTER 5

Phil strode along the Promenade, breathing in deeply, despite the damp, raw-feeling November day. Wednesday afternoons were supposed to be set aside for sporting activities but surely this brisk walking could be construed as such. Fortunately, his two companions were of a like mind. All of them were glad to escape the parochial confines of the camp for a few hours. Many of the National Servicemen practised Egyptian PT, a euphemism for lying on your bed and doing nothing. Others might have left the camp carrying a rolled up towel tucked under their arms, claiming they were going swimming when they got to Blackpool. Few of them ever did; it was just an excuse to lounge around in a café or go to the cinema. As regulars, he, Chipper and Fred were no longer under such tight restrictions and could come and go as they pleased as long as they had a pass to leave the camp.

'This is the life, eh, lads?' asked the Chipper of no-one in particular. 'Beats walking down the 'ammersmith Road.'

'I'd rather be walking in Snowdonia,' Fred said gloomily.

'Cheer up, Fred. You're only feeling that way after having a bollocking off the Sergeant this morning,' consoled Phil.

The three had been walking briskly in the direction of Central Pier, coming from South Shore. As they drew level with the Golden Mile with its assortment of amusement attractions, and candy floss booths, most of them closed for the season, Fred spied a lone sea food stall. 'The smell of those whelks is making me feel hungry. How about it, lads?'

Chipper shuddered. 'No, way too cold.'

'Then what about a cup of tea and a bun?' Fred persisted.

The other two laughed. It was a standing joke between the three of them that Fred, despite being stick thin, was always hungry. Phil clapped him on the shoulder. 'Good idea, Fred. Let's go to Bob's.'

Coming towards them was a blonde-haired young lass clutching her coat to her body. Her face was pinched with the cold. Phil stopped and stared, unable to believe it. 'Sally? It is you, isn't it?'

She glanced quickly from Phil to the other two and a shuttered look crossed her features. 'Oh, hello.'

'You remember Chipper and Fred from the dance, don't you?' She nodded and gave them a tentative smile. 'We're all off to Bob's café for a cuppa to warm up. Want to come along?'

She seemed hesitant then, as if common sense won out, she shrugged and said 'OK then.'

The warm fug of the café was welcome. They settled themselves at a table by the window and Chipper went to order the tea.

'How do you two know each other anyway?' Fred asked. 'You never did say.'

'I picked her up – literally – off the floor at Central Station. She were running away from home.'

'I was not,' she protested.

'You didn't deny you were running away from summat,' Phil said.

'No, I didn't,' she conceded.

'So you came here, not knowing where you were going to stay, what you'd do for a job?' asked Fred. As she nodded, he said, 'Phew! That was a brave thing to do.'

Chipper returned with the tray. 'Here we are, four cups of char and some sticky buns.' He took a cup and placed it in front of Sally, deftly offering her the plate of iced fingers, while balancing the tray he was carrying. Sally looked impressed.

Phil laughed. 'Chipper's an expert at this,' he explained. 'He works in the Sergeant's Mess.'

'What do you do at the base, then?' she asked Phil.

'I'm a Pay Clerk, mostly checking rolls of comptometer readings and presiding on Pay Days. Fred here is attached to Motor Transport.' Fred was already munching on his own iced finger and merely nodded in agreement. 'What about you? How's it going at the hotel?'

She put her half-eaten bun down on her plate. 'It's not working out. I'm leaving at the end of the week.'

'Oh, sorry to hear that. What will you do now then?'

'I've been trying to find work in a boarding house but having no luck. Wrong time of the year.'

'Well, Bob were quite interested that time I mentioned you to him. Do you want me to have a word with him?'

Again, a variety of emotions flitted across her face before saying, 'If you don't mind.'

Bob, after what had happened last time, was understandably dubious. 'I don't know … on the other hand, we are busy right up to Christmas. I'll just go and have a word with Betty. It's quiet enough now and I won't be long.'

Phil strode back to the table where Sally sat alone, Chipper and Fred having wandered over to the juke box. 'You might be in luck. Bob thinks they might need a bit of extra help, at least until Christmas.'

Her face was suddenly transformed with a warm smile. 'Oh, Phil, that's good news. If I could get a job, I'm sure I could find lodgings somewhere.' The strains of Paul Anka singing 'Diana' filtered from the juke box.

A few minutes later, Bob emerged from the doorway which seemed to adjoin the house and came towards them. 'Good news, lass. The wife could do with some help. She's run off her feet at the moment but she'd like to see you before she agrees. Is that OK?'

'That's wonderful, Mr …?'

'Parrott. But just call me Bob, everyone does.'

'Thank you, Bob.'

'Come on then, I'll take you through to meet the wife. Keep an eye on the café for me, will you, Phil? Help yourselves to another cuppa if you want.'

Bob came back in a few minutes, giving Phil a thumbs-up sign, but Sally was gone for a good half-hour. When she came back, she had that warm smile on her face. 'I've got the job! And there's a room thrown in.' She sat down and slurped some now cold tea, pulling a face as she did so.

'So when do you start?'

'Saturday. Oh, I can't wait. A boarding house is so much friendlier, isn't it?'

'What'll you do after Christmas?'

Again, she hesitated before answering and he sensed she was hiding something. Well, he had no intention of prying. 'I have no idea but perhaps something will turn up,' she said.

'You could always go home,' Phil said. 'No one would blame you if you did.'

'No, I shan't be doing that.' From the emphatic tone of her voice, Phil knew how determined she was to go through with this. 'What about you? Do you get back to Horwich often?'

'No. The last time were for my brother's funeral. He died in a road accident.'

She shifted on her seat and looked to where the others were by the juke box. 'That's so sad.'

'Aye, there's a hole in our lives where Brian used to be. Oh, and I were supposed to go home for my brother's wedding a few weeks ago but it were called off at the last minute.'

To his surprise, she stood up quickly and said, 'Is that the time? I said I'd be back before now. Must go.' And, with a quick wave in the direction of Chipper and Fred and a nod to Phil, she was gone leaving him gaping at her retreating back.

'What's up with her?' Fred wandered back to their table, followed by Chipper looking puzzled. 'Did you say something to upset her?'

'Not that I'm aware of. I were just telling her about my family when she decided she had to leave. She didn't even finish her tea,' Phil said, indicating the half-empty cup on the table.

40

'And she's left her iced bun,' said Fred, pulling the plate towards him. 'Ah, well, mustn't let it go to waste.'

* * *

On the Sunday morning after starting work at the Shangri-La, Sally woke, unsure, for a few seconds, where she was. Then she remembered. She'd been given an attic bedroom, smaller than the one she'd shared with Sandra at the Moncrieff but it was much more comfortable. She guessed it might be used when the season was in full swing for there was a washbasin in the room. On the floor below was a bathroom and toilet which, having only a tin bath and an outside toilet at home, was something she could appreciate.

Initially, she'd been unsure of the wisdom of taking the job at the Shangri-La in case she came across Phil Roberts more than was wise. But what choice did she have? She had to live and work somewhere. Like so much else in her life at present, she'd face that problem when she had to.

Shortly afterwards, there was a knock on the door. 'Sally, are you awake? Time to get up. There's a cuppa for you outside the door,' came Mrs Parrott's voice.

'Thanks, Mrs Parrott. I'll be down directly.'

'No rush. You've time to have something to eat yourself before we tackle the guests' breakfasts.'

Hearing Mrs Parrott on the creaky stairs down to the next floor, Sally rose, stretched and opened the door for her tea. She didn't want the landlady seeing her in her pyjamas in case she noticed the tell-tale bump. Thankfully, she had passed the morning sickness stage a few weeks ago.

Within twenty minutes, she was downstairs in the spacious but cluttered kitchen, rinsing her mug at the sink. 'What do you want me to do, Mrs Parrott?'

'If we're going to be working together, I'd rather you called me Betty. Mrs Parrott reminds me of my late mother-in-law,' she said, 'and I'm not a bit like her. How Bob ever found the courage to propose, I'll never know.' She indicated a chair at the large scrubbed kitchen table. 'Sit yourself down, lass, and have some toast and another cup of tea. We'll be busy enough once we start. You'll need something in that belly of yours to sustain you.'

Involuntarily, Sally glanced down at her belly. Was her pregnancy obvious at this stage? She'd chosen to wear her one loose sweater over a plain black skirt. The waistband was a little tight but the bump didn't show too much at this stage. What she would do for clothes when she became bigger, she didn't know. The few clothes she possessed were nearly all tight-fitting and totally unsuitable for pregnancy.

As she munched on toast, Betty, cutting the rind off bacon rashers and laying them on a wooden board, gave her a run-down on what would be expected of her in a normal day's work. 'First of all, obviously, there's the early morning tea for those who want it. Bob and I have done those this morning, it being your first day, but in future the three of us will take it in turns. Either Bob or I'll give you a knock every morning like I did this morning. Minus the cup of tea, of course. That was a treat for today.'

Sally looked at her new boss intently, taking stock of her. Tall, thin, but wiry looking, Betty radiated a sense of energy, as if she might spring into action at any time. Somewhere in her forties, she had a lively-looking face, topped by coarse grey-peppered dark hair, cut in a straight bob just below her ears. She had about her a no-nonsense sort of attitude that seemed so typical of seaside landladies. 'Then it's breakfast, cereals, porridge, bacon and egg. You'll be going into the dining room taking the orders and bringing them back to me. That's why it's been so hard since my other girl left, I can't be in two places at once, and my place is in the kitchen.'

'I'll be glad to help in any way I can, Mrs …Betty.'

'Well, if you've finished your tea and toast, we'd better crack on,' Betty said, washing her hands at the sink. 'Some of the guests will be in the dining room already.'

'So early?' She saw from the clock on the wall that it was barely half past seven. She took her cup and empty plate to the sink under a window overlooking the back yard.

'One of our guests, Mr. Wolfit, will have been up since about six. Goes for a brisk walk along the Promenade every morning, then buys his newspaper. You'll find he's a proper gentleman, always raises his hat to me when he sees me outside.

'Right, lass, if you're ready, you can take the cereals and this milk jug through to the dining room. I'll tell you about the rest of your duties as we go through the day.'

After a busy morning seeing to the breakfasts, clearing up afterwards and some routine cleaning, Sally felt more like a lie-down than going for a walk. Yet she was determined to keep up with her afternoon walks as long as she could.

Later, coming through the front door after a brisk walk on the Promenade, she met Betty coming downstairs, her cheeks flushed from the nap she'd been having. 'You're back early, Sally. Did you have a good walk?'

Sally looked up and smiled. 'Yes, thanks. It's a bit fresh out there but pleasant enough.'

'Come through to the kitchen and we'll have a cup of tea before we start thinking about tea for the guests.'

The large, airy, old-fashioned kitchen still smelled pleasantly of the baking Betty had done this morning but everything had been cleared away, ready for the preparations for what Sally guessed would be a salad tea. Like most boarding houses, Betty only served breakfast and high tea. Guest were expected to vacate their rooms after breakfast, returning only in time for tea.

Without being asked, Sally went to the sink and filled the kettle up, while Betty took the cups down from the large open dresser where all the pots were stored. 'Take some of that fruit cake from the tin, love. I don't see why the guests should have all the fun.' As Sally busied herself cutting the large slab cake, Betty said, 'Will you cut a piece for Bob and take it through to him?

He'll make himself some tea.' While Betty brewed the tea, she placed a piece of cake on a side plate and took it through the doorway under the stairs linking the boarding house to the café.

Bob took the plate from her. 'Thanks, love. This'll put me on nicely until we have our meal later. You settling in OK?'

'I think so, Bob.' She liked Bob. He had an easy, avuncular manner that made you feel you could trust him. His kindness was apparent from the moment you met him, but she was willing to bet he could be firm when the need arose. He was about the same height as Betty but had a tendency to corpulence, probably a tribute to Betty's cooking. Bespectacled hazel eyes twinkled in a round face capped by thinning sandy hair.

Some customers came in then, a young couple with a small child. 'Excuse me, love, must see to the customers,' Bob said, then turned to the young man who had come up to the counter. 'Now, what can I get you?'

Back in the kitchen, Betty had poured the tea. 'Come and sit down, love, take the weight of your feet while you can. We've a bit of time to kill before we need to start and I'm glad of the chance to have a chat.'

Sally pulled the cup towards her and took a sip from its contents, wondering what Betty had to say to her.

'Do you think you'll like it here, Sally.'

'Yes. I like meeting people and think I get on OK with them.'

'The guests seem to take to you too and that's always a good thing. But what are your plans after Christmas? Will you go home?'

Sally didn't need to think before replying. 'No. There's nowt for me there now.'

'Forgive me, love, for an interfering old biddy but I can tell you're unhappy about something. Was it a broken heart that made you leave everything behind?'

Maybe it was the soft-spoken way in which Betty said it. Whatever the reason, tears threatened. She kept them at bay with fierce determination. 'Summat like that. I loved someone but he

loved another girl. It would hurt to see them together so I …
left.'

Betty leaned over and put her hand on Sally's forearm. 'Oh,
love, I am sorry. I shouldn't have asked.'

'It's all right, really. It did me good to actually tell you. I've
told no-one, you see, not my family, certainly not … him how I
felt. As far as everyone was concerned, I wanted a fresh start
after working six years in the mill.'

'Well, your secret's safe with me. I shan't breathe a word to
anyone.' Taking her hand away, she indicated Sally's now-cooling
cup of tea and the generous piece of cake awaiting her. 'Now
drink up then we'll think about making a start, getting ahead of
ourselves.' She took her own cup and plate across to the sink
then half-turned back to Sally. 'And I'll have a word with my
fellow landladies, see if anyone can come up with something for
you after Christmas.'

CHAPTER 6

Phil was late going to the Mess for his evening meal and the canteen was almost empty. Chipper was probably already on duty in the Sergeants' Mess but Fred was sitting at their usual table enjoying a post-tea fag. He waved Phil over.

'How-do, Phil,' Fred said as Phil sat down and took his eating irons out of his pocket. Despite Fred's normal Welsh sing-song accent, he occasionally came out with Lanky talk which amused Phil.

'How-do, yourself,' replied Phil before taking a mouthful of beans and chips. The contents of the plate were lukewarm at best but unless he went hungry, he'd have to eat up. 'Food doesn't get any better, does it?'

'Should have had the curry, it was half decent today.' Fred indicated his empty plate.

'Didn't have much choice. It were either chips and beans or beans and chips.'

'At least that's always edible. Unlike some of the stuff they dish up.' Fred rose and picked up his mug. 'I'm off for another cuppa. Do you want one?'

'Might as well. Help wash this muck down.'

By the time Fred returned with two mugs of steaming tea, Phil was mopping the plate up with a slice of bread and thinly spread butter. He pushed the now empty plate away as Fred sat down. 'Thanks, mate. Have you heard the latest buzz, by the way?'

'No, what's that?'

'That the Egyptians have scuttled a load of ships in the Suez Canal, blocking it.' On Bonfire Night, the Anglo-French invasion of Egypt had commenced, with the combined naval fleet anchoring off Port Said.

'Bloody hell, no! That could lead to petrol rationing.'

'Already been talked about, I believe.'

'Bugger! I've got some leave due in the next few weeks. Wonder if I can wangle some through MT. You can bet the military won't be rationed.'

'Could be worse, Fred. You could be looking to get out of Hungary.' At the local cinema, they had all seen horrific pictures of the fighting on the streets of Budapest on the Pathé Newsreel.

Fred was no doubt thinking of those scenes when he said, 'Poor buggers! They didn't stand a chance against the highly disciplined Soviet troops.'

Phil pulled his cigarettes out of his jacket, and after offering the packet to Fred, lit their cigarettes. 'Hard to imagine owt like that happening in London or Manchester.'

'I did hear there was a public meeting in London earlier this month and demands made for Anthony Eden to resign because of his handling of the Suez crisis,' Fred commented. 'Hardly a riot, though.'

'I've heard he's a broken man. I feel sorry for him, in a way, because he thought he were from the same mould as Winston Churchill,' Phil said.

'No way! There'll only ever be one Winnie.'

Phil stood and pushed his chair back. 'I'm off to phone Pam, see if she wants to go out Sunday afternoon.' In the malodorous phone booth, he gave the operator the Gregory's phone number. After a couple of minutes, he found himself speaking to Pam. 'Hello, love, it's Phil.'

'Phil! What a nice surprise.'

'I wondered if you fancied a trip to Stanley Park on Sunday. I can wangle a couple of hours or so in the afternoon before I'm on duty in the evening.'

'Sorry, Phil. My Auntie Beryl and Uncle Alf are coming for tea for Gran's birthday and Mum and Dad will expect me to be here.' Pam was part of a large and close family with many brothers, sisters, cousins and various great-aunts and uncles and they always seemed to be celebrating some event or other. 'Perhaps we can make it to the pictures one day next week?'

Phil sighed. 'I'll have to let you know. They seem to be giving me more responsibility these days. Makes it difficult to make arrangements in advance.'

'It's all right, love, I do understand,' Pam said. 'It's a good job we're on the phone so you can get in touch quickly.'

'That's why, when I knew I could get some time off Sunday, I thought I'd see what you were doing.'

'I am sorry I can't make it.'

'Not to worry. It can't helped.'

After chatting for another few minutes, Phil rang off, feeling disgruntled. He hated being cooped up on the camp when he didn't need to be and somehow it wasn't as much fun doing things on your own. Fingering the book of matches bearing the name of the Shangri-La in his pocket, he contemplated his next action. Sod it, it was worth a try. Eventually, he was put through and when a voice at the other end said, 'Shangri-la Guest House,' he pressed button A and heard his coppers clink down into the receptacle.

'If it's not too inconvenient, can I speak to Sally, please?'

'Speaking.' Sally sounded guarded. Maybe she didn't recognise his voice.

'Sally, it's Phil Roberts. Is it all right to talk for a few minutes?'

'Yes, we've just finished clearing up after tea.'

'I thought ...' He realised he didn't know how to continue. 'How have you been? Enjoying working at the Shangri-La?'

'Very much so. I like seeing to the guests.'

'Do you fancy going to Stanley Park on Sunday afternoon?'

'Why?' Her curtness caught him off guard.

'I've got a few hours off and thought you might enjoy getting out a bit yourself,' he said. 'And you can tell me how it's all going.'

'What if it's raining?'

'If it is, well, maybe we could go to the Tower or something.'

'I'd have to be back by four, to help with the teas.'

'That's not a problem. I'd need to get back to the camp anyway.'

'OK, then. What time?'

'How about if we meet about 12-ish? Maybe have a sandwich if the café's open.'

Back in the Mess, Fred was still sat at the table, the ashtray now full to overflowing. 'Manage to speak to Pam?'

Phil nodded. 'Not that it did me much good. They've got visitors on Sunday afternoon so she can't get out.'

'That's your plans buggered then.'

'It was with Pam but I rang the Shangri-La and asked Sally What's-her-name if she'd come out with me instead.'

Fred raised a quizzical eyebrow. 'Two-timing the lovely Pam?'

'A walk in Stanley Park's hardly a date. Anyroad, I wouldn't do that to Pam.'

He sat back and took a cigarette out of the packet of cigarettes Fred had left on the table. Despite his reassurances to Fred about Pam, he found, to his surprise, that he was looking forward to seeing Sally again.

* * *

Sally awoke before the alarm on Sunday morning. Her attic room was shiveringly cold and still as dark as night. She was warm enough under the blankets and eiderdown but one hand had dislodged itself from and was ice-cold. She withdrew it under the covers and tucked it between her warm thighs. The luminous hands of the alarm clock on the bedside table told her it would soon be time to get up but for the few moments left to her, she luxuriated in the warmth of her bed.

She thought back to the phone call she'd had from Phil. She'd vowed to avoid him if she could yet she'd agreed to see him again. What had made her do that? Because he reminded her of Nick. Not in looks, of course, but by the fact that they were brothers.

She recalled the night she had spent in Nick's arms during Horwich holidays and the contrast between this freezing bedroom and the heat of that summer day and night. They'd been in each other's company all day, first of all on the trip to Haigh Hall, near Wigan, then in the pub and onto a party. To Sally it had all been magical. It was only later when she woke in the frowsty bed, with her make-up smeared over her face, her hair like a bird's nest, that she realised Nick had used her, probably imagining she was Kathy Armstrong. Admittedly, he had offered to marry her as soon as she told him she was pregnant but she'd known even then his heart wasn't in it.

She was saved from more introspection by the alarm ringing and she shot out an arm to turn the strident noise off. Throwing back the bed covers, she edged her way out of bed and reached for her clothes, dressing as quickly as she could, shivering as she did so.

She was already laying out the trays for early morning teas when Bob came yawning into the kitchen. 'Morning, Sally, love. My turn for teas today. Betty'll be up soon enough for breakfasts.' He lifted the huge kettle off the hob where Sally had had it boiling and brewed the tea in the small teapots each room was entitled to. 'Eeh, it's a bit parky this morning. Can't see out at the moment but I bet there's been a frost.'

'You're right. There was frost on the windows when I opened my curtains.'

'You'll freeze up there this weather. It's the coldest room in the house. Must have a word with Betty about moving you to another.'

He left the kitchen with the first tray as she was about to remind him she was only here for about another month and would cope. She picked up another tray and followed Bob up the stairs.

By the time they'd finished with breakfasts, a watery sun had appeared so at least the weather would be fine for that afternoon. The café didn't open until later in winter and Bob had disappeared upstairs with the Sunday paper. Sally guessed the bathroom would be occupied for some time to come. She was just enjoying a second cup of tea when Betty spoke. 'I'm glad of this time alone with you, Sally. In fact, I asked Bob to disappear for a while as I wanted to have a chat with you.'

'Oh dear, that sounds ominous.' Sally tried to be flippant but her heart was pounding, dreading what Betty would have to say.

'You've been here a couple of weeks now and I've noticed you've put weight on. There's no easy way to say this, love, so I'll be blunt, are you pregnant?'

The words hit Sally like a douche of cold water and despite the cosy warmth of the kitchen she shivered. Should she deny it? No, it was no use pretending. She could no longer hide it. She was getting too big. Already she was struggling to find anything to wear that hid her belly. 'How … did you guess?' She was suddenly fearful. Would Betty sack her? What would she do then?

To her surprise, Betty leaned forward and patted her hand as it clutched the cup. 'It wasn't hard. Don't look so worried, love, I'm not going to throw you out. In fact, I'd like to help you if I can. Is that the reason you ran away?'

She had carried the burden of her pregnancy alone for so long that having someone to share it with would be a relief. 'In a way, yes. But, as I told you before, the lad concerned didn't love me and I realised it would be no use going ahead. I told him … told my family … I'd had a miscarriage and that he didn't need to marry me.'

Betty looked at her approvingly. 'That was a brave thing to do. Most girls in your position would have gone through with it.'

'That's why I came here. Horwich is a small town, everyone knows everybody else's business and I couldn't stay for obvious reasons,' she said, pointing to her belly.

To her surprise, Betty rose and came to put her arm round Sally's shoulder. 'Oh, you poor girl! What will you do now? You can't hide your pregnancy for ever.'

Comforted by the contact, she leaned slightly against Betty's supporting arm. 'I haven't been doing too much thinking about it but you've made me realise I have to face up to things and decide what I'm going to do.'

'Well, don't do anything for the moment. I've had an idea but I need to talk to Bob about it. And don't look so worried, lass. You're not the first and you certainly won't be the last.' Betty moved away and sat down again. 'Now, aren't you off out later with that nice young RAF chap? Does he know?'

Should she tell Betty that Phil was the brother of the lad whose baby she was carrying? She decided not to. That was a complication too far. 'No, I've managed to hide it so far.'

'It might be an idea to tell him. He comes into the café regularly and you wouldn't be able to avoid him forever. How far on are you, by the way?'

'I'm guessing about four and a half months.'

'Oh, how lovely! You should be feeling the baby move any time soon.'

Sally found herself thinking about how positive Betty had been about her situation as she prepared for the outing this afternoon. She wondered what the baby moving would feel like and how she would know. Although she was fearful about what the future held, she knew she could no longer conceal her pregnancy. She wished now she wasn't going out this afternoon. With her fate hanging in the balance, she didn't feel up to facing Phil, especially with what she was going to tell him, but she'd promised and she had no way of getting in touch with him.

* * *

The late November day was now bright with varying bursts of sunshine, the ever-present Blackpool breeze sending white clouds scudding across the sky. Phil had arranged to meet Sally by the bus stop to Stanley Park and he watched her as she approached, apparently deep in thought. A red scarf and mittens brightened the somewhat dull grey coat she was wearing. Their vividness was reflected in the pink of her cheeks, giving her face a wholesome glow. Practicality had won out over vanity for she was wearing flat ballet-style shoes. As she saw him, a wavering smile curved her mouth. She looked, he thought, about fifteen and again he felt that crazy desire to protect her though he knew she was quite capable of looking after herself.

'Hello, Sally. You look nice,' he said, cringing that he sounded so pathetic.

She gave a grimace as if she found that hard to believe. 'Thanks.'

'We've been blessed with the sunshine today, haven't we?' And cursed himself for more inane remarks.

'We have, though there's still a stiff breeze.' Her voice sounded odd, a little stilted. Perhaps she'd been having second thoughts about meeting him today. Or any day come to that.

He laughed. 'All part of Blackpool's charm.'

'Along with the smell of fish and chips, winkles and candy floss.'

'Summat like that.' The green and cream livery of a Blackpool Corporation bus came into view. 'That were good timing. Shall we go upstairs or down?'

'Down, I think. It's not very far, is it?'

'About ten minutes. It's ages since I've been. What about you?' he asked as they clambered aboard.

'I think we came on a rare day out, probably a chara outing.' A wistful look crossed her face. 'We could never afford a proper holiday.'

He gave the fare to the conductress and watched as she pulled two tickets from her ticket holder and punched them.

'Neither could we, there were always too many of us and my Dad had a weakness for the horses.'

She laughed then. 'My Dad didn't believe in spending money on what he called frivolities. Not that there were much money, he were only a labourer at … a clay works.'

'Tell me about your family. Do you have any brothers and sisters?'

Did he imagine it or did she hesitate before replying? 'Two sisters, both younger than me and an older brother. My Mam, of course. My Dad died a couple of years ago.'

'Oh, sorry to hear that.'

'He were very strict with us kids so he weren't much missed. Mam went to pieces a bit though.'

'Whereabouts in Bolton did you live?'

Again, there was a slight hesitation. 'Daubhill,' she said.

'Winter Street, Horwich, for me,' he said. 'Though we've got a council house now on the Brazeley estate. I've only been once, in September, and that were for my younger brother's funeral.'

'How's your … family coping?' she asked, though he had the feeling she had been about to say something else.

'Pretty well, all things considered. My youngest brother were with him at the time and it affected him badly. He seems to be getting over it a bit now, so Mam tells me.' He grinned. 'She writes faithfully every week. It's more or less always the same format. "How are you, Phil? We are all well though your Dad has had a cold and don't we know it!" I'm not very good about replying, I have to admit.'

He half expected her to ask him how many brothers and sisters he had but she fell silent and turned her head to look out of the window. In fact, she seemed deep in thought and he had to tap her on the arm when the bus approached Stanley Park. 'We're here, Sally.'

The park was busy on this rare fine day, with mums and dads pushing prams and trailed by older children, older couples walking their dogs, or young people, like themselves, out for a stroll. Phil and Sally chatted in polite fashion, saying no more than they needed to, until they reached the more sheltered Italian

Garden. Finally, Phil decided he had to speak. 'Is summat up, Sally? You seem a bit … quiet.'

'No, I'm OK.' Nevertheless, he detected a catch in her voice.

He indicated one of the benches overlooking the Garden. 'Let's sit down here. Looks as if it might be more sheltered from the wind.' As they sat, she hunched further into her coat. 'Whatever is bothering you, you can tell me. I like to think we're friends now.' He sat some way apart from her, not wanting to crowd her, to feel she was under any kind of pressure.

'You might not want to be my friend when I tell you what I have to.' Her face against the scarlet of her scarf was now pale.

'Try me. It can't be that bad.'

'The fact is … the reason I came to Blackpool … is because I'm pregnant.'

He gaped at her stunned, unsure whether she was joking but the look of anguish on her face told him she wasn't. He had a vision of her as she had looked in that pink dress when they had gone to the Halloween Dance. She certainly hadn't shown then. 'Bloody hell, Sally, you kept that quiet!'

'I haven't wanted to face up to things before now,' she admitted. 'Betty forced me to do so earlier by asking me outright.'

'I presume the lad concerned didn't want to know.'

Her head came up and there was a defiant tilt to her chin. 'No, he offered to marry me. I turned him down because I knew he didn't love me.'

'But you wouldn't have been the first to go through with a marriage for the sake of the child,' he pointed out. 'He might have come to love you given time.'

She shook her head. 'No, he would never have loved me. He were in love with someone else.'

He felt helpless in the face of her predicament, unsure how he could help her. But then again, why should he? She wasn't his responsibility. 'What will you do now?'

'I don't know. Betty wanted to have a chat to Bob first. Then she's going to talk to me when I go back.' Then, in a small voice, she said, 'Presumably I'll have to go into a Mother and Baby Home at some point.'

'What then? Will you have the baby adopted? Most girls in your situation do.'

She sighed and looked, if anything, sadder than before. 'I'd like to keep it but I don't suppose I'll be able to. I mean, how would I support myself and a baby?'

He could tell she was near to tears but fighting against it and, despite his misgivings a moment ago, he was moved more than he would have thought possible. Shuffling closer to her, he put his arm round her shoulder. 'And why would you think I wouldn't want to be your friend anymore?'

She looked at him then. 'Do you mean that?'

'Of course, I do. Don't forget for every girl like yourself, a lad has been behind her trouble.' He felt like giving the lad responsible a punch on the jaw for ducking out of the situation, no matter what Sally said in his defence.

She smiled and her relief was visible. 'Not many people think like you. Most people would disapprove.'

'I like to think I'm not like that.' The sun had gone in and a cold wind was swirling round them. 'Let's see if the café's open. I'm ready for a warm drink.'

As she stood, her hand flew to her belly and she let out an exclamation.

'What is it, Sally? Are you in pain?' Concern made his voice sharp.

'Nothing, that is – I think I just felt the baby move.'

'What did it feel like?' he asked, with interest.

She laughed. 'Like a bit of wind, actually.'

CHAPTER 7

When Sally arrived back at the Shangri-La, the kitchen seemed more warm and welcoming than ever. Despite the temporary nature of her residence here, the boarding house was starting to feel like home. She hesitated in the doorway, taking in the Welsh dresser piled high with pots and dishes of all sizes, the huge range that was the hub of the kitchen, the smell of newly baked scones on a cooling tray on the scrubbed wooden table. She couldn't help but compare it to her own home in Horwich. The two-bedroomed terraced house in Mary Street West was always cluttered and untidy. Her Mam had never been much of a housekeeper but since her Dad had died, even those limited skills had deteriorated. What it would have been like lodging there while married to Nick, given the antagonism between him and Jud, she couldn't begin to imagine.

Betty greeted her warmly. 'Sally, love, pull up a chair and get yourself a cuppa while we have a chat.' She nodded in the direction of Bob who, sitting at the table with his wife, was obviously going to be part of the discussion. To her relief, neither of them looked particularly stern or cross.

As she reached for a cup from the dresser, Betty continued, 'Did you enjoy your walk? Not too cold for you?'

She poured herself some tea from the teapot. 'No, providing you kept moving or found a sheltered spot to talk. I told Phil about the baby, by the way.'

'Good. What did he have to say?'

'He were a bit stunned to begin with but at least he didn't condemn me.'

'Nice lad, that,' Bob said. 'Wouldn't have expected anything else from him.'

'Which brings us neatly to what we want to talk about,' Betty said, a more serious look on her face. 'Bob and I have had a good long discussion while you've been out and this is what we're suggesting.' Taking a deep breath and sitting back in her chair, she turned to Bob. 'Do you want to tell her or shall I?'

'No, I'm happy for you to carry on.' He turned sideways to Sally and gave her an apologetic grin. 'I'm not much of a talker, love, and Betty can say it all better than me anyhow.'

'If you're agreeable, we'd like you to stay here until such time as you have to go into a Mother and Baby Home. We'll see how you feel after the baby's born but if you still want to come back here after the baby has been adopted ... I presume that's what you plan to do?'

A lump had come in Sally's throat at the kindness of this homely couple. 'I'd like to keep the baby but don't see how it would be possible.'

'Well, no need to think about that at this stage,' Betty said. 'What Bob's suggested, and I think it's a good idea, is that for appearances' sake, we say you're our niece, come to stay with us while your husband is serving abroad with the Army.'

'You'd need to buy a cheap wedding ring from Woolworth's, lass,' Bob put in, 'sooner rather than later.'

Looking from one to the other of them, Sally said, 'But why are doing all this for me? You don't owe me owt. And you said yourself, there'll be no work after Christmas.'

Again Bob spoke. 'That's true but you can give us a hand with the decorating and spring-cleaning we always do then. It also means that when we take our holiday in January, there'll be someone here to keep an eye on the place. As for why we're doing it, Sally, we've had experience of the same thing.'

Sally didn't miss the look of love and sadness that passed between Betty and Bob.

60

'It's a long time ago now and I was younger than you, barely eighteen. And the baby was Bob's in case you are wondering.' Sadness clouded Betty's eyes but her voice was steady and calm. 'We were childhood sweethearts, Bob and I, but his mother was a bit of a martinet and wouldn't agree to our getting married. My parents sent me away to stay with my grandmother in the Lake District but ...' There was a sudden catch in her voice, '... The baby died soon after he was born.'

'Oh, Betty, I'm so sorry,' Sally said, moved by this glimpse into Betty – and Bob's – past life.

'It's a long time ago, I know, but we've never forgotten our son. Not a day goes by without we don't think of him.' Her eyes had filled with tears.

Bob reached across for her hand which he held in his own. 'What made it harder to bear was that, for no apparent reason, we've never been able to have any more children.' Then he grinned. 'And it wasn't for want of trying.'

To Sally's amusement, a blush came to Betty's face and neck. 'Oh, you, Bob Parrott!' She gave her husband a playful tap on his hand. 'Anyway, in the short time you've been with us, we've become fond of you. You are always cheerful, have a ready smile and will muck in with anything.'

Touched by Betty's words, Sally fell silent.

'Do you need time to think it over?' Betty said. 'After what we've suggested, you might want to go home again.'

She thought briefly of her brother's reactions should she go home. 'No, I don't need to think about it. I can't anyway. Don't forget, my family think I've had a miscarriage. I'd like to accept your offer.'

Betty and Bob exchanged a swift look then Betty said, 'Have you been to see a doctor yet?'

'Once. He confirmed I were pregnant.'

'You'll need to register with a doctor here. You can do that first thing tomorrow. I think you'll find he will arrange for you to go in a Home,' Betty said, getting up to fill the kettle for yet another cup of tea.

'Do you know what these Homes are like, Betty?'

61

The older woman shook her head. 'For me, it was all done unofficially but my grandmother never let me forget that I was a bad girl in trouble and deserved all I got. She treated me like a skivvy.'

Sally voiced her own reservations. 'It's just that I've heard these places are more like a prison, lots of strict rules and regulations.'

'I think they were more like that at one time but I'm sure they'll have improved since then. You'll cope, I'm sure.'

'I won't have much choice,' Sally said.

* * *

The weather was cold, even for December, and Joyce shivered in the penetrating wind that whistled down from the moors surrounding Horwich. When she had set out that morning, the blue sky and fitful sunshine had fooled her into thinking it was warmer than it actually was. She pulled the collar of her coat closer round her neck and held it there with one gloved hand. The other held the battered shopping basket they'd had for years.

As she passed Ferretti's ice cream parlour and the sports shop next door, she saw Jud Simcox turn into Lee Lane from the Princes' Arcade and her heart sank. He'd started to pester her whenever he saw her, wanting her to go out with him and there would be no way of avoiding him.

As she suspected, he stopped when he reached her. 'Well, if it isn't Nick Robert's little sister,' he said, a huge grin on his pitted face, 'though not so little as she once was.' His eyes flicked to where her fitted coat outlined her breasts.

'Hello, Jud,' she said and made to walk on.

Seeing her manoeuvre, he side-stepped so she couldn't get past him. 'Where you off to, Joyce?'

'It's nowt to do with you,' she snapped.

'Ooh, getting a bit snooty now, are you? Taking lessons from your brother's girl-friend?' he jeered.

'Don't come your bully-boy tactics with me, Jud Simcox,' she said. 'I'm not easily intimidated.' She did a swift half-turn past him and marched on.

He trotted after her. 'I'm sorry, Joyce, I were only teasing, honest.' The trouble was whatever he said somehow held a hidden menace. Or at least that's what it felt like to her. 'Can I walk with you for a while?'

She shrugged. 'Please yourself, it's a free country.'

'How's your Nick? I haven't seen him for a good few weeks. He doesn't come in the Long Pull much nowadays.'

'He's been busy settling into his new job.'

'Ah, yes, he's working for that Jock what's got the poky garage by the Crown, isn't he?'

They had reached the top of Winter Hey Lane and she was pondering how she could get rid of him.

'Where are you off to?' he asked now.

'I've still got a few errands to do then I must get home.' She nodded to the contents of the basket. 'Mam's waiting for these.'

'When are you going to stop pussy-footing around and come out with me?' Although his tone was quiet, she sensed the threat behind his words.

'You don't half fancy yourself, Jud,' she said through gritted teeth.

'Not as much as I fancy you,' he retorted. 'I'll keep asking until you say yes.'

'Then you're in for a long wait. Hell will freeze over before I'd go out with you.'

He grabbed the wrist that was still holding her coat around her ears and the strength of his grasp surprised her. 'I usually get what I want in the end.'

'Let go of her, Jud.' Relief flooded her as she heard Dave's voice behind them.

Jud wasn't intimidated by Dave's superior height; if anything his grip tightened. 'Why should I? She's not your girl-friend anymore.'

'No, but I still care what happens to her and I can tell you're scaring her. Besides, she's my mate's kid sister and I know Nick won't be happy about you bothering her.'

Jud released her wrist but only slowly, grudgingly. 'We were only chatting, weren't we, Joyce?'

She was about to agree in order to defuse the situation but Dave forestalled her. 'No, you weren't. I've been behind you for a while now. I heard you ask her out and I heard her refuse. Now push off.'

'Get you!' jeered Jud. 'Coming the big guy now! Well, let me tell you you're nowt without Nick Roberts.'

'Then we're quits, aren't we, Jud? Because without Bill Murphy and Jim Stephens, you're just a little squirt.'

Jud's face flushed a dark red and the muscles around his jaw tightened. 'You'll be sorry for that remark, Bragger Yates, you'll see.'

As he stalked away, Joyce saw that his fists had clenched by his side. 'I think you've made an enemy there,' she said. 'You know how sensitive he is about his lack of height.'

'I'm not worried about him.'

'I were thinking of the beating Jud and his mates gave Nick a little while ago. I don't want the same thing happening to you.'

'I'll watch my back, don't worry,' he tried to reassure her. 'Tell me, has he bothered you before today?'

She didn't know what to say. She didn't want to inflame the situation any further. 'Let's say, it weren't the first time he's asked me.'

'He's a funny lad, that Jud Simcox. He's never got over being turned down for his National Service because of his acne. It's weird,' Dave said, 'most of us would do owt to get out of going. He's the only lad I know who actually wanted to go.'

'Our Phil were the same. Couldn't wait to go,' she reminded him. 'Now he's made it his career.'

'Enough about other people,' he said. 'How about making the most of this opportunity and going to Harry Stocker's?'

'Oh, dare we? What if Jud's there?'

'I don't give a toss. He won't be likely to start owt there. Harry wouldn't stand for any nonsense.'

Harry Stocker's Temperance Bar was, as usual, an oasis of warmth and light. Seated at one of the pitted and worn tables, Joyce cupped her hands round the mug of hot Vimto gratefully and took a sip of the scalding liquid. 'Oh, lovely!'

He leaned over and touched her cheek, his finger straying to a lock of hair that had fallen in a tight curl on to her forehead. 'Oh, Joyce, love, I miss you so much.'

Such was the powerful intensity of feeling between them at that moment that she looked around to see if anyone else had noticed but a group of lads and lasses hovering round the juke box, none of whom she knew, were the only other customers. The haunting sound of Elvis Presley singing 'Love Me Tender' came from the juke box and seemed to touch her heart. She knew whenever she heard that song again, it would remind her of this particular moment.

'I think of you all the time. Maybe if we were allowed to see each other more often, I could get on with life better.' There was a touch of bitterness in his voice. 'Have you thought any more about – you know?'

Joyce looked at him, puzzled. 'No, I don't know. What?'

He glanced around as if checking no-one else was in the vicinity then leaned closer. 'About going to Scotland to get married.'

Her heart began racing. 'Yes, I've thought about it but … I mean, people like us don't do things like that, do we?'

'Why not?' He reached for her hand across the table.

'Is it really possible?' she whispered.

'Honestly? I don't know,' he said, 'but I'll look into it. It's too risky meeting you in Horwich even if today was accidental. Meet me in Bolton next Saturday afternoon and I'll let you know what I've found out.'

CHAPTER 8

The NCO Mess was a welcoming haven of warmth and light from the cold and frosty December night. Phil and Fred had already eaten their meal of mince, mashed potato and cauliflower by the time Chipper came to join them. 'Watcher, chums! How's things?' he said, plonking his behind on a chair opposite Phil and immediately tucking into his meal.

'Pretty good considering. How's yourself?' asked Fred, pulling on the cigarette he had just lit.

'Fine and dandy,' Chipper mumbled, his mouth full of food. 'You, Phil?'

'I'm OK too.' Suddenly, he grabbed Chipper's wrist, halting the forkful of food on its way to his mouth. 'Don't eat anymore!'

Chipper gaped at him. 'Why not?'

'Because I can see what looks like a caterpillar in your cauliflower.'

The fork and its contents clattered to Chipper's plate. 'You're having me on, right?'

Phil pointed to where the carcass of what had obviously been a caterpillar before it had been bleached by the boiling water it had been cooked in. 'Wish I were, mate.'

Chipper clapped his hand to his mouth. 'Oh, shit! I feel sick now.'

Fred, who was staring at Chipper's plate with fascination, said, 'You're not the only one. We've both had the same meal.' He clutched his stomach and pretended to retch.

Phil and Fred waited while Chipper took the remains of his meal back to the duty sergeant, fortunately not Wilko. 'What did he say?' Phil asked when Chipper re-joined them with a new helping of mince and mash without the cauliflower.

'"Don't shout about it, son, they'll all want one,"' Chipper said gloomily, 'then as I went to get another meal, he said, "Good source of protein, caterpillars."'

Despite the seriousness of the situation, Phil couldn't help laughing. 'He was probably right. I've heard about these survival courses where participants are encouraged to scavenge for insects.'

'I shan't be volunteering for any of them then,' Chipper said, returning to his meal but this time more gingerly, prodding the mince and mash with his fork, as if expecting some other foreign body to be lurking in their depths. 'I think I've been put off cauli for life.'

'I suspect that if your survival depended on it, you'd eat it,' Phil pointed out.

'Wouldn't like to be in the same billet as you if you'd had to eat a whole cauli,' said Fred.

They were still laughing about this when the duty sergeant came over to their table. 'Corporal Roberts? There's a phone call for you outside.'

Phil rose, his throat suddenly dry. 'Thanks, Sarge.' Then, as he turned to leave, he said to the other two. 'Bloody hell! Last time this happened, my kid brother had been knocked down.'

'Fingers crossed then that it's something of a nothing,' Chipper said.

In the phone booth in the lobby, he picked up the phone with some trepidation. 'Hello?' he said.

There was a click as the operator connected him. 'Caller, you're through now.'

To his relief, it was Sally on the other end of the line. 'Phil?' She sounded breathless as if she had been hurrying or was anxious. 'Sorry to ring you only you did say it would be all right between 6 and 7 o'clock. Did it cause you any problems?'

'Hello, Sally. No, we were only chatting after our meal when the Duty Sergeant came over.'

'Good. Only Betty and Bob are giving me a little party for my 21st and I wondered if you – and Pam, of course – would like to come. Chipper and Fred as well if they're free as I've asked those girls I used to work with and they're coming too.'

He felt a start of surprise at her words. 'I'd love to if I can. When is it?'

'This coming Sunday.' He realised that the breathlessness was because of excitement and guessed the Parrotts had sprung this on her as a surprise.

'I'll have to ask Pam. And I won't know about Fred and Chipper until I've spoken to them.' He hesitated, then said, 'Will any of your family manage to get there?'

'I won't be asking them,' she said shortly. 'Will you ring me to let me know if you and the others can make it only Betty needs to know because of the catering?'

He was still musing on the phone call when he went to re-join his two friends.

'Well?' Chipper asked.

'It was Sally. Her 21st birthday is next week and she's asked us all to a little party.'

Chipper leaned back in his chair and slapped his hands together. 'Great! It's ages since I've been to a party.'

'Don't get too excited. Bob and Betty Parrott will be there as well as those girls from the dance.' He wondered why she wasn't asking any of her family. 'Think you'll be able to make it?'

'More than likely for me,' said Fred.

'I'll need to check the Sergeants' Mess duty rosters but if there's a problem I might be able to swap with someone,' Chipper said.

Phil thought for a moment then said, 'Look, there's summat you ought to know about Sally before Sunday. She's expecting.'

Chipper rocked back in his chair. 'Blimey mate, that was quick work! You've only known her a couple of months,' he quipped.

'Daft bugger! It's not mine. Being pregnant were the reason she came to Blackpool. She's about five months gone.'

Fred whistled. 'So she was up the duff when she came to the dance? I'd never have known.'

'She were only about three and a half months then so she still weren't showing much.'

'Why didn't the lad who'd done the deed marry her?' Chipper asked.

'Apparently he were all set to do so but she realised he didn't love her.'

'That took some guts. There's not many girls who'd have let him off the hook easily.'

Phil checked his watch. 'I'd better go and phone Pam. Ask if she wants to come.' Even as he said it, he realised he'd rather she wasn't able to. Then his conscience kicked in and he rose before he could change his mind.

It was Pam herself who answered the phone. He told her about Sally's phone call and that she was included in the invitation. 'Sounds lovely. I'd love to go.'

He hesitated before saying, 'There is one thing. The reason Sally came to Blackpool is because she's pregnant.'

There was a long moment of silence and Phil's heart sank. He knew what Pam was thinking. Believing that there should no sex before marriage, she hadn't let Phil progress beyond certain agreed limits.

'I see,' she said finally. 'Why hasn't she married the lad concerned?'

'He offered but she chose not to.'

'I wouldn't have thought she was in a position to be choosy,' Pam said, a brittle edge to her voice.

'I'm sure Sally will understand if you don't want to go …'

'No,' she interrupted. 'Of course I'll come. It'd look bad if I didn't … and she's got enough problems to contend with.'

As he thought, Pam's innate decency came through and he was genuine when he said, 'Thanks, love. She'll appreciate that.'

* * *

Sally held the rose pink taffeta dress, now way too tight, in front of her. The last time she'd worn it was for the Halloween Dance. She couldn't help but think of Phil as she did so. He had become a part of her life, almost without her realising it. He was coming tonight together with Pam, Chipper and Fred. As were the three girls from the Moncrieff. She hadn't seen them since she'd left and it had taken all her courage to phone. She remembered there'd been a public phone in the staff canteen and she'd had to wait a few minutes for someone to find Sandra

'Sally!' the girl had said, gasping for breath as if she'd dashed down the stairs. 'I'd almost given up hope of hearing from you and, of course, I didn't have a phone number for you. Where are you working now?'

'A boarding house on Central Drive. The Shangri-La.' Sally drew in a deep breath before continuing, 'I've a good reason for not getting in touch. The fact is, Sandra, I'm pregnant.'

After only a slight pause, the other girl had scoffed, 'That's a poor excuse. Surely now's the time when you need friends.'

'What about Ruth and Barbara?'

'I'm sure they'll think the same. After all, it could just as easily be any of us,' Sandra had said.

'You'd be surprised. Different people have had different reactions. When I went to the doctor's, his nurse treated me as if I had some contagious disease, looking down her nose at me.'

'Probably a dried up old prune,' Sandra said. 'How far on are you?'

'Five months,' Sally said.

'What happened to the lad? Wouldn't he stand by you?'

'He offered but I knew it wouldn't work.'

'Didn't stop him putting you in the club, did it?'

Sally laughed. 'Anyway, the reason I'm ringing is to invite you to a party for my 21st this coming Sunday.'

71

'Count me in. I'm always ready for a bit of a knees up. I'll speak to Ruth and Barbara and ring you back if you give me the phone number.'

Now it was Sunday evening and she was preparing for the party. With reluctance, she put the rose pink taffeta dress back in the wardrobe and drew out the purple maternity dress she'd managed to buy. With long sleeves, a fitted bodice and a panel gathered at the front under the bust to accommodate her growing bump, she knew the style and colour suited her though what she would do with it afterwards, she hadn't a clue. Peering in the mirror on the dressing table, she applied eye shadow and some mascara. She rarely bothered these days. At one time she wouldn't have gone out of the house without make-up. She was letting the bleached blonde grow out too, leaving her natural blonde to show through.

Downstairs, she found Bob in the resident's lounge. From somewhere, bunting from the Coronation had been found and strung along the ceiling of the lounge. Candles had been placed in sturdy bottles and when lit would provide an intimate atmosphere. For the moment though, the wall-lights were on and Bob was rigging up an old wind-up gramophone in the corner. 'Ah, there you are, love. Don't you look a bobby-dazzler?'

She laughed and patted her belly. 'Hardly likely to set any pulses racing with this, am I? Where's Betty?'

'In the kitchen as usual.'

The kitchen was welcoming with light, warmth and the smell of baking. Betty looked up, a tray of sausage rolls she taken from the oven in her hands, her face red in the heat, as Sally entered. 'Anything I can do to help, Betty?'

'You can wrap the knives and forks into some napkins, if you will. Apart from that, everything is ready. What do you think?' She indicated the table in front of her.

It was loaded with the sandwiches the pair of them had prepared this afternoon, a bowl of salad, ham on the bone ready to be sliced, a dish of crisps and a huge trifle in Betty's best fruit bowl. 'It looks fantastic, Betty. I can't thank you and Bob enough for what you're doing for me.'

72

'Sounds like your first guests have arrived, Sally,' Betty said as the doorbell jangled. 'Don't bother coming back in here, go straight through to the lounge with them.'

Phil, Pam, Chipper and Fred were the first to arrive, Phil carrying a carton of bottled pale ale. All the lads were in civvies and looking very smart.

Sally tried to take the carton from him and, in resisting her attempt, his fingers lingered on hers and she looked up at him in surprise. 'You look lovely, Sally, in fact you're blooming. Pregnancy suits you.'

She pulled a face at him. 'I don't plan on it being permanent.'

She focused her attention on Pam who was fussing with the buttons on her coat. Was she imagining it or did Pam look slightly uneasy, maybe because Phil had drawn attention to Sally's pregnancy? Perhaps, deep down Pam didn't approve. She could understand that. Lots of people didn't. 'Hello, Pam. Let me take your coat.'

In the lounge, the wall lights had been dimmed and the candles lit. In the semi-gloom, she could see they had already been joined by the residents, the Jamiesons and the Olivers, and who had been invited out of courtesy, since it was their lounge being taken over. Mr Wolfit, who liked to come and stay every couple of months or so, was there too. Sally introduced the three young men to the two elderly couples but when she got to Mr Wolfit, he winked at her and said, 'Which one is your young man, Sally?'

'None of them, Mr Wolfit. Stop trying to get me into trouble.'

The old man laughed heartily and put a fatherly arm round her shoulder. For some reason, the gesture touched her and she wanted to lean into him for comfort. 'Sorry, love, for a moment I forgot about your husband. In the Army, isn't he?'

Behind her, she heard Fred whisper to Phil. 'You never said anything about a husband,' and Phil's reply, 'Ssh, Fred. That's just to save Sally unnecessary embarrassment.'

Her cheeks burning, Sally was glad to turn away and answer the doorbell again. This time it was the three girls, Sandra, Ruth and Barbara and they handed her a bottle of Chianti with its distinctive raffia casing. Sandra leaned forward and gave Sally a quick hug. 'Happy birthday, Sally.'

'It's not actually till tomorrow,' she pointed out.

'Doesn't matter. The sentiments are the same,' Sandra said. She was wearing a black circular skirt and a white *broderie-anglaise* blouse. Sally envied her slender figure. It helped that Sandra was tall. Even when not pregnant, she would never be that slim.

'Sandra said you were pregnant. How are you feeling?' Ruth asked, her plump face alive with interest.

Sally patted her bump. 'Getting enormous.'

'I must say you look well,' Barbara said, bringing up the rear as the girls crowded into the hall. 'Have you felt the baby move yet?'

She took their coats and hung them over the newel post at the bottom of the stairs. 'Yes, a couple of weeks ago.'

'Ooh, what does it feel like?' Ruth asked.

'A bit like a butterfly rustling its wings to begin with,' Sally said. 'Now it feels like fairy doing a high kick routine. I expect by the end, it'll feel like a miniature football team.'

She took the three girls through to the lounge where they exchanged greetings with the three RAF lads and Pam who looked relieved to see the girls. Bob set the bottles on the top of the small cocktail bar and said, 'Now, who would like a drink?'

The party, from that point on, took on a life of its own. No one drank to excess, the food all but disappeared and the old scratchy records playing on the wind-up gramophone made everyone roar with laughter. With the rug usually in place on the floor taken up, there was even some dancing. At one point, Sally found herself bopping with Phil, not always easy with someone whose style was not familiar. To her surprise, though, their steps matched and he swung her round in an expert and efficient way. 'I didn't know you could bop,' she gasped, slightly more out of breath than she would be usually.

'There's lots of things you don't know about me,' he said, an arm still round her waist. 'You know what they say about the quiet ones.' There was an intensity in his voice that, for some reason, disturbed her.

She pulled away from him abruptly. 'I must go and get a drink of water,' she said, making for the kitchen to compose herself.

'You're not feeling faint or owt are you?' he asked, concern in his voice.

'No, just thirsty.'

To her surprise, the kitchen door was locked. 'Betty, are you in there?' she asked as she knocked.

'You can't come in. What is it you want?'

'A drink of water please,' she asked, curious as to what was going on behind the locked door.

There were movements from the kitchen, the sound of running water, then the door opened a few inches, the space between blocked by Betty's body, a glass of water in her hand. 'Here you are,' she said, handing the glass to Sally.

Sally tried to peer round the door but was thwarted by Betty laughing and shutting the door quickly. She had a feeling she knew what Betty was up to but, not wanting to spoil the surprise, she shrugged and made her way back to the lounge.

She was sat chatting to the girls when, about ten minutes later, Betty appeared in the doorway, carrying a beautifully iced cake glowing with candles. But when had Betty have time to bake such a cake when most of the time Sally herself was around? She guessed it must have been when Sally had gone to bed and she was touched anew. No one had ever done such a special thing for her before. Bob hastily pulled out a side table and Betty placed the cake carefully on it. 'Happy birthday, Sally.' Then, with Bob conducting the impromptu choir now clustered around her, they all sang 'Happy Birthday,' with out-of-tune enthusiasm.

'Blow out the candles,' someone called out to her, 'and make a wish.'

'I can't think of anything,' she gasped.

'Never mind, blow them out anyway.'

After that, the party seemed to slow down. The residents left for their own rooms, warmly thanking Sally for inviting them. Mr Wolfit even gave her a kiss on her cheek and wished her lots of luck with the baby. He would not be visiting now until well into the spring, he said. Bob rummaged around his record collection and found some war-time ballads which he put on the gramophone. The others were taking the opportunity to either chat among themselves or to smooch to the slow records. Pam was deep in conversation with Barbara. Sally sat a little apart and, with her pregnancy, not feeling quite a part of the group.

'Dance with me, Sally, if you're not too tired?' It was Phil and he was holding his hand out to her, a questioning look on his face.

She put her hand in his and let him pull her up. 'I think I can manage to stagger round the room though I feel I've put on pounds after all that food and birthday cake.'

He made exaggerated gestures with his arms as if he was dancing with an elephant. 'I'm not that big,' she protested. They wove their way around the room to the sound of Frank Sinatra singing, 'I'll Be Home For Christmas.'

'It must have been terrible, during the War, not to know when your loved one was coming home,' she murmured, looking up at him.

'I should think the thought of home was the only thing that kept most soldiers sane, especially during the First World War.'

They continued to move sedately round the room for a couple of minutes then Phil spoke again. 'Come out into the hallway, Sally,' he whispered. 'I've got something for you. I wanted to give it to you privately.'

The Moncrieff girls had given her a joint present, a pair of earrings and some nylons while the lads had given her a silk scarf and she'd thought Phil had been included in that. She looked at him in surprise but, being near the door into the hallway, led him through it. 'What is it?'

'This,' he said, producing a small elegantly wrapped package from his pocket.

76

She tore off the wrapping and opened the blue velvet box. Inside was a silver pendant in the shape of two clasped hands which she immediately took to be a symbol of friendship. 'Oh, Phil, it's beautiful!' she breathed, holding it between her fingers up to the light.

'Let me put it on for you,' he said, taking it from her hand. She turned with her back to him and let him fasten it round her neck. As his fingers touched her neck, a pleasurable shiver shot through her and she felt his fingers tremble. 'My hands are a bit big for this.' He turned her round to face him and touched the pendant where it lay at the neck of her dress. 'I know it's not quite midnight but happy birthday, Sally.' And leaning down, he kissed her, a tender touching of his own lips to hers.

The kiss took her by surprise but, to her amazement, she felt herself responding and the kiss became deeper, longer. She lost herself in the feelings he was arousing in her, feelings she had never known before, not even with Nick. Then reality kicked in. She pushed her hands against his chest and leaned back. 'No! Don't!' She couldn't believe what had just happened. What was she thinking of?

He looked down at her, his own eyes troubled. 'Sally, I know you felt something too …'

'We mustn't... We can't … ' she babbled, stepping back from him. 'There's Pam …'

The door to the lounge opened – she didn't even realise Phil had closed it after them – and the others piled out into the hallway, Pam at the forefront. She must have sensed something of the tension between Phil and Sally for she said sharply, 'What's going on here?'

Sally's face flamed while Phil put his finger under his collar as if it was suddenly too tight. 'Just wishing Sally a happy birthday for tomorrow seeing as it's nearly midnight.'

Fred diverted attention by looking at his watch. 'So it is. Time we were getting back to camp.'

'Proper little Cinderellas, we are,' quipped Chipper. 'You ready for the off, girls? If so, we'll walk you back to the hotel.'

Bob and Betty had followed them out and Sally realised the gramophone had been turned off. In the flurry of retrieval coats and goodbyes, she didn't have chance to speak to Phil again but as the group left, Phil turned round and gave a last wave of his hand. Her own hand flew to the pendant as if in acknowledgement.

CHAPTER 9

Phil walked up the alley between his parents' house and the neighbour's, the sound of his footsteps echoing against the walls. The last time he'd been here had been for his brother's funeral back in September. The atmosphere then had been one of numb shock, of tears shed and unshed. He couldn't help wondering what it would be like now.

Taking a deep breath and hoisting his kit bag higher on his shoulder, he opened the back door of the house. 'Hello Mam,' he said to the figure standing at the sink, peeling potatoes. Mary Roberts turned, her grey eyes lighting with pleasure at the sight of her second son.

'Phil, lad, good to see you!' She came forward to give him a swift hug and leaned back to look at him. 'You're looking well. RAF life is obviously suiting you.'

'I'm OK, Mam, but how have you been?'

She made a see-saw movement with her hand. 'I have bad days and good days.'

He didn't know what to say to that and chose not to say anything. 'Any chance of a brew, Mam?'

She indicated the cooker where a kettle was simmering on the hob. 'I'll brew up in a minute. You go through to the front room. Your Dad's there with Nick. Our Joyce is upstairs getting ready to go out.'

'Do Nick and Dad still fall out?'

'Not as much as they used to. Your Dad's calmed down a lot since coming out of prison.'

Phil grinned. 'I heard about you tipping his cold tea over his head when he came home drunk after gambling his wages away.'

She laughed. 'Aye, that were funny. Don't mention it to your Dad though. He's a bit touchy about it. And about the time Nick gave him a good hiding.'

'Weren't that because he'd hit you?'

'Yes, after I met him at the Works Gates demanding he hand over his pay packet. He'd never done it before or since.'

Phil was still smiling when he walked into the front room. 'Hello Dad, Nick.' Danny Roberts, a big-bellied man with thinning hair and a jowly face, was sitting in his favourite chair by the fireplace, a day old racing paper in his hands, though he put it down to greet Phil. 'Hello, son.' He hawked a globule of spit into the fire, a habit Phil despised. He and his Dad never had much to say to each other.

Nick, wearing a vivid turquoise shirt with drainpipe trousers, jumped up and shook Phil by the hand. 'Good to see you. How's things in the RAF?'

'Much the same. It's busy with servicemen coming and going all the time. It's slackened off now though until the New Year.'

'Good to have you, especially over Christmas. It'll help Mam get over it being the first Christmas without our Brian.'

'Where are the kids?'

'Out playing somewhere, I think. They've made friends with some other children now which takes Derek's mind off losing Brian. Lucy helps a lot too.'

'Mam said she's turning into a tomboy.'

Nick grinned. 'She's shot up and filled out a bit. Much more outgoing than she used to be.'

The front room had been hung with the same tatty old streamers, though he noticed a couple of paper chains among them, probably made by Derek and Lucy. The fake Christmas tree they'd had for years stood on Mam's old treadle sewing machine, its sparse branches decorated with tarnished tinsel, the few fragile baubles that had survived and pipe cleaner snowmen. The sight gave Phil a sense of nostalgia for the good Christmases that Mam, no matter how tight money had been during the war, had managed to give them as kids.

He heard footsteps coming down the stairs and Joyce burst through the door into the front room. Wearing a dressing gown too small for her and her hair piled high on her head, she looked much younger than her sixteen years. 'Phil! I thought I heard your voice.' She gave him an affectionate hug and he caught a whiff of scented bath salts.

'Hello Joyce. Mam said you were going out tonight. Where are you off to?' He sat down on the sofa and she plonked herself down beside him.

'The Band Room at Wingates.'

Mam came into the room carrying two mugs of tea in her right hand, one in her left. Nick went to take one from her and passed it to Phil.

'Mam, can I stay a bit later tonight with it being Christmas Eve? There's extra buses laid on.' Joyce asked.

'I suppose so but only half an hour, mind.'

'Oh, thanks Mam.' She gave her a quick peck on the cheek causing tea to slop out of one of the mugs.

Dad closed the paper in an exaggerated gesture. 'I'd just said no earlier,' he snapped. 'But don't mind me, I only live here.'

'Little madam! She didn't tell me that. But, Danny, it's only fair with it being Christmas Eve. And she is nearly seventeen.'

Danny heaved himself up, and shoved his shirt back into his trousers from where it had come adrift while he was sitting. 'Nobody listens to owt I say anymore,' he grumbled and left the room with a burp.

Joyce covered her mouth trying not to laugh but when she saw Nick doing the same, she took her hand away and let the laughter out, to be followed by Nick and Phil. 'Stop it, all of you!' Mam said though Phil noticed her own mouth twitching. 'Joyce had no right to go against his word.'

'Come on, Mam,' Nick reasoned. 'Dad's had no authority in this house since he were in prison.'

Mary sighed. 'I know and it's partly my fault because I told him straight I weren't going to be a doormat any longer.'

'He's certainly not the bully boy he used to be, is he?' said Phil.

Nick was seeing Kathy later so Phil changed into civvies and went in search of a couple of his former mates. He tried a couple of the pubs where he thought they might be, had a half of bitter in each in case they came in later but when no-one turned up, he finished his beer and wandered up to the Long Pull. It wasn't a pub they'd frequented previously but he knew it was popular with some lads, his own brother for one.

The Long Pull was packed and, being Christmas Eve, there was a spirit of revelry in the air. He saw many people he knew by sight if not by name, but then Horwich was that sort of place. Isolated as he was from the crowd around him, an unexpected wave of loneliness overcame him. It wasn't a feeling he was familiar with. It was his own fault he hadn't kept in touch with his mates. Once he'd started his National Service, he found he was more comfortable in service life than he had been when he'd been in Civvy Street. The rules and regulations, the parameters all servicemen had to work within, suited his methodical and logical mind, hence him deciding to make it his career. He missed Chipper's cheerful grin and Fred's dry wit.

And, he had to admit, he missed Sally too. The memory of that kiss lingered in his memory. The tenderness of it, the depth of feeling that had arisen as their lips met, had taken him by surprise and, he thought, Sally, hence her withdrawal. Even in the dim light of the hallway, with that purple dress outlining her bump, her blonde hair shining with good health, her face flushed and rosy from the wine and the laughter, she had looked so adorable that he couldn't resist kissing her. He should never have done it, not when he was supposed to be going out with Pam.

'Can I get you another drink, lad?' came a Scottish voice at the side of him. He was an older man, stocky with thinning grey hair and a cheerful smile on his round face. He had a pipe in his hand and he used it to gesticulate to Phil's glass, now nearly empty. 'You look as if you could do with some company.'

'Thanks, I will. Just a half though.'

'Not much of a drinker then.'

'No, not really.'

As they waited for their drinks to be brought, the man turned to Phil. 'How come a young lad like you is on his own on Christmas Eve. Stood you up, has she?'

Phil laughed. 'Nowt like that. I'm home on leave and haven't been in touch with my mates for months.'

'What service are you with? I'm ex-Navy myself.'

'The RAF. I started as a National Serviceman but signed on as a regular some months ago.'

The man picked up his drink from the bar and indicated the other glass to Phil. 'Where are you stationed?'

'Kirkham.'

The older man looked at him speculatively, his head to one side. 'You wouldn't happen to be Nick's brother, would you?'

Phil gaped at the man. 'You know our Nick?'

He laughed. 'I should say so. I own the garage near the Crown and he works for me. The name's Mac, by the way.' He held out his hand which Phil shook.

'Phil. Phil Roberts.'

'Let's get away from this crush,' Mac said indicating the queue at the bar. 'Unless you've other plans?'

Phil picked up his drink and followed Mac away from the bar. 'Nowt that won't wait.' As they sat down at the table Mac had indicated, he said, 'How's our Nick doing? Is he settling in okay?'

'He's doing grand but then he's been working for me on Saturdays a while now. It's been good for me too. I was just drifting before, not really interested in the business. He's helped me build up it again.'

They talked for some time about Nick and Mac's plans for the business and Phil found himself warming to this stocky Scotsman, wishing he'd more time to get to know him. The talk drifted on to what was happening in the world and Mac showed a rare insight that made Phil feel he should take more of an interest. As it was, he and his mates tended to rely at best on the

Pathé News at the pictures; at worst on the scuttlebutt of the Mess. Rarely did he read a newspaper. It was obvious that Mac did. From him, Phil learned that Anthony Eden had flown to Jamaica to 'to rest and recuperate,' it was said, Mac reported disparagingly. He clearly didn't think much to Anthony Eden. He learned, too, that British troops had been leaving the Middle East and that salvage crews were due to start clearing the ships scuttled in the Suez Canal.

While they talked, the hubbub of the pub swirled around them, the cigarette smoke getting thicker, the noise rising to a crescendo. If anything, the pub was becoming more crowded than ever and Phil wondered how he was going to push his way through to the toilets at the rear of the pub. He mentioned his need to Mac who shook his head. 'I wouldn't if I were you. Jud Simcox has just gone there and for some reason he's been giving you dirty looks all the time you've been sitting here.'

Phil blinked. 'I can't think why, I've no particular argument with him.'

'From what I've heard, he's always been a bit of a funny bugger but that business with Nick and Sally didn't help.'

Phil picked up his glass to take a drink. 'Sally?'

'Jud's sister, Sally. The lass Nick got in the family way.'

Phil choked on his drink, smashing his glass down on the table with a force that slopped most of the contents over the sides and puddled on the table. He coughed, gasping for air. Mac, a look of alarm on his face, thumped Phil on the back.

'What did you say?' Phil managed to gasp when the worst of the coughing was over.

'About Sally? She was the lass who was going to marry Nick until she miscarried.'

Now that the initial shock had passed, Phil had gone cold and the hand that reached for the glass was shaking. His brain was whirling. Sally? The girl he'd kissed and who had kissed him back? The girl he had been thinking of almost constantly since her party? Who hadn't really miscarried and was still carrying Nick's child? It was too much of a coincidence to be anyone but her. He felt revolted and sickened.

84

'You OK, lad?' Mac's voice was concerned. Phil shook his head, too numb to speak. Mac gave him a shrewd look. 'You've met her, haven't you? In Blackpool?' At Phil's nod of the head, he said, 'Of course, it stands to reason. You probably spend most of your off duty time in Blackpool.' Still Phil said nothing, staring at the puddle of beer on the table, the need for the toilet completely forgotten. 'It's obvious you didn't know. Let's get out of here, lad. I live just round the corner and I can make you a cup of tea.'

He stood and with his hand under Phil's arm, guided him towards the door. The fresh air revived him a little and he gulped it in eagerly. 'Sorry about that, Mac,' he said, 'but it were a bit of a shock.'

'No need for explanations, Phil. Not unless you want to, of course.'

Minutes later, Phil was ensconced in a shabby but comfortable armchair in Mac's flat above the garage. While Mac pottered in the kitchen, he took in his surroundings. Scattered around the small sitting room were piles of newspapers and magazines and it was easy to see from where Mac had gained his extensive knowledge. A pre-war Bakelite radio stood atop a cluttered sideboard while the table top was covered with more newspapers and a few books. Overall there was a stale smell of old pipe tobacco, made obvious by the ashtray overflowing with the dottle from his pipe.

Mac returned at that point bearing two mugs of tea. 'Hope you don't mind condensed milk, lad. Being on my own, it's not worth buying milk.' He sat down on one of the chairs at the table and pushed a cup towards Phil. 'Get that down you. It'll do you good.'

'Thanks, Mac.' Phil took a grateful sip of the highly sweetened milky tea. 'You said you live alone. Have you no family then?'

A shuttered look came on Mac's expressive face. 'I did have, son, lost them both just after the war.'

'I'm sorry, Mac.'

'It's OK. I can actually say that now, partly thanks to your Nick. He found me dead drunk one night, brought me home, looked after me until he was sure I was all right,' he explained. 'I'd been drinking, you see, because it was the anniversary of my wife and kiddie's death in a fire. I found myself talking about it to Nick and it's been easier since. And Nick's never said a word to anyone.' He had been lighting his pipe while talking and he used it now as a pointer to Phil. 'I'm not prying into your business, Phil, but if you want to talk, you'll find me a good listener.'

Phil was no longer numb with shock; instead anger was filling him. 'There's not much to tell to be honest. I met her the day she arrived in Blackpool and have sort of taken her under my wing since then.'

'And you've taken quite a fancy to her,' Mac surmised.

'I suppose I have,' Phil admitted, 'but I hadn't appreciated how much until I realised the Sally you were talking about and the Sally I know is the same person.'

'She must have had her reasons.'

'I know why. She lied to me because she knew I was Nick's brother and didn't want me to tell him she's still pregnant.'

It was Mac's turn to gasp. 'She didn't have a miscarriage?'

'No,' Phil said grimly. 'She's most definitely still carrying Nick's baby.'

'And that hurts?'

'More than I care to admit. I thought her an innocent lass taken advantage of by some heartless sod and felt sorry for her,' Phil said through gritted teeth. 'You won't tell our Nick, will you? It'd muck his life up if he found out.'

'Very wise, lad. Course not.'

Phil gave a snort of disgust. 'Some bloody Christmas this is turning out to be!'

CHAPTER 10

Sally had thought she might miss her own family, this being the first Christmas she'd ever spent away from home. Instead with the boarding house busy for the festive season, Christmas had been full of warmth, laughter and conviviality. Betty and Bob had striven to make the atmosphere as homely as possible to ensure the guests had a good time and Sally had enjoyed contributing to that. And there were times when it was just the three of them settling down to a meal or sitting in companionable silence listening to the Light Programme on the wireless. During those restful moments, she had found herself thinking of Phil, hoping he was enjoying his Christmas as much as she was enjoying hers. It had crossed her mind that someone in the Roberts' household might speak of her but dismissed the thought as a remote possibility. Nick would be too wrapped up in his first Christmas with Kathy to mention Sally to his brother. The thought of Nick no longer disturbed her as it did. When he did cross her mind, it was usually in the context of carrying his child.

The baby had been unduly vigorous over the Christmas period as if he or she was enjoying the festivities too. After the first few months of barely putting any weight on at all, she now seemed to be expanding every day. She had long since given up trying to fit into her pencil skirts even with a piece of elastic between buttonhole and button. Betty, who was a couple of dress sizes larger than Sally, had given her an old gathered skirt.

That, and a couple of maternity smocks she'd bought in the Market Hall sufficed for day wear. She hated feeling so frumpy.

Now it was New Year's Eve and Phil had phoned to ask if he could come and see her. She didn't question her motives for wearing the purple dress again. The Parrotts were spending the evening with the guests in the Residents' Lounge, determined to see out the last of the old year and the start of 1957 on the television Bob had recently had installed. She and Phil would be able to use the small but cosy sitting room the Parrots used during their rare free times. After the kiss they'd exchanged on the night of her party, she was a little anxious about this meeting. She'd tried hard to ignore the sudden flare of passion between them. Had Pam questioned Phil after catching them close together in the hall? She knew Pam had been suspicious.

He was late which surprised her. It seemed out of keeping with what she knew of Phil's character and sparked a niggling worry that she tried to dismiss. He arrived some moments later but offered no apologies and the worry became a snake of suspicion. One look at his face as he moved from the dimness of the hall into the light of the sitting room told her. 'You know, don't you?' she said in a quiet voice.

'What? That the kid you're carrying is my brother's? Yes, I know.'

'Who told you? Was it Joyce?'

He appeared flummoxed. 'Joyce?'

'She and I got to know each other when we had looms next to each other in the mill.'

'I take it she doesn't know you're still pregnant?'

'No, of course not. You're the only one who knows.'

'Not quite,' he snapped. 'It was actually Mac, Nick's boss, who let slip who you were in the course of a conversation over a beer. He knows now.'

'He won't say owt, will he?' she asked in consternation.

'He's said he won't tell Nick, if that's what you're worried about.'

As she realised the import of what he was saying, she whispered, 'It must have been hard for you over Christmas, knowing what you know, and I'm sorry for that.'

'It bloody well ruined my Christmas,' he said. 'All I could think was that Nick had had his way with you and got you pregnant.'

'It weren't all down to Nick,' she said. 'I could have said no.'

'All this time I'd thought of you as having been taken advantage of by some lad who couldn't have cared less about the consequences.'

'It were never intended to happen. We took precautions.'

'I don't want to know the sordid details,' he said, his voice sharp. 'Whatever happened, however it happened, you lied not just to my brother, but to me. How did you think you were going to get away with it?'

She ignored his question. 'Funny how it's all right for lads to get their end away with girls but those same girls are expected to remain virgins. Bit of a contradiction that.' She was pleased to see her remark had taken him aback and he didn't know what to say.

'Besides,' she continued, 'I hadn't been with anyone else. And I'd loved Nick for years. I thought at long last we were getting together.'

'You were fooling yourself then, weren't you? He were using you.'

'Don't you think I didn't know that when I woke up and found him gone,' she said, tears clogging her throat. 'I felt cheap then but it were too late.'

Seeing her distress, he too calmed down. 'How do you think it makes me feel knowing my brother has … put you in the club? Especially after what happened on the night of your party … Well, never mind that. Do you still love him?'

'Honestly? I don't know. My whole life at the moment seems to be bound up with getting through this pregnancy. Beyond that I can't think.'

He stood and straightened his tie. 'Well, I guess there's not much else to say so I'd better be on my way.'

She knew she couldn't let him go like this. Admittedly, her interest in him had initially been because of his connection with Nick but over the last three months, he had become a part of her life and she would be saddened if they were to part like this. 'I'm truly sorry for spoiling your Christmas and for misleading you.'

He gave a half-hearted grin. 'Well, it weren't all bad. There were times when I could put what had happened behind me and enjoy being with the family.'

'How are they all? Has your Dad settled down after being in prison?' It was a strange relief to be able to ask him questions like this, now her secret was out. Well, at least one of her secrets. The other she had told no-one and never would.

'He's OK. I think Mam's had a harder time of settling down than he has. She got used to being independent.'

'And of course, losing your Brian wouldn't have helped.'

'No, that were hard for all of us. It were like a bright light had gone out of our lives.' He looked across at her as if it had dawned on him, too, that he could talk openly about his family now, knowing that she knew them all through Nick and Joyce. She thought she saw a softening in his face though that might have been with talking of Brian. 'By the way, when did you first realise it were me?' he said now.

'When you introduced yourself as Phil Roberts. It all clicked into place and I remembered seeing you years ago in the park when me and some other lasses were mucking about with your Nick and his mates.'

'I wondered why you dashed away so quickly that first day,' he said, realisation dawning. 'Do the Parrotts know your real name, by the way?'

'I had to tell them because of it being on my P45.'

'Look, Sally, I've said my piece and there's nowt else to say. Except that I'll stand by you in whatever way I can. After all,' he said, his voice sharpening, 'it's my nephew or niece you're carrying.'

'Thank you, Phil,' she whispered.

There was a discreet knock on the sitting room door and Bob poked his head in. 'Hello, lad. Betty said she thought you were here. We wondered if the two of you wanted to join us all in the Residents' Lounge.'

Phil looked at his watch. 'Thanks, Bob, but I'm meeting Pam.'

'Bring her back here if you like,' Bob offered.

'Thanks all the same but there's a few of us from the camp, with our girlfriends, and it wouldn't be fair on you.'

He left then, without mentioning seeing her again and she sensed something had disappeared from their budding friendship. That saddened her. The confrontation with Phil had left her feeling bereft, as if she'd lost something precious. Yet, in a contradictory way, she was glad she didn't have to pretend with him anymore. In only a short while, it would be a new year and, she hoped, a new start, though in what way, she could not envisage. All her thoughts now were centred on the soon-to-be-pressing problem of the baby.

* * *

The house in Lancaster Avenue was quiet when Joyce got back home on New Year's Eve but there was a note from her mother. 'Have gone round to the Browns with your Dad,' Mam had written. 'I've kept popping back but will you keep an eye on the kids when you get in? You know where to find me if you need me.' The Browns were a lively family a couple of houses down and the two families had become friendly. She had been able to hear the revelry coming from their house as she had walked up the street and was glad for her parents' sake. Better by far than her Dad going off to the pub by himself.

The emptiness of the house reinforced the resentment she felt that she'd had to leave the New Year's Eve dance at the Wingates Band Room. It didn't seem fair, somehow, that she and her friends had had to leave the dance in full-swing simply because of the need to catch the last bus back to Horwich. But

91

they'd all been under strict instructions to be back home by half past eleven at the latest and that had been a special dispensation because it was New Year's Eve. She supposed it made sense because everyone still had to work tomorrow, despite it being New Year's Day.

Disconsolately, she stirred the fire with the poker, causing the coals to flare up with renewed vigour and, reaching for her Picturegoer magazine, settled herself on the sofa. Moments later, she was totally immersed in an article, looking up only when the door to the front room opened and her mother entered.

'Ah, you're home,' Mary Roberts said. 'Did you have a good night, love?'

'Yes, thanks, Mam,' she said, then looked at her mother in amazement. Gone was the drab woman of every day. Instead Mam was wearing a raspberry-coloured tailored dress which Joyce remembered as hanging in the dim reaches of the old wardrobe in Mam and Dad's bedroom. The vivid hues of the dress had brought colour to her cheeks and her greying fair hair, normally worn in a wispy bun, now hung loose but pinned back at the sides with gold-coloured combs. 'Mam, you look lovely. What have you been doing with yourself?'

Mary smoothed the fabric over her hips. 'I thought I'd make a bit of an effort, it being New Year's Eve. And I've had this dress years.'

'The colour suits you, Mam. And I like your hair like that.'

She patted her hair self-consciously. 'Aye, I thought I'd let my hair down a bit. Literally. I've moped around long enough.' A shadow passed momentarily over her face. 'Our Brian wouldn't have wanted that.'

'You'd never have got him to bed quietly like Derek,' Joyce laughed. 'He'd have been wanting to go to the party with you.'

'It's hardly a party, love,' Mary protested. 'Just a bit of a get-together with the Browns and a few of their friends. And,' she said with a mischievous twinkle in her eyes, 'it means I can keep more of an eye on your Dad.'

'I'm surprised he agreed to go.'

'I said I were going and I don't think he liked the idea of me going on my own.'

'You do right, Mam.'

'I'll go and check the kids are all right then I'll be getting back before midnight. Your Dad'll be letting the New Year in later,' she said, then was gone.

Despite the warmth from the now-glowing fire, the room felt colder without Mam's glowing presence and Joyce wondered what her Dad thought to his invigorated wife. It was a pity the same couldn't be said about her father. Big-bellied, loud, with a deeply lined face and thinning dark hair, he largely went his own way and to hell with everyone else.

A thunderous knocking on the front door roused her from the light doze she'd fallen into. She grinned. That'd be her Dad, First Footing round the neighbourhood, as he usually did. Except when she glanced at the clock, she saw it wasn't midnight yet.

When she opened the door, it was to find Dave on the doorstep with a semi-conscious Nick draped over his shoulder. 'Let me in, Joyce, love. Your Nick's a bloody dead weight,' he gasped, his good-looking face showing obvious signs of strain.

Without questioning him further, she held the front room door wider so that Dave could struggle in with his burden. He laid Nick carefully on the sofa and stretched up, his breathing heavy.

She bent over Nick, loosening his bootlace tie and collar. 'What's happened? I thought Nick were seeing Kathy this evening.'

He blew loudly through his lips. 'He were, but at the last minute, Kathy had to stay behind. You know her father's seriously ill? Well, he's taken a turn for the worse. So Nick came looking for me.'

'But how did he get this bad so quickly?'

He grimaced. 'Someone slipped him a Mickey Finn.'

'Don't tell me, Jud Simcox.'

'I think it were meant for me only Nick grabbed my drink by mistake.'

93

She put her hand to her mouth. 'Oh, no!'

'Fraid so. That's why I had to bring Nick home. Least I could do.'

'I'm glad you were there. What should we do with him though?'

'Leave him, I guess. He doesn't seem too distressed, does he?'

She looked at her brother critically. Nick had a beatific look on his face and she had to smile. 'No, wherever he is, he's completely out of it.'

'So, Joyce?' Dave said, a querying note in his voice.

As she turned to look at him, she caught her breath at the intensity of his look. He opened his arms and she stepped into them. 'Happy New Year, love,' he whispered, his lips against hers.

'Happy New Year,' she whispered back. If they didn't count the near-comatose form of Nick on the sofa behind them, they were alone for the first time in ages, and they were intensely conscious of it, kissing and whispering words of love.

Finally, she leaned back in his embrace. 'Nice though this is, Dave, you really ought to go before my Dad comes First Footing it.'

'Just another few minutes,' he begged, stopping her whispered protests with yet more kisses.

They were roused, finally, with a firm knock at the front door, followed by a raucous rendition of 'Auld Lang Syne.'

'Too late,' she said. 'You'd better leave by the back door.'

'Damn, I were hoping to stay a bit longer.'

'Come on, I'll let you out but you'll have to wait in the alley until I've let Dad in.'

There was a more persistent knocking on the door. 'Come on, Joyce, let me in. I know you're in there. Your Mam said so.'

They were creeping through the hallway when the letter box rattled and her father peeped through it. 'Who've you got in there, Joyce?' he said, suspicion in every word. They heard him trying to put his key in the lock, his judgement flawed with the drink. With a despairing look at Dave, she opened the door and her father stumbled in. 'What's going on, then?' He was shaking his head from side to side as if to clear it. Then, as he caught sight of Dave, he yelled, 'What the bloody hell is he doing here? Have you been sneaking him in behind our backs?'

They stood, the two of them, as if paralysed, not knowing what to say, afraid to say anything in case they incriminated themselves further.

'Well?' her father demanded, his head turning from one to the other of them, his hands hanging limply by his side. He'd obviously had quite a lot to drink for he was swaying slightly.

'Bragger brought me home, Dad.' This came from Nick, who must have been roused by all the commotion. He stood in the doorway, his hands holding on to the door jamb on either side for support. 'Oh, bugger! I'm going to be sick' With a hand over his mouth, he pushed past the three of them and dashed up the stairs to the bathroom.

'What's up with him?' Danny spluttered.

'Someone slipped him a Mickey Finn, Dad,' Joyce explained, her voice not quite steady, 'and Dave had to bring him home. He's not been here long and he was just going when you knocked.' She darted a quick glance at Dave and he took her meaning.

'That's right, Mr Roberts. Nick were in a bit of a state and I couldn't leave him, could I?'

'I suppose not,' her father conceded grudgingly. 'But I'm not going until you've gone down the street. And Joyce, you're coming back to the Browns with me.'

She shook her head. 'No, Dad. I'll stay here with Nick. He shouldn't be left alone.' She could hear him retching in the bathroom. 'And Mam asked me to keep an eye on the kids.'

'All right, then. But he's out of here now,' he said, pointing first at Dave then at the open door. In his semi-inebriated state, his finger wavered between them and Joyce had to bite back the laughter.

'It's all right, Mr Roberts. I'm on my way now.' With a last lingering look at Joyce, he went through the doorway, then turned at the last minute. 'Say ta-ra to Nick for me, will you? Not that he'll be in a fit state to appreciate it.'

'I will, Dave, and thanks again for bringing him home.' She gave him a last look, trying to put as much emotion and feeling into it as it suddenly dawned on her that she didn't know when she would see him again. She shut the door behind him and turned to face her father, expecting him to say something further.

Instead, he gave her an inane grin and said, 'Happy New Year, Joyce.' It was only then she saw he was holding the traditional offerings of a knob of coal and a chunk of bread.

CHAPTER 11

A few days before the Parrotts were due to go on holiday, the phone rang. 'Oh, who the hell is that?' Betty said, in the middle of making a list of what she wanted to take.

'I'll get it,' Sally said, reaching for the receiver. 'Shangri-la Guest House.'

'Can I speak to Mrs Parrott, please?' a woman's voice said.

'Who's speaking, please?'

'Val Drake. She'll know who I am.'

Sally held the receiver out to Betty. 'Someone called Val Drake for you.'

'Oh, she's Aunt Lily's neighbour. I hope nothing's wrong.'

Betty listened for a few minutes before sitting down suddenly on a chair, then said, 'Thanks for letting me know. I'll ring you back once I know what we're doing.' She replaced the receiver then turned to Bob. 'Aunt Lily's died, Bob. We're going to have to go up there and sort things out.'

'Miserable old sod never did have any sense of timing,' Bob grumbled.

'I don't see what we can do, love. You know I'm Aunt Lily's next of kin.'

He sighed. 'Well, that's buggered our holiday up right good and proper.'

Within only a short time, the holiday was cancelled and arrangements made for the Parrotts to go to the Lake District to sort out the funeral arrangements and clear the house.

By the time they were ready to leave, Betty was in a rare flap and worried about leaving Sally completely alone, with her being pregnant.

Bob attempted to soothe her. 'Stop worrying, Betty. It's no different than if we were going on holiday.'

'Bob's right. I'll be fine, honestly,' Sally said, hoping she sounded more confident than she felt. If she was truthful, she'd been dreading this for the past few weeks.

'Betty, love, we need to go now,' Bob urged, indicating the waiting taxi outside the open front door. 'Otherwise we're going to miss the train.'

'I'm coming! I'm coming,' was Betty's exasperated response. 'Now you're sure we've remembered everything?'

Bob took hold of Betty's arm and propelled her closer to the street. 'What we've forgotten, we'll have to do without.'

She shrugged her arm away from his. 'I meant have we remembered to tell Sally everything.'

'If you haven't, there's always the telephone,' Sally consoled.

'The Robinson's telephone number!' Betty said. 'Did I write it down?'

Sally laughed and picked up the lengthy list Betty had made from where it lay on the hall table. 'It's on here, Betty. Now go!'

The silence, once the door had closed behind them, seemed immense and she stood, absorbing it, for long moments, aware for the first time of her complete solitude. Betty and Bob would be away for the best part of two weeks and for most of that time, she would be alone, something she'd never experienced before. Although her family situation hadn't been ideal, there'd always been someone there.

Then, straightening her shoulders, she marched through to the kitchen where she made herself a cup of tea. She sat at the table, nursing the mug in both hands, as she took stock of her situation. Sandra and the other girls had promised to come and visit and Mrs Robinson had said she'd pop in from time to time but there was no one to rely on but herself and her own resourceful nature.

The first night, she barely slept, so frightened was she. Now there no guests, the boarding house seemed larger than ever, the dining room and residents' lounge echoing emptily. Heightened emotions meant that even slight noises were magnified. She was glad when a lightening of the room told her it was morning and she could get up and make herself a much-needed cup of tea. She was so exhausted the following night that she slept straight through, rousing only when her bladder starting screaming for relief.

To keep herself occupied over the next few days, she tackled some of the items on Betty's 'to do' list. When she realised that she'd got a fair way through the list, she slackened off, allowing herself to rest more often with her feet up on the sofa, a mug of tea to hand, a book to read and the wireless playing softly in the background. The quiet rhythm of the days took over and she found she was falling asleep more easily and more often. She felt cocooned, she and her baby, in an oasis of warmth and security.

As if to remind her she wasn't completely alone, the baby gave her a swift kick under the ribs. She smiled softly, stroking the area where a small foot might be. In response, there was another kick, more gentle this time, under her fingers. She lay on the sofa, stroking her belly, in silent wonderment at the miracle taking place under the layers of skin and muscle. She tried to guess what the baby would look like. A miniature version of Nick would be nice, she thought. She was no longer thinking of Nick with an ache in her heart. Her feelings for him had been transferred to this precious bundle she was carrying.

Thoughts of Nick led to thinking of Phil. He hadn't been in touch since New Year's Eve and she missed his quiet strength and dependability. Although their contact had only been infrequent, he had been there in the background. Somehow she had known he would have come if she'd needed him. Still, the rift had occurred and there was no point in fretting about it. She rose and rinsed her mug out at the sink, stacking it on the drainer.

Later that evening, as she was making scrambled egg for her tea, the phone rang. With a sigh of annoyance, she pulled the pan off the stove and answered. The caller proved to be Bob. 'Sally, are you okay?'

'Yes, I'm fine.'

'Listen, love, there's a storm coming tonight and by all accounts, it's going to be a bad one. Will you make sure all the windows and doors are secure?'

'I will, Bob. Thanks for warning me.'

'If you've any problems, say windows smashing or loose tiles, Mrs Robinson will have telephone numbers of tradesmen you can contact. And give us a ring if there's anything you're not sure of. Val's said we can use her phone any time we need it.'

'Bob, I'll be fine. I'll cope.' She didn't tell him of the jolt of fear she'd felt with his words.

'I'll pass you over to Betty. She wants a word.'

There were whispered words between Betty and Bob then she took over the phone. 'Hello, Sally, love. How are you? Coping okay?'

'Yes thanks. I went a bit mad to begin with but I've slowed down now,' she said. 'How's it going up there?'

'Slowly. The funeral's fixed for next week. In the meantime, we've made a start on the house.' Sally heard Bob say something in the background and Betty gave a short laugh. 'Bob's just saying that with the clutter Aunt Lily's left behind, it'll take us weeks. He's got a point though. There's so much stuff here that I don't know how we're going to sort through it in the time available.'

'If there's a lot of paperwork, why don't you pack it all in boxes and bring them back with you to go through at your leisure?' she suggested.

'That's a good idea.' Sally heard Bob say something else then Betty spoke again. 'Better go, love, Auntie's neighbour's made us a cup of tea and it's going cold.'

So's my scrambled egg, thought Sally, but said nothing. She threw it away and had a boiled egg instead. By the time she was ready for bed, the wind had risen only slightly and she couldn't help wondering if Bob had panicked more than necessary. To be sure, she checked all the windows and doors, not only of the boarding house but the café. All seemed safe and secure.

She woke sometime after midnight to find the wind was now howling, rattling both the window and the bedroom door. She got up to peer outside but could see nothing for the rain now lashing against the glass. She shivered in the draught from the window and scooted back to the warmth of her bed. Not to sleep though. Sleep was impossible, the noise from the wind and the rain was thunderous. The force of the storm was so intense that, for the first time, she felt fear at its power and very much aware of her isolation. She yearned suddenly for the comfort of her sister's body next to her, as she had when she'd been at home with her family. A few tears of self-pity trickled out of her eyes and she swiped them away. This wouldn't do at all, she told herself. She had to get through this night as best she could.

At that point, there was such a fierce gust it seemed the whole house shook. With it, came the sound of crashing glass and she shot down in her bed, clutching the eiderdown closer around her. Yet she knew she had to investigate, despite wanting to stay under the covers. She pulled on the dressing gown the Parrotts had bought her for Christmas and thrust her feet into slippers then, her heart hammering, she climbed the stairs to the attic, intending to start there and work her way down.

The broken window proved to be her old attic room and was glad she wasn't still sleeping there. The problem appeared to be a piece of guttering that had come loose and smashed against the glass, breaking it. She inspected the damage as best she could, being wary of the jagged remainder of the window and any glass on the floor but there was nothing she could do until morning. In the meantime, rain was coming in through the hole and already pooling on the floor. Then she remembered the pile of old and threadbare towels Betty kept against such emergencies. Gathering an armful from the huge cupboard on the landing below, she climbed back to the attic again, wadding them over the pool of rainwater to soak up the worst.

The wind had reached such ferocity by this time that she knew there would be little chance of sleep in her bedroom. She'd be better off by the range in the kitchen, curled up on the one shabby armchair for what remained of the night. Pausing in her own room long enough to grab her eiderdown from the bed, she went downstairs to the still warm kitchen. The fire in the range, banked up for the night, took a little time to perk into life again but she succeeded in the end. Down here, the wind was audible only in the chimney as it whistled and whined down, causing the newly revived flames to dance in agitation. After making a mug of cocoa, she snuggled in the eiderdown and the armchair until both were moulded around her body. Here she felt safe from the worst of the storm. There was nothing more she could do but wait out the night and hope too much damage wasn't being done.

She woke some time later as it was getting light to find the fire had nearly died down. Putting fresh coal on, she reflected on the night just past. The fear she had felt at being so alone on so wild and night was, to her surprise, already fading from her memory. Alone, she had survived one of the worst storms she could ever remember.

Mrs Robinson was her first caller that morning. She came round early, while Sally was still enjoying her first cup of tea. When Sally, mug of tea in her hand, opened the door to her, she bustled in. One of the no-nonsense breed of Blackpool landladies, she was plump and capable and Sally was glad to see her.

'Eeh, love, I've been that worried about you, all on your own in your condition, I had to come round straight away. How are you?' she asked, concern on her round, open face.

Sally, still feeling the remains of the euphoria at having come through the night, laughed. 'As you can see, Mrs Robinson, I've survived.'

'What a storm that was!' The older woman leaned against the sideboard. 'Have you any damage?'

'Some of the guttering came loose and smashed an attic window, but I don't know if there's owt else,' Sally reported.

'My Joe went out into the street and, by the looks of it, you've lost a couple of ridge tiles. Same as us. He'll get onto our roofing man this morning for both of us. And we've the number of a glazier who'll put you new glass in. I'll get Joe to ring him for you if you like.'

'Yes, please, Mrs Robinson. Has there been much damage that you know of?'

'Most of it'll be roof tiles lifting, I'm guessing. Oh, and the milkman said a chimney had come down in Palatine Road. He reckons it's made a right mess of their roof, gone right through into one of the bedrooms.' Mrs Robinson had an air of self-importance to be relaying this information which made Sally smile.

She was glad nothing like that had occurred at the Shangri-la. The crash from the broken window had been enough of a shock as it was.

'I'd better get back home now, love, but come round if you've any more problems or need me. Promise?' The older woman lifted her eyebrows in a query.

'I will and thanks for sorting out the tradesmen for me.'

'No problem. Mind you,' she lifted a finger as if in warning, 'whether they'll be able to come today remains to be seen.'

'It'll depend on how much structural damage there's been, won't it?'

'It will that but the ones we use are all good blokes so they'll do their best for us, I'm sure.' As she made to exit the kitchen, she stopped by the back door. 'I do think you're brave, Sally, staying all on your own in this big house, especially with you expecting a baby. When is it due?'

Sally put a protective hand to her belly. 'Mid-April, the doctor thinks.'

'Not so long now, then. Will your husband be able to get back in time?'

For a long moment, Sally was flummoxed then remembered she was supposed to have a husband in the Army. 'I don't know,' she said, the lie sitting uncomfortably with her. 'It depends on circumstances.'

'Caught up in this Suez affair, is he? Well, that's understandable though it does seem as if it's on the way to being resolved.' She was having to hold the door to stop it banging to. Although the wind had dropped considerably, it was still gusting from time to time. 'Now don't forget, me and Joe are only next door.'

Soon after Mrs Robinson left, the phone rang. It was Bob checking first of all to see if she was all right and secondly, if there had been any damage. She told him about the guttering and the window, mentioned the ridge tiles, but that the Robinsons had it all in hand. Reassured on all counts, he rang off.

It turned out to be a busy day with tradesmen calling to check the damage. None of the repairs were urgent, they said, and priority had to be given to people with more substantial damage. In the meantime, the glazier sent one of his lads round to fix some hardboard to the window so no more rain could come in.

By early afternoon and after her broken night's sleep, Sally was beginning to feel tired and had just settled down on the sofa when the front door bell rang. Groaning with the effort, she heaved herself up and went to answer it. To her surprise, her caller was Phil, in his RAF uniform.

He looked nervous, twisting his cap round in his fingers. 'Hello Sally. I had to come round and see if you were all right after the storm.'

She gaped at him from the open door.

He grinned. 'Aren't you going to let me in?'

'Sorry, yes.' She held the door open for him and he stepped inside the hall. 'How did you know I was on my own?'

'I remembered the Parrotts were due to go on holiday round about now.'

'The holiday was cancelled. Betty's aunt died and they've had to go and sort things out.' She led the way into the kitchen, glad of its welcoming warmth. She felt awkward in his presence after their confrontation on New Year's Eve.

'How long have they been gone?' he asked from inside the kitchen door.

'I can't remember. Five, six days?' The days had a way of blurring into each other. 'The funeral is sometime this week though so they should be back soon after that.'

'I don't like to think of you being on your own.' He was looking at her, a thoughtful look in his blue-grey eyes.

'Why should you care?' she snapped. 'You made your feelings plain enough last time you were here.'

He shifted his weight from one foot to the other, still running his cap between his fingers. 'Yes, I know I did. But, then, last night, with all the wild weather, well, I couldn't settle. I had to come over as soon as I could get away, to make sure you were all right.'

She stood stiffly, both hands on her belly. 'Well, as you can see, I'm fine and so is your nephew or niece.'

He winced. 'Ouch, I deserved that.' He gave a rueful grin. 'I see you're still wearing my necklace.'

Her hand flew to her neck and she turned to face him. 'Yes, I wear it all the time.'

'Nice to know you haven't completely forgotten me.'

No, she hadn't forgotten him. The rift between them had niggled. She knew now she should have been honest with him in the beginning, at least about who she was. What was that saying – something about what a tangled web we weave when first we practise to deceive? That had certainly been true for her. Now, though, they had a second chance at this bittersweet friendship with the barriers removed. That is, if Phil could overcome the hurdle of her carrying his brother's child. 'Would you like a cuppa and a slice of Betty's fruit cake?' she asked eventually.

'I'll take that as a peace offering then, shall I?' he asked grinning and sat down on the sofa, putting his cap down beside him.

* * *

105

Phil had thought that healing the rift with Sally would sort out his mixed emotions. It hadn't. If anything, he felt more confused than ever. He was supposed to be going out with Pam Gregory, yet he was having feelings for another young woman, who was pregnant with his brother's child. The knowledge was like a burr trapped between his clothes and his skin, pricking when he least expected it. It would have been easier if he could have ended their friendship yet he found he could not. He thought back to the time he had gone to see her after the storm. It had not been easy to go but on the night of the storm when the wind had howled through the billet finding any gaps around windows and floorboards, he had been unable to sleep for worrying about her alone in that big house. He'd rushed through his work that day and asked permission of the duty officer for a couple of hours off camp and been given a 1250 pass to discover that Sally was not only unperturbed but proud of the fact that she'd survived the night alone.

Now he and Pam were seated in the Bellisima Coffee Bar where they'd come to escape a biting wind. Here, everything was too slick, with gleaming Formica tables, chrome stools anchored to the floor, a hissing espresso coffee machine and the walls covered with scenes from Naples, Venice and Rome. It was the 'in' place to come if you were young but if he was honest, Phil preferred the homely atmosphere of Bob's Café.

'You're not much company this afternoon, Phil,' Pam said. There was no hint of censure in her voice, merely concern. Pam was one of the sweetest natured girls he'd ever come across, generous and warm-hearted, which made him feel even more guilty about his feelings for Sally. He knew Pam was more than a little in love with him and he wished, sincerely, he could feel the same about her. 'Sorry, love, I was miles away.'

'Anywhere interesting?'

He groaned inwardly. If only she knew. 'I was thinking how everything has changed in this last year and wondering what the future might hold.'

Instantly, her eyes brightened and he could see she'd put the wrong interpretation on his remark. 'It were summat I heard on the wireless the other day, some current affairs programme, I think,' he said quickly. 'One of these programmes that takes a look back at the year just gone.'

'I didn't know you were interested in current affairs.' The light had gone out of her eyes but at least he had diverted her.

'I met someone at Christmas who impressed me by his knowledge of what was going on in the world. Since then, I've been taking more of an interest by reading newspapers.'

'What was it that made such an impression on you then?'

'The commentator were saying what a cataclysmic year 1956 had been, what with the Suez Crisis and the Hungarian Revolution.'

'But haven't they petered out with no satisfactory conclusion to either?'

'Aye, but there'll be repercussions for years to come. And we still have petrol rationing to remind us about Suez.' Looking across the table at Pam, he could see her eyes had glazed over. He put his hand over hers. 'I'm sorry, love. I'm boring you.'

'No, no! It's just that ...'

'What?'

'I thought you might be thinking about our future,' she said in a small voice.

Feeling suddenly uncomfortable and a little hot under the collar, he said, 'In what way?'

'Well, we've been going out together now for six months and I wondered ...' Her voice tailed away and a flush had crept up her face from her neck.

'Go on,' he urged.

'Whether you ... what you feel ...about me.' Her face was fiery red now.

Alarm bells rang in his mind. At the same time, he didn't want to upset her. She was too nice a person for that. 'If I'm honest, Pam, I don't really know.' Her face fell and he thought he saw the glisten of tears in her eyes. 'I'm very fond of you, really I am, but I hadn't thought too much about a future for us. Not at this stage. I mean,' he hurried on, 'I'm bound to get posted somewhere else sooner or later.'

'Move away from Kirkham, you mean?' She looked shocked, as if she'd never thought of the possibility before.

'Yes, I'm unlikely to be stationed there forever. I've been there much longer than I thought as it is.'

'Couldn't you buy yourself out? Make a new life for yourself here in Blackpool. I'm sure Dad would be able to find you a job somewhere.'

'Pam, love, I'm a regular. I'm in for the duration,' he pointed out. 'It's what I want to do. I can't really see myself working on a building site. My brother used to be a labourer and he hated it.'

'Do you want us to finish then?' she asked in a small voice.

'Not see each other again, you mean?' When she nodded, he continued, 'Of course not. I'm quite happy to carry on the way we are. I just can't think of a future for us at the moment. I mean, we're both only twenty.' He knew what the problem was, of course. Girls of Pam's age were under pressure to either be seriously courting or engaged by the time they were twenty-one. If they weren't, they were considered to be 'on the shelf.' Part of the courting ritual was visiting your girlfriend's parents for Sunday tea and he'd done that several times already. Yet he'd never taken Pam home to meet his parents and he knew she'd probably wondered about that too. It wasn't as easy as taking tea with the Gregory's because of the distance involved and the need to get a pass for long enough.

He sighed, thinking back to the time when they'd met. It had been at another dance at the camp some time last year. He'd seen her standing with some other girls and been taken with her ready smile, her slim figure and curly auburn hair. He'd asked her to dance, they'd hit it off straight away and had been going out together ever since. It was a comfortable, easy-going relationship, built on mutual liking and respect. Only since Sally had come into his life had he questioned his feelings for Pam. Which wasn't fair on the girl sitting opposite him now. She deserved better than that. He made a determined effort to put his often-ambivalent feelings for Sally into proper perspective.

CHAPTER 12

Sally held on to the arm of the chair as she lowered her now-bulky body into its depths. She seemed to have put on so much weight since the New Year and she still had another couple of months to go. Although she loved this baby as much as it was possible to love it, she couldn't wait for her time to come. Everything was getting to be an effort and she hadn't been able to help the Parrotts with the decorating as much as she'd hoped. Instead, she concentrated on the lighter tasks and prepared meals for them. They'd been so good to her, despite her circumstances, and she knew she was lucky to have found them. And it was all down to Phil rescuing her that day.

He had taken to coming round whenever he happened to have any free time. Knowing who she was, seemed to have brought an unseen barrier down and they were more able to relax in each other's company than previously. Occasionally, when he came, they would go out for a drink or, if it was an afternoon, he would accompany her on her usual stroll. No more striding out for her these days. Instead, she waddled, which she hated. Still, she enjoyed getting out of the house whenever the weather allowed. She had now seen Blackpool in all its moods, the Edwardian gentility of the tightly packed guest houses, the soaring splendour of the larger hotels, the tackiness of the Golden Mile and the Pleasure Beach, the old-fashioned trams that trundled up and down the Promenade and had come to love it all. Would she settle here permanently? She liked to think so but much depended on what she decided about the baby. Until he or she was born, her life was on hold.

She looked across to where Betty and Bob were wading through a box of Betty's aunt's papers. There'd been seven boxes in all and they'd been going through some of the paperwork each evening. This one, the largest, was so old the sides were bending inwards. It seemed to be taking an inordinate amount of time to sort through, especially as they kept getting distracted by the box's contents. Mostly they were old bills or receipts, some of them dating back to the early part of the century, cuttings of recipes or articles from wartime newspapers or an occasional postcard or letter.

'Do you want me to give you a hand?' Sally asked now, pointing to the pile of papers in Betty's hand.

'Would you? That'd be a big help,' Betty replied, passing her the wodge of papers from her hand. 'If you come across anything legal, it could be to do with the house so save those. Any old bills or receipts can be thrown out, no point in saving those, but put the letters to one side and we can read them later. I'd like to keep some of them.'

The house in Kendal had been left to Betty but, rather than sell it, they had decided to keep it. The intention was to do it up then rent it out as a holiday home. It was added security for their future. When they eventually retired, it would be to the house in the Lake District, which they both loved.

The three of them sat contentedly, music drifting out from the old wireless on the sideboard in the sitting room, sifting through the papers. It was a slow process; one or the other of them would be distracted and read something out. By the looks of the pile of discarded papers at their feet, Bob would be having a good bonfire at some point.

'What's that envelope?' Betty pointed to where a letter had fluttered from Sally's hand on to the chair at the side of her.

Sally picked up the envelope. 'It's a letter addressed to a Mrs B Hutton.'

'That was my grandmother. Read it to us, love, will you?' Betty said.

Sally drew the single sheet of paper from the creased envelope and scanned the signature. 'It's dated 1932 and it's from someone called Ada Thompson.'

'That's the year our baby was born,' Betty mused. 'And Thompson's not a name I'm familiar with. Go on, read it.'

The writing was looped and scrawling and she had a little difficulty with some words. 'Dear Mrs Hutton. This is just a brief note to let you know that the baby has …' When she got to the word 'baby,' she stopped, looking across at Betty, who had gasped and dropped the papers she was holding. Clutching at Bob's hand, she waved at Sally to continue. '… Settled in well. We love him dearly already and have decided to call him Peter. Thank you so much for arranging it all. You have made our lives complete. As promised, I shan't write again.' Sally looked over to where Betty had paled while Bob looked stricken.

'My baby … he didn't die! Grandma lied to me.' Betty gasped now. 'Bob, our baby, our son … somewhere he's alive.'

'I can't believe this! That old witch … Sorry, love, I know she was your grandmother, but to do such a thing … how could she?' Bob exclaimed.

'I'll go and make us a cuppa,' Sally said, pushing herself up out of the armchair. She handed the letter to Bob who stared at it, as if unable to take in its contents. When she left them, Bob was shaking his head in bewilderment.

By the time she came back into the sitting room, a tray of tea balanced for stability on her bump, the couple had had time to compose themselves and Bob was reading the letter again to Betty, as if to glean more from its sparse contents. Betty was clutching a handkerchief in tense hands. 'One thing has occurred to me, love, your grandmother couldn't have been as hard-hearted as all that,' he said.

'How do you reckon that?' Her voice was thick with unshed tears.

He tapped the letter. 'Well, she'd obviously asked the Thompsons to let her know how the baby was settling in.'

Betty nodded in agreement 'No, she wasn't a bad woman. It would have all been my mother's idea, I'm sure.'

111

'I wonder why your grandmother didn't destroy the letter.'

'Could it have been in the hope it would be discovered one day?' Sally asked.

Betty held out a trembling hand for the cup of tea Sally had poured. 'I doubt that, Sally. My aunt looked after my grandmother till she died and then stayed on in the house. These papers would have been there long before she died. If Auntie had known about this letter, she would have destroyed it. She and Mum were very close and would have supported each other through everything.'

'What will you do now?' Sally handed Bob the mug he always used.

The couple looked at each other, seemingly of one mind as usual. 'We'll hire a private detective,' Bob said.

'With a name like Peter Parrott, he shouldn't be too hard to track down,' Betty said, then gave a short laugh. 'What a name to saddle a child with! Peter Parrott!'

'Except he won't be called that, will he?' Sally pointed out. 'He will have been registered under the name of Peter Thompson.'

'Of course, I'm not thinking straight. Where was the letter sent from, Bob?'

H scrutinised the sheet of paper again. 'It's an address in Kendal.'

'Not too far from Auntie's house. My guess is the Thompsons must have been known to my grandmother, if not well, at least enough to know they wanted to adopt a child.'

'I wonder whether it was done officially?' Bob mused.

'I don't suppose my grandmother, being of a different generation, would worry too much about formal adoption. There would have been the cost implication too.'

Sally picked up her own cup from the tray and made as if to leave the room. 'I'll go to my room and leave you both to discuss what's happened.'

Betty put out a hand to stop her. 'No, love, stay. You're part of this family now and you've as much right to be here with us, better in fact, than our son.' She pointed to the letter, still in

Bob's hands. 'After all, you've become part of our lives and, like it or not, he hasn't.'

'Even if we do find him, Betty love, it's been 25 years and he may not even know he was adopted.'

'I know that, Bob. But just knowing he's alive somewhere helps. If we can find him, it would be even better.'

'We'd have to decide if, or how, we can approach him.'

The three of them talked long into the night about the implications of the situation until the fire died down and they were forced to their beds. Even Sally found her mind was too full of events to sleep well and she found herself thinking of her own baby. She tried to imagine how it would be to be told your baby had died, the anguish Betty must have gone through, but she couldn't and deliberately turned her mind to more positive things.

* * *

The hot and steamy atmosphere of Harry Stocker's Temperance Bar in Horwich was welcome after the bitter cold of the late February day as Joyce and her three friends laughingly piled in from the street. Someone obligingly moved up for them and the four girls were able to squeeze onto one of the corner tables. 'Phew! It's busy in here this evening,' commented Brenda.

'Everyone must have had the same idea, to get out of the cold,' Joyce said.

'I don't mind,' said Maureen, the girl next to her. 'Adds to the atmosphere.'

'Anyone we know in here?' queried Sheila, peering round the fuggy, smoky room.

'There's always someone we know,' laughed Joyce, while casting a quick glance round the room in case Dave was in. 'Horwich is that sort of place.'

'Too much so, if you ask me. You can't get away with owt here,' sniffed Brenda.

'Don't look now, but Jud Simcox and his mates have just come in,' whispered Sheila, giving Joyce a nudge in the ribs.

Joyce hung her head and buried her nose in the distinctive white Vimto mug, breathing in the rich blackcurrant fumes. 'Oh, no! I can't get away from him these days.'

Maureen had seen her furtive action and leaned closer to Joyce and Sheila. 'What are you two whispering about?'

Sheila gave Joyce a questioning look to which Joyce nodded her assent. 'Jud's been mithering Joyce to go out with him'.

'Ugh, horrible!' Maureen gave a mock shudder. 'He's creepy.'

The three older lads, Jud and his two mates, Bill Murphy and Jim Stevens, stood out among the crowd of younger lads and lasses, most of whom were in early to late teens. The three stood in the doorway, a sneering look on their faces, and a deep silence fell over the crowd of youngsters. Then everyone started chattering at once. Joyce had kept her head down all the time but it was to no avail. 'Hello, Joyce. How are you?' Jud stood at the side of the table. Bill and Jim had stayed in the doorway, positioned so she could not have made her escape without brushing past them. Not for the first time, she felt trapped in Jud's presence and wished desperately he'd leave her alone.

She didn't answer his question, merely forced out the words, 'Er, hello, Jud.'

He cast disparaging looks over the other three girls. 'These your mates?'

'Yes, we bloody well are,' snapped Sheila. 'What's it to do with you?'

'I don't give a shit. I was just making conversation,' Jud retorted. 'You off to the pictures?'

'Yes, eventually.'

'Might go there ourselves. Which one are you going to?'

Joyce looked at the other three and gave a small shake of her head. 'We haven't made our minds up yet.' Although they'd already decided they were going to Johnny's, the other three kept quiet and she blessed them for it.

Sensing perhaps he wasn't going to get anywhere with her friends there, he turned to walk away. Then he stopped and faced her again. 'By the way, have you heard owt from our Sal recently?'

'No, I haven't.' She wasn't lying. She'd received only the one letter at the beginning and Joyce was now a little worried about her former workmate.

'OK. See you around some time,' he said over his shoulder as he walked away.

'Not if I see you first,' hissed Joyce but not loud enough for him to hear.

The four of them giggled, as much with the release of tension as anything else, as they watched the three older lads leave. 'Good riddance to bad rubbish, I say!' muttered Maureen.

'I suppose their mothers must love them,' Sheila said, laughing.

'Happen the only way any of them can get a girl is through intimidation.' Joyce shivered as she remember what Kathy had told her about Jud and Bill Murphy grabbing her one night in Coffin Alley. No harm had come to her because Nick had come to her rescue.

A short time later, the four girls were heading up Lee Lane towards the Princes' Arcade, where the run-down cinema of Johnny's was located. She had deliberately led them this way so they wouldn't have to go through Coffin Alley, the quicker route. The small incident in Harry Stocker's was too recent and she wasn't taking any chances.

All to no avail because as they turned into the Arcade, they were faced with Jud and his two mates, all of them looking smug. In what was clearly a planned approach, Bill and Jim moved in between them cutting off Sheila, Brenda and Maureen from Joyce, who'd been on the outside. Somehow they got the other three girls backed into a corner and held out their arms to stop them forcing a way past. Joyce looked round for an escape route but the Arcade was too busy to push a way through, laughing gangs of lads and lasses probably thinking this was a bit of horseplay. Jud grabbed Joyce's arm. 'Got you now, my girl,' he whispered, lunging closer to her.

She struggled against his grip but he hung on. 'I'm not letting you go until you give me a kiss.'

'Never,' she said, casting desperate looks around her but there was no-one to help her. The last of the groups were disappearing into the cinema.

'It's no use you looking for Bragger Yates. He's not here tonight. Now, are you going to give me a kiss?' In answer she clamped her lips together. 'Well, if you're not going to co-operate …' He yanked her closer to him until she was within inches of his pock-marked face, his grip on her arm now so tight she was surprised later to find she hadn't been bruised. She deliberately turned her head away.

Then, suddenly, Brenda was there and she was batting Jud about the head with her handbag. 'You bastard! Leave her alone.'

Under her continued assault, he was forced to let Joyce go. 'You crazy bitch, give over!' he yelled, holding his hands above his head in an attempt to stop Brenda.

'You're depraved, you are, lusting after young girls like us,' Brenda said, continuing her assault. Jud's two mates, taken by surprise by Brenda's escape, now gave way to an incensed Sheila and Maureen who had followed Brenda's example and were using their own handbags as assault weapons.

'Enough, enough!' cried Jud. 'I'm out of here, come on lads.' With a venomous look back at Joyce, he sprinted off towards the Billiard Hall, Jim and Bill lumbering after him.

'Are you all right, Joyce?' There were two bright spots of anger on Brenda's cheeks.

Sheila and Maureen came up to them and the four of them clustered together. 'Yes, thanks to you,' Joyce said, clinging to her friends. 'How did you manage that, Brenda?'

The other girl giggled. 'There's a lot to be said for being thin and wiry. I were in the middle and it only took a second to duck under their arms. I think they were too busy watching you and Jud to realise what I were doing.'

'Seriously, love, you're going to have to watch yourself with that little slime ball, Jud Simcox,' Sheila said.

'I never thought he'd try a trick like that, with all four of us being together.' Joyce shuddered as she thought of those thin mean lips intending to kiss her.

'Does Bragger know?' Sheila asked now.

'Yes, he overheard him once. He'd go mad and I don't want him to get hurt.' Joyce squared her shoulders. 'No, I'll just have to make sure I'm never in a vulnerable position again.'

'You weren't today,' Maureen pointed out, 'but that didn't stop those thugs.'

'Do you mind if we don't go to the pictures tonight?' Joyce asked the others. 'I don't really feel like it now.' Where would it all end? Why was Jud so determined to pursue her, particularly when she had shown him how distasteful she found his advances?

CHAPTER 13

As Phil and Fred drove into Blackpool to pick Sally up to take her to the Mother and Baby Home at the beginning of March, Phil was feeling edgy on Sally's behalf. Now the time had come for her to go into the Home, she must be wondering what the future held for her.

'Everything all right, Phil?' Fred asked, one hand on the steering wheel, the other on the gear stick.

'Just thinking about Sally, how she's feeling right now,' Phil answered.

'Nervous, I should think. Not knowing what's to come. You'd think they'd let prospective … patients? inmates? Whatever they're called … visit to get a general idea of the place.'

Phil laughed. 'Might put them off, then where would they go?'

'How long does she have to be in for?' Fred swung skilfully onto Central Drive.

'Supposed to be six weeks before and six weeks after, depending on what she decides about the baby.'

'Has she thought about what she wants to do?'

'She'd like to keep it but she's realistic enough to know how difficult life would be if she did.'

And you don't know the half of it, Fred, old chum, Phil said under his breath, thinking of his brother's part in Sally's predicament. He gave a deep sigh as Fred pulled up at the Shangri-la. 'Give me a couple of minutes, Fred. I'll see if Sally's ready.'

She opened the door to his first ring as if she had been waiting for him. She was pale but composed, only the determined set of her mouth and the tightening of her fingers on the straps of her handbag betraying her tension. Behind her, with Sally's single suitcase, stood Betty, a worried look on her own face.

'Ready, Sally?' Phil asked though it was patently obvious she was, even down to her coat, which she now buttoned. It wouldn't meet all the way down and her belly protruded from its folds.

'As I ever will be,' she said quietly then turned to Betty. 'Bye, Betty.'

Betty put the suitcase on the floor and pulled the young woman into her arms to give her an enveloping hug. 'Bye, love. Keep your chin up.'

'I'll try,' Sally said, her voice muffled in Betty's shoulder.

Betty leaned back and looked into Sally's eyes. 'We'll be over to see you as soon as we can arrange it.'

Once settled into the back seat of the Austin, Sally said very little on the journey. In reply to Fred's query as to whether she was nervous, she gave a forced smile and said, 'Terrified.'

The directions Sally had been given to find the Mother and Baby Home were clear and, with Phil reading them out, Fred found it easily enough. Heywood House proved to be a large Victorian house set in its own grounds, a mile or so from the centre of Preston. The stone gateposts topped by ornamental balls were all that remained of what must once have been an imposing entrance. There was no indication it was a Mother and Baby Home, just a painted sign at the entrance announcing that this was Heywood House.

As Fred pulled up on the circular drive, Phil turned to Sally. He noticed that, if anything, she had gone even paler and her lips were clamped shut. 'Well, Sally, this is it.'

She gave him a quick smile and put her hand on the door handle. 'I know. I just want to get it over with now.'

He leapt out of the car and helped her out, knowing her bulk would make that difficult. Once she was out, she shrugged his hand away and marched up to the front porch, her back straight, her bump thrust forward. He couldn't help but admire her in the face of what must be a daunting prospect.

'Gutsy little madam, isn't she?' Fred said, leaning forward to speak to Phil and nodding towards Sally who was ringing the doorbell.

'She certainly is,' Phil agreed. 'All right if I go in with her?'

'Course. I'll be here when you come out.'

By the time Phil reached the porch, the door had opened to reveal another heavily pregnant girl with a round dumpling of a face lit up with a huge smile. 'Hello, are you Sally Simcox? I'm Mavis Johnson. Come in,' she held the door open to admit Sally. 'Is your boyfriend coming in too?'

A flush suffused Sally's face as she said, 'Oh, Phil's not my boyfriend. He's just a friend.'

'It doesn't matter. He can still come in, at least for a short while. Boyfriends – or male friends come to that – aren't usually allowed until Sunday afternoons, but it's OK for anyone who's brought you here to come in for a while,' Mavis explained.

Phil followed Sally with her suitcase. The entrance hall was large, with a tiled floor, the tiles broken and chipped in places, and an imposing staircase with heavy wooden newel post and banisters. 'Come through to the Common Room while I tell Matron you're here.' She turned to Phil and gave him an appraising look. 'I should warn you, the other girls are in there and you'll probably cause a bit of interest, especially wearing your uniform.'

He was glad she'd warned him because the Common Room held about half a dozen young women, all in an advanced stage of pregnancy, and they all stopped talking when Sally and Phil walked into the room. Faintly in the background, he caught the sound of a baby crying and guessed there must a nursery somewhere close. The Common Room must have previously been a large sitting room and there were still vestiges of its former glory in the curtained bay window overlooking a bedraggled front garden. Several armchairs and a couple of sofas made the room seem crowded. An old-fashioned sideboard held

121

books and boxes of board games. On the open leaf of a gate leg table, was a half completed jigsaw and a pile of magazines. In an alcove was old television set in a wooden cabinet. All this he took in while the conversation had stilled.

'Everyone, this is Sally Simcox, our new girl,' Mavis said, waving her arm around the room.

'Hello Sally,' came the chorus back.

'Sit down while I find Matron.' Mavis indicated one of several dining chairs ranged round the back of the room. 'Shan't be long.'

Phil didn't take the proffered seat though Sally did, lowering her bulk carefully. Her mouth, he noticed now, was trembling a little though she was making a determined effort to control it. His heart went out to her and he put his hand on her shoulder. Gratefully, she looked up at him and placed her hand over his, giving it a squeeze.

Mavis was gone only a couple of minutes before she re-entered the Common Room, followed by a bustling figure wearing a crisply starched uniform whom she introduced as Matron. 'Welcome to Heywood House, Sally.' Then she turned to Phil. 'And is this the young man concerned?'

Sally blushed again. 'Oh, no, Phil's the friend who's brought me here.'

'Come through to my office, both of you, while I explain a few things.'

'I'll go if you like,' Phil offered.

'I'd prefer it if you would stay then you can be reassured that Sally, your friend,' and here she hesitated, looking at Phil over her glasses, 'is in good hands.' He couldn't help a rueful smile. She obviously thought he'd been responsible, despite Sally's protestations.

Glancing at each other, meekly they followed the bustling woman down the hall and into a much smaller room containing a desk, a couple of chairs and a filing cabinet. 'Sit down both of you.' As they did so, she pulled a file towards her and opened it. 'Now Sally, your baby is due around 14th April, is that right?'

At Sally's nod of agreement, she continued, 'Well, as you know you will be here approximately 6 weeks until the baby is born. I understand from the doctor's letter that you plan to have it adopted.'

Sally's chin came up again. 'I haven't decided definitely yet.'

She gave Sally an appraising glance. 'During the next few weeks, I'd like you to think about the difficulties you will face should you decide not to have the baby adopted. Not least the difficulty in obtaining work with a young baby to care for. And National Assistance isn't enough to bring up a child.'

Matron closed the file. 'You'll find that discipline here, although strict, is not barbaric. Sister and I are very much aware that young women like yourself are to be helped not condemned.' She leaned back in her chair, and Phil saw that there was a kindly gleam in her eyes. 'You will be expected to help out in the kitchen and in keeping the Home clean. There is a roster in the dining room for such chores. I won't go through the daily routine with you, I'll leave that to Mavis with whom you'll be sharing a bedroom.'

'After your baby is born, you will be expected to care for him or her in the normal way for about another six weeks. Your baby will be bottle fed from the beginning to make it easier for any adoptive parents. It won't be easy caring for your child, knowing you will have to give him or her up. Our advice is that you treasure this time with your child, knowing it is all you will ever have.'

'What happens if I decide to keep him or her?' Sally said defiantly.

'You will be allowed to leave after your lying-in, providing we are satisfied you and the baby are going to a suitable home. Now, have you any more questions?'

'What are the arrangements for visiting Sally?' Phil asked. Sally looked at him in surprise. She obviously didn't think he would come and see her.

'Boyfriends are allowed to visit for three hours on Sunday afternoons. Then you will be allowed to meet only in the Common Room in the company of others. Other visitors can come then, too, and also on Wednesday afternoons.' He could tell by the tone of her voice that she still suspected he was the father. 'What about you, Sally? Any more questions?'

She shook her head. 'Not that I can think of at the moment.'

'Please feel free to seek out Sister or myself at any time. If we can't see you immediately, we'll make a time for later.' Matron pushed herself up from the chair with both hands on the desk. 'Now, after you've said goodbye to your friend, Mavis will show you round.'

There was an awkward silence in the hall after she'd closed the door of her office as Sally and Phil stood, not knowing how to say goodbye. Finally, Phil said, 'I'd better go. Fred will be frozen by now.'

'Thanks for bringing me. Thank Fred too, will you?' Then her face crumpled and he guessed she was on the point of tears. 'Oh, Phil, I'm scared.'

He couldn't help it, he pulled her into a comforting embrace. She seemed to welcome the contact. 'I know, Sally. But you'll come through it, I know you will.'

'Did you mean it, about coming to see me?' she asked, her voice muffled by her proximity to his chest.

'Course I did. If you don't mind, that is.' As he looked down at her, he could see that her eyes glistened with unshed tears and again he was struck by her vulnerability. 'I don't know when because of getting time off but I'll come when I can.'

The door to the Common Room opened and Mavis stood in the doorway. 'Sorry, Sally, but we need to get you settled before we have tea at half past five.'

Sally took a deep breath and picked up her suitcase. 'I'm ready.' With a last glance at Phil, she walked with Mavis towards the imposing staircase. At the half landing, she turned and gave him a last wave as he was going through the door.

* * *

Sally was unprepared for the sense of isolation she experienced as Phil left Heywood House by the front door. He was, she realised, her last and only link with her life as she had known it. From now on, she had little control over what happened to her, apart from the overwhelming decision about whether to keep her baby. Until that decision was forced upon her, she knew the best way to get through this unnerving experience was to accept whatever came her way and to take each day as it came.

She followed Mavis upstairs into a large bay-windowed bedroom which she guessed was over the Common Room. 'This is our room, Sally. That's to be your bed over there.' Mavis pointed to the bed in the far corner of the room almost behind the door. At the side of the bed was a locker with an in-built single wardrobe. 'Bathroom's at the end of the corridor on the right. We all share that so it can be a bit of a scrum sometimes. There's a further two bedrooms and another bathroom on the next floor.'

Sally hefted her suitcase onto the bed. 'How many girls are there in the Home?'

'There's ten of us, eight who are pregnant and two girls who have already had their babies.' A shadow passed over Mavis's face. 'One of the girls is due to give her baby up in the next few days and that's always hard. We get to know each other so well that we all feel her pain.'

'Does everyone get on well here?' That had been one of her areas of concern.

Mavis did a see-sawing movement with her hand. 'There's always the odd difficulty.'

As Sally opened her case, Mavis said, 'Look, I'll leave you to unpack. When you hear the gong for tea, make your way down to the Dining Room, just behind the Common Room. I'll introduce you to Margaret and Jean who share with us.'

After Mavis had gone, Sally eased her way on to the bed and took a deep breath, looking round the large room. It was cluttered, with four beds and four lockers. There was pleasant light green wallpaper on the walls with a border of darker green leaves at picture rail height. Behind the door were the instructions on what to do in the event of a fire. She smiled at the thought of eight lumbering girls making their way to the fire exit which was apparently at the end of the corridor and easing their respective bumps down a steel ladder. None of them would be waddling anywhere in a hurry.

She turned to her unpacking. Not that there was much of it. She didn't have many clothes and she hadn't seen any point in bringing much anyway. Especially as she couldn't get into her old clothes now. She sat on the bed when she'd finished, undecided what to do next. Should she wait for the gong, as Mavis had suggested, or should she make her way down to the Common Room? She guessed that with much of what would unfold over the next few days, she would feel a little lost.

Making her mind up, she wandered down the corridor to check out the location of the bathroom – thankfully it had a separate toilet – then made her way down to the Common Room. In the doorway, she hesitated, to be greeted by Mavis. 'Ah, there you are, Sally. Come and meet Margaret and Jean.'

Margaret was a cheerful outgoing sort of girl, tall and, except for her prominent bump, slim with long hair swept into a pony tail. Jean, on the other hand, was small, quiet, shy. Truly, she didn't look old enough to be having a baby yet her bump stated otherwise. Sally learned later from Mavis that, at 15, she was the youngest of the residents, and everyone else mothered her a little. She wondered how they had come to be having a baby and supposed that, as they got to know each other, their respective stories would emerge.

From the time the gong for tea sounded, Sally was hurled into a round of activities that filled the evening till bedtime and was glad of it, for it gave her less time to think. Tea proved to be adequate and nourishing, if unimaginative. Afterwards, she helped the others, whose turn it was, clear away and wash up, amid much laughter about Margaret not being able to get close to the deep sink because of her bump. 'You wait until it's your turn to mop the hall,' threatened Margaret.

126

'Why, what do you mean?' Sally asked.

'You've seen that massive tiled floor in the hall?' To Sally's nod of agreement, Margaret continued, 'We all have to take our turn at mopping it. On our hands and knees.'

Sally stopped in the middle of wiping one of the large dinner plates. 'Surely not.'

'Oh, yes,' said Mavis, a grin on her round face. 'Sister reckons it's good for positioning the baby. Happens once every couple of weeks or so. Can you imagine how uncomfortable it is on your hands and knees with a large bump swinging below?'

Sally stroked her belly. 'Vividly.'

Just before bedtime, Mavis took Sally into the Nursery to meet June who would be giving up her baby within the next few days. She was a sweet-faced girl, who already had lines of sadness around her mouth. She was giving her baby, a little girl, a last feed before settling her down for the night. Watching her tenderly holding her child against her shoulder as she gently patted the baby's back, Sally was overcome with the poignancy of the scene. Unable to stop herself, she whispered, 'How can you bear it?'

'With great difficulty,' June said, gently turning her head to kiss her baby. 'But I don't have any choice.' The baby gave a huge burp and a trickle of warm milk leaked from its mouth onto June's shoulder. She looked back to Sally. 'Would you like to hold her?'

'Oh, could I?' June nodded, and passed the baby over to Sally, who cradled the child's head with one hand as she had seen June do and the other under the baby's bottom. She was surprisingly solid for such a small scrap of humanity but incredibly vulnerable for all that. She had never been so close to a new born baby before. In wonderment, she gazed down at the tiny lips, pursing in and out in some imitation of a suck, the way her star-shaped hand waved in the air and her little legs came up in an involuntary movement as a spasm of wind passed through the small belly. With a gentle kiss on the child's forehead, she passed her back to June. 'She's gorgeous,' she whispered in awe.

June looked down at the baby's face, now at peace, and said, 'Isn't she just? Her new parents are going to be ...,' there was a sudden catch in her voice, '... are going to be so lucky.'

Lying in bed that night, Sally reflected on her first few hours in the Mother and Baby Home. It hadn't been as frightening as she'd feared. Not that she'd known what to expect. As Matron had said, the regime, though strict, didn't seem too harsh, if the friendliness of the girls she had met today was anything to go by. She had been surprised by that. Somehow she had thought the incumbents of such a place would be girls hardened by life. She had voiced aloud her thoughts to Mavis, to whom she already felt close, but the other girl had shaken her head. 'No, it's the innocent girls who get caught and have to come in here,' she'd said. 'The other sort of girl knows the right thing to do to avoid unwanted pregnancies.'

In the dark quietness of the bedroom, Sally was overcome by acute loneliness. The other girls were only a matter of yards away, seemingly sleeping peacefully. At the moment, she had no connection with them although she was realistic enough to know this might change as they all got to know one another. She suspected that any friendships made here might be like holiday friendships. You meet, in similar circumstances, find a sense of kinship, exchange addresses, full of good intentions of keeping in touch. And you do for a while until finally the Christmas cards stop. Here it would be no different, particularly with girls coming and going all the time.

Suddenly, she missed the comforting familiarity of her family, the known safety of the streets and buildings of her home town, even the 33 and 35 buses trundling up and down Chorley New Road between Bolton and Horwich. Irrationally, she longed for the life she had known before she became pregnant, the irregular meetings with Nick, the pictures a couple of times a week, going to the pubs or dance halls with the lads and lasses. Just then, she'd have given anything to return to that life, away from this unknown world she had been thrust into. She cried then, silently so as not to wake the others, tears oozing from her eyes and soaking into the pillow she was clutching. Then, gulping to contain the tears, she pulled herself together. This wouldn't do. Whatever was going to happen to her here had to be endured as best she could. Unbidden, the thought of Phil as he'd waved her goodbye, popped into her mind. He looked, as always, steady and dependable, smart in his RAF blue, someone you felt you could rely on. Eventually, she fell asleep, one hand fingering the friendship necklace he had given her.

CHAPTER 14

The routine at the Mother and Baby Home soon became familiar to Sally and she settled in quickly. Admittedly there were rules and regulations, petty though some of them might seem, but it was logical to abide by them. It made life easier for everyone in the long run.

One of the rules, with Heywood House being a Church of England Mother and Baby Home, was that they should all to go to church on a Sunday morning. This meant walking to the nearby church accompanied by either Sister or Matron. Not surprisingly, there were disapproving looks on the faces of the locals at the sight of several heavily pregnant young women walking into church.

The vicar, also chaplain to Heywood House, was a tall man, spare-framed, with an expressive face, dark Brylcreemed-hair and a reassuring presence. When he began his sermon, she found her attention wandering back to June, who had remained at Heywood House. Mothers were excused church attendance. She was jolted back to the present by the vicar rapping loudly on the lectern in front of him and saying to his congregation, 'Am I boring you?' A titter of laughter ran through the congregation but at least he now had their attention.

'Is he always like this?' she whispered to Jean, her nearest neighbour.

'Well, let's say he's not your conventional clergyman,' she whispered back. 'A couple of weeks ago, he stopped the organist mid-hymn and told us all to sing with more gusto.'

From further along the pew, Sister leaned forward and with a finger to her lips, told them to be quiet.

'Sorry, Sister,' they both mouthed back.

The girls with whom she shared a dormitory soon became fast friends and they often giggled and chatted together long after 'lights out' at ten o'clock. Inevitably, she came to know their stories as they came to know hers. Mavis had fallen pregnant by her long-standing boyfriend. She was now seventeen, as was her boyfriend, but as he was an apprentice earning a pittance, there was no chance of them marrying.

Twenty-year-old Margaret's boyfriend was a sailor on an extended tour in the Antipodes. She planned to keep the baby so that when he did eventually come home, they could be married. Her parents were supporting her in this and she would be able to take her baby back home.

Jean's story was perhaps the saddest of all. At fifteen, her innocence had been taken advantage of by an older lad. Because she was still under age, the police were involved and the young man, pleading innocence, had been taken to court. It was all very messy and Sally's heart went out to her. She was a sweet, loveable girl with a winning nature and would do anything for anybody.

Since that first day, Sally had been drawn to the Nursery, calling in to gaze at June's baby. Because June herself was often there, seeing to her little girl, she and Sally became friendly. Always, a hint of sadness lingered in June's eyes as she looked at her baby and Sally knew the other girl was storing up every precious moment of this time. Despite this, she let Sally help with her baby's care, showing her how to change a nappy and how to hold her properly. Sally loved the feel of the tiny mite in her arms and couldn't wait to hold her own.

Because it was one of those sudden friendships that flare up in shared circumstances, Sally found was able to tell June about Phil and how, being Nick's brother, it had caused some friction between them.

'Is he the young man in RAF uniform who brought you here?' June asked, while changing her baby's nappy. 'I saw him briefly from the back of the hall as I came out of the Nursery.'

132

Sally wondered if June had seen her enfolded in Phil's arms. 'Yes, that's him.'

'He seems a nice lad, good-looking too.'

Sally looked at her in surprise. 'Good-looking? I suppose he is, in a solid dependable way.'

June looked at her appraisingly. 'I think you're fonder of him than you realise.'

'Don't be silly,' Sally said, but felt her face colouring up. 'It's because he's Nick's brother. And besides, he's already got a girlfriend.'

June laughed. 'Pity that. There's not many of his type around.' Her face darkened. 'And I should know.'

Then June told her how the lad she'd been going out with had told her one day that he'd been going out with someone else at the same time and that he was going to have to marry her because she was pregnant. Shortly after, she'd found out she was pregnant herself. When she'd told her parents, they had packed her off to stay with an aunt in Cleveleys until such time as the baby was born. There was no question, she said, of keeping her baby. Her parents were too strait-laced and strict.

Sally leaned across and touched June's hand. 'Oh, I'm so sorry, June. I know how much you love this little cherub.'

'Hold her for me, will you, while I get rid of this dirty nappy and wash my hands.' She passed the sweet-smelling baby to Sally. 'I don't know how I'm going to bear it, Sally.'

She took the baby from June with now expert hands and tucked her up against her shoulder, rubbing the tiny back. 'How long is it off now?'

June sighed. 'Three days … and counting.'

'How does it work?'

'The new parents arrive at the front entrance and go into Matron's Office, where they sign some forms. I'm allowed a few minutes to say goodbye, then either Sister or Matron will take little Ruth from me. I have to stay in the Nursery until the new parents take my baby …,' and here her voice broke a little, '… their new baby out of the front entrance. I will be expected to leave the Home as quietly and as quickly as possible afterwards, no prolonged goodbyes or opportunity to recover from the shock of the parting.'

June was crying now and Sally rose, baby and all, and leaned down to hug her. 'I'll be there for you, I promise.'

'That's sweet of you, Sally, but they won't let you.'

Sally was horrified. 'That's cruel!'

'Another of the rules,' she said, shaking her head regretfully. 'It's to save anyone like yourself who has still to have your baby dwelling on the outcome too much.'

Over the course of the next three days, they all shared in the agony of the young mother as she prepared mentally and physically for the parting. On the day of the handover, Sally said a tearful goodbye to June and the baby, who would leave as Ruth but an hour later would have a new name, chosen by her adoptive parents. She didn't see June again but thought about her all day, winging silent thoughts to her as she returned home where she would be expected to behave as if nothing had happened. Sally didn't see how it would be possible, not when June would be grieving for baby Ruth.

* * *

As Fred wasn't able to take Phil over to Preston, he'd been planning to go by bus to visit Sally. Then, when the three mates had gone into Blackpool and were having a cup of tea in the café, Bob himself asked Phil if he would like to accompany him and Betty the following Sunday to see Sally as he'd recently bought a car.

It proved to be one of those grey, dismal days the North West specialises in, with a fine, drizzling rain. All the way to Preston, Bob had to lean forward to peer out of the misted-up windows. 'Bloody rain!' he muttered, swiping the inside of the window with the sleeve of his jacket. 'I'd rather it rained heavy than this bloody drizzle.' Phil, in the front of the car with him, fervently hoped they'd get to their destination in one piece. Bob had bought the car so they might travel up to the Lake District, once petrol rationing was lifted. Although Bob had been a staff car driver during the War, Phil suspected he hadn't driven since he'd been demobbed.

'For goodness sake, Bob,' Betty said from the back, 'stop moaning and just get us there.'

'That's what I'm trying to do, woman,' Bob said through gritted teeth. He looked at Phil, raising his shoulders slightly, but Phil didn't react. He had no wish to get involved in this husband-and-wife bickering. Despite the momentary disagreement, he could tell Betty and Bob were deeply fond of each other.

At Heywood House, they were admitted by a young girl of about fourteen or fifteen, her bulging belly at odds with her still youthful features and slight girlish frame.

'Can I ask who you've come to see?' she asked.

'Sally Simcox,' said Phil.

'You'll find her in the Common Room, I think. If she's not there, someone will go and find her for you.' In the Common Room, Phil saw immediately they were not the only visitors. At one of the tables sat the young woman who'd let them in the first time, holding hands with a young lad who didn't look old enough to father a child, let alone take on responsibility for one.

Sally's face lit up when she saw them. As pushed herself upright from the deep armchair to greet them, she winced and pain flitted across her face.

'Are you all right, love?' Betty asked in concern.

'Just a bit of back-ache,' she said, rubbing the area with her hand. 'Let's sit at the table by the window then we can talk better. And Phil, you've come too.'

'I said I would, didn't I?' For a second or two, as she acknowledged his presence, he had the feeling the two of them were frozen in a moment of time. She seemed to sense something too for the laughter went briefly from her eyes.

'I'm glad you did,' she said softly then turned to the Parrotts. 'How did you all get here? It can't have been an easy journey.' She looked from one to the other of them.

135

'I've bought a car,' Bob said, dangling the keys from his fingers, obvious pride in his voice.

'It's only a Ford Popular, Bob, not a Rolls Royce,' Betty said.

'As long as it gets us from A to B and is economical to run, that's what counts, eh, Phil?' he said, as if appealing to him man to man.

Phil chose to back him up on this one. 'Quite right, Bob.'

Once seated at the table, Phil asked Sally how she had settled down.

'Oh, fine,' she said, 'and I get on well with the girls in the dormitory, though Margaret has moved out now she's had her baby. We're expecting a newcomer tomorrow.'

'Who was the young lass who let us in?' Betty asked. 'She didn't look much above thirteen.'

'That would be Jean.' She nodded to where the younger girl sat reading a Picturegoer magazine.

'She doesn't look old enough to know what it's all about, let alone be lumbered with a baby,' Bob said.

'It was an older lad who got into trouble over it apparently. Poor girl! She's in our dormitory.'

'Do you all get on with each other? Not just in the dormitory, but in here,' Betty said, gesturing to the other girls in the Common Room, most of whom, if they didn't have visitors, were reading or chatting quietly among themselves.

'Mostly we do, but there's bound to be some disagreements. Usually, they get sorted out after a few minutes.' She giggled. 'I think we'd get our ears boxed by either Sister or Matron if we let it develop into a row.'

'Are they very strict, then?' Phil asked.

'It might seem that way but they're both nice people underneath their starched uniforms. I think it's more a question of not standing for any nonsense.'

The door opened and two girls came in pushing a trolley laden with tea things. 'Ah, tea time,' Sally said. 'Are you all having a cup?'

Chatting over cups of tea and biscuits, the time passed quickly and almost before they realised, it was time to go. As the Parrotts said their goodbyes in the hall, Bob said, 'We'll wait for you in the car, Phil, give you two a few minutes together.'

'There's no need, Bob,' Sally said, blushing a little.

'Nonsense, you don't want a couple of old fogeys like us around,' Betty said.

The two of them didn't know what to say to each other once the older couple had gone. 'So, you're really all right then, Sally?' Phil said finally.

'Apart from this nagging backache and the strain on my bladder, I'm fine.'

The tension stretched between them until Phil said, 'Look, I'd better go, it's not fair to keep Betty and Bob waiting.' Yet still he hung back. Then, on impulse, he pulled her as close as he could, given the bulk of the baby coming between them, and gave her what he hoped was an affectionate, almost brotherly, hug. 'You take care of yourself now,' he said.

* * *

Standing alone in the cavernous hall, after Phil had left, Sally felt again that sense of utter loneliness she had experienced when he'd first brought her here. This wouldn't do at all. It was simply that Phil was a connection to her past, to real life. To think of him in any other way was not to be considered. As she had done that first day, she straightened her shoulders and turned to go back to the Common Room.

In the doorway, Mavis was coming out, half turned towards someone still in the Common Room and laughing at whatever what was being said. She did not see Sally and barged into her, knocking her sideways. Sally tried to avoid the collision but the force of their two bulky bodies threw her back against the doorjamb and she felt a wrenching pain in her back and reaching round her side. She doubled up, two hands on her lower belly, gasping with the ferocity of the pain.

'Oh, Sally! I'm sorry, I didn't see you. Are you all right?' Mavis clutched at Sally's upper arm. 'Come and sit down.'

The pain was subsiding now and she allowed Mavis to lead her to the nearest chair. 'Jean, be a love, get Sally a glass of water.' Mavis pulled a hardback chair to the side of Sally's chair and said, 'How are you feeling now? Shall I go and get Sister or Matron?'

She shook her head, though she still felt a little faint. 'No, I'll be all right. I think I must have twisted something when I tried to avoid you.'

Mavis took hold of Sally's hand. 'I'm such a clumsy clot. I've been told often enough to look where I'm going.'

Jean returned, carrying a glass of water, which Sally accepted gratefully. After a few minutes, she felt more normal and turned to Mavis. 'I really do feel OK now, Mavis, you can stop looking so worried.'

'Look, when we do the washing up after tea, you're not to join in. I'll take care of that.'

'Don't be silly! I'm fine now, honest.' Mavis took some convincing though. When they'd finished tea and were clearing away, Sally had literally to grab a tea towel from the other girl's hands. They ended up laughing, having a tug of war with the tea towel until Jean, who was actually doing the washing up, had to speak sharply to them.

'Will you two behave yourselves? You're carrying on like a couple of kids.' They stared at her in amazement and, as she saw their faces, she too burst out laughing. 'See what you've done, you've started me off now.'

'Let's talk about something else then or we'll never finish clearing away,' Sally suggested, endeavouring to keep her face straight. 'I take it that were your boyfriend who came this afternoon,' she said to Mavis. She and the young man in question had sat at one of the smaller tables, holding hands and gazing into each other's eyes.

Mavis sighed and contemplated the plate she was drying. 'It were. Because it's such an awkward journey he can only come every couple of weeks or so, but I do miss him.' She added the plate to the pile of clean ones and picked up another. 'People don't take us seriously because we're so young but we really do love each other.'

'The girl I used to work with is only seventeen and she's in a similar situation. No one takes her relationship with her boyfriend seriously. In fact, they've been forbidden to see one another,' Sally said.

Mavis looked at her with interest. 'Do they stick to that?'

Sally laughed. 'I suspect they don't.'

'Nor would I. At least we're allowed to see each other.'

'Actually, that couple who came to see me this afternoon have been in the same position as you and your boyfriend,' Sally said, taking the plate Mavis had been intent on polishing to a high sheen, and placing it with the others.

'Really?'

Sally nodded. 'They were very young when they found she was expecting. This was years ago of course,' she added. 'She was packed off to her grandmother, who lived in the Lake District, to have the baby.'

'What happened to the baby?' Mavis asked, picking up the last plate on the draining board.

Sally suddenly realised the implications of what she was telling Mavis and decided not to frighten her unduly. Nor did she feel it was appropriate to tell her that Betty and Bob had always yearned after the baby they believed had died. 'Oh, the grandmother arranged for a private adoption and Betty went back home as if nothing had happened.'

'But they did eventually marry?'

'Yes, a couple of years later, I believe.'

'And they're happy?'

'Very much so. A proper Darby and Joan.'

'Who was that nice-looking young man who came with them?' Jean asked, wiping down the draining board.

'That was Phil, a friend.'

'Just a friend?' said Mavis, quirking her eyebrows.

'Definitely,' said Sally perhaps with more emphasis than she had intended.

Later that night, as the three girls were preparing for bed, Sally paid a last visit to the toilet. There, to her alarm, she discovered blood in her knickers. Not just blood, but thick clots. Immediately, her body started to shake with nerves. What was happening to her? Was the baby coming early? She'd always thought that labour was preceded by the waters breaking, not with blood, but she knew she would have to check. Going back to the dormitory, she said to Mavis and Jean, 'I'm going to have to go and see Sister or Matron, I've started bleeding.'

Mavis clapped a hand to her mouth. 'Oh, I hope it's nothing to do with what happened this afternoon.'

Sally shook her head. 'I'm sure it's not. I had backache earlier today, remember?'

It happened to be Matron on duty that evening. She took Sally into the examination room and checked her and the baby over. After she'd finished, she said, 'Baby's heartbeat is a little fast so it's possible some of the placenta has broken away.'

'Is that dangerous?' Sally asked in a small voice.

'Not at this stage. If you continue to bleed, we may have to induce you, but don't worry about it for tonight. Try and get some sleep and we'll have another look in the morning.'

It proved not to be so, for, sometime in the early hours, Sally woke to what she thought might be a contraction. She waited, uncertain as to whether she'd imagined it or not, but when, a few minutes later, another wave of pain flowed over her belly, she knew she had to get help. There was a bell near the door to summon either Matron or Sister but when she tried to reach it, she doubled over with another contraction.

'Sally, is something wrong?' came Mavis's voice through the darkness.

'Yes,' she gasped. 'I think the baby's starting. Could you get to the bell for me?'

'I'll do it,' Jean whispered. 'I'm nearer than Mavis.' She swung out of bed and padded across to the emergency bell, switching on the light as she did so.

'Sorry I woke you both,' Sally said, sitting on the side of her bed clutching her belly.

'Don't be silly, we'd want to know. Is the pain very bad?'

Sally knew Matron wouldn't want her to alarm the other girls so she simply said, 'Like a very bad period pain.' She drew in a deep breath as another pain lanced through her.

'They seem to be coming pretty often though, don't they?'

'I would have thought so for the early stages of labour, but I'm no expert.'

Just then the door opened and Matron bustled in, a fluffy candlewick dressing gown bulking out her ample proportions. 'What's the problem here?' she asked a little snappily.

As another spasm of pain shook her, Mavis said, 'Sally thinks the baby's starting.'

Matron gave a deep sigh and said, 'You'd better come along to the examination room then.' She waited until Sally had struggled into her dressing gown and helped her towards the door, turning off the light as they left. 'And you girls, go back to sleep.'

'Good luck, Sally,' Mavis called.

In the examination room, Sally could tell that Matron was a little put out at having been disturbed but as soon as she'd examined Sally, her manner changed and she became all concern. 'Well, Sally, you'll be having this baby sooner than we anticipated. In fact, from the look of things, it won't be very long at all.' She washed her hands in the adjoining sink then said, 'Will you be all right here while I get dressed?'

Between gritted teeth, Sally nodded her assent. Alone in the examination room, Sally started to shake with nerves. So this was it, the moment she had anticipated and yet dreaded. Nick's baby was coming, and in a hurry to get here by the look of it. Typical of Nick's offspring, she thought. Then, irrationally, she wished Phil was here with her. His presence alone would be calming; just holding his hand would have soothed her. But men weren't allowed in delivery rooms. This was women's business.

By the time Matron, now fully dressed, returned, time had begun to blur. She helped Sally into the delivery room and onto the hard, uncomfortable bed. The pains, she knew without being told, were coming so fast now there was hardly any time to draw breath. She longed to scream but she had already been warned by Matron to be quiet so as not to frighten the other girls who had still to have their babies. Concentrating on that and on the waves of pain as they gripped her left her with little breath anyway. The gas and air helped but she barely had time to breathe normally before she was grasping the nozzle again. At one point, Matron left her and minutes later Sister, also fully dressed, joined them. Sally had no idea what was going on between her legs but it certainly seemed to concern both midwives if their look was anything to go by. Her body, by this time, was telling her to push and obediently she obeyed the instinct.

'No, no! Don't push yet!' Matron said.

Sally tried hard not to do so but the urge was so strong she had little option. Her body seemed to want to expel all its contents and she pushed with all her might. 'I have to,' she muttered through gritted teeth. Her whole life seemed to be focused into this one moment.

'The head's through, Sally, now one more big push when the pain comes,' Matron said.

Sister had one hand on Sally's belly and must have felt the contraction start for she said, 'Now, love, now!'

With another almighty heave, Sally felt the baby slither out and tears stung her eyes. 'That's it, Sally, the baby's born. Now the next contraction will expel the afterbirth.'

As she did so, it occurred to Sally that she hadn't heard the baby cry. She thought babies always cried with the shock of the big wide world after the warmth of the womb immediately they were born. She managed to push herself up onto her elbows. 'My baby, is he all right?' she gasped.

142

She caught the look that passed between the two women and noticed, for the first time, the limp blanket-wrapped bundle in Matron's arms. A cold feeling of dread filled her.

Sister put her hands on Sally's shoulders, pushing her back on to the delivery bed. 'I'm sorry, Sally, your little boy didn't survive.'

'My baby's dead?' She looked from one to the other of them. 'He's dead?'

'I'm afraid so. From the look of the afterbirth, too much of the placenta had come away for him to be able to survive the trauma of the birth,' she said, still holding Sally down.

Bearing in mind what had happened to Betty, she said harshly, 'I want to see the baby.'

'Are you sure?' Matron asked.

'Yes,' she said emphatically. Sister moved away allowing Matron to bend and show her the bundle. She forced herself to look at the perfect but blue-tinged lifeless face of her baby, topped with a tuft of dark hair. Just like Nick's.

That's when her heart broke.

CHAPTER 15

Phil was sitting with Fred and Chipper in the Mess after the usual indifferent offering that passed as their evening meal when he was called to the telephone again. The caller was Betty Parrott and she sounded upset. 'Phil, I'm glad I caught you. This won't have got you in any bother, will it?'

'No, I'm off duty. What can I do for you? Is owt wrong?'

There was a slight pause as if she was gathering breath. 'We've had word from the Mother and Baby Home. It's Sally.'

His heart started racing and his throat went dry. 'What's wrong with her?'

'She went into labour last night and, well, in the early hours of the morning, she had the baby, a little boy ...' She hesitated then said, her voice breaking a little, '... It was stillborn.'

Phil couldn't believe what he was hearing. There was a ringing in his ears and he had to take a deep breath to overcome the feeling. 'But we were only there yesterday afternoon.'

'She must have started after we'd left, I think. Matron didn't go into any details.'

'How is she? Do you know?'

'Devastated, apparently. She'll be coming home in a few days. Matron said she'd ring when Sally's well enough to leave.'

'Will you be able to go and get her? Do you want me to come with you?'

'No, it will probably be best if we go alone.'

They talked for a couple more minutes before ringing off and Phil walked back into the Mess stunned, his face set in grim lines.

'What's up, mate? It's not the family, is it?' Fred asked. They both remembered the devastating news he'd received last year when his brother had been knocked down. Ironically, this was family, too, wasn't it? That somehow made it harder.

'That were Betty from the Shangri-La,' he said, as he joined them at their table. 'They've had a phone call from the Home. Sally's lost the baby.'

'That was careless of her, wasn't it?' Chipper said. Then, as if realised his London sense of humour wasn't appropriate in this case, said, 'Sorry, mate. Me and my big mouth.'

'She wasn't due for a few weeks yet, was she?' Fred asked now.

'Her date were mid-April, I think, so she were a month early. Poor Sally. I think I'll pop over and see her on Wednesday afternoon.'

'I'd offer to take you,' Fred said, 'but I daren't risk taking the car out at the moment, with this intermittent fault. Some problem with the fuel pump, I think.'

Both Phil and Chipper looked at each other and shrugged. Then Chipper deliberately crossed his eyes which made Phil smile despite the heaviness in his heart. He and Chipper hadn't a clue about the innards of the motor car and fooling about was a standard practice whenever Fred mentioned them.

Sally was much on his mind over the course of the next couple of days. He had no idea of the kind of torment a young mother would have to deal with to be told her child had died at birth but he could imagine. Sally must be devastated. Her whole life since she had come to Blackpool had been bound up in the baby. Now reality must be faced. He wondered what she would do with herself. Would she stay in Blackpool? Or would she return to Horwich and take up her old life again? Somehow he doubted it.

After a tedious journey involving two buses and a lengthy walk to Heywood House, he was met initially with disappointment. The girl who answered his ring on the doorbell was an unfamiliar face and she refused to let him in. 'Boyfriends are only allowed on Sunday afternoons,' she said, crossing her arms over an ample chest and emphasising her bump.

'I'm not Sally's boyfriend.'

'Well, male friends then,' the girl prevaricated.

'Look, Sally's a good friend. She's just lost her baby and I'd like to see her now I've come all this way,' he said. 'Please will you ask Matron or Sister if they will bend the rules for once?'

The girl heaved a sigh but uncrossed her arms. 'All right, then. Wait here, will you?' With that, she shut him out on the doorstep. He stuck his tongue out at the closed door.

It was Sister herself who opened the door to him and ushered him inside. 'I'm sorry about that. Of course, you can see Sally. It will probably do her good.' She ushered him into the tiled hall. 'She was in the Common Room last time I saw her.' At the entrance to the Common Room, she laid a hand on his arm. 'Be patient with her. She's taken the loss very hard. In fact, it would do her good to cry but she doesn't seem able to.'

There were several groups of visitors in the Common Room but Sally was sitting alone at a table by a side window, staring at some daffodils tossing their heads in the wind outside. About her was an air of isolation and Phil sensed this was deliberate. He sighed, not knowing what he was going to say to her or even if he would be welcome but he had to try. 'Sally?' he said, gently touching her shoulder.

She yanked away as if she'd been touched by a hot poker. 'Leave me alone!' she cried without looking at him.

'Sally, it's me, Phil.' He pulled up a chair at her side but didn't try to touch her again.

Her eyes focused on him for the first time. 'What are you doing here?'

'I've come to see you, to tell you how sorry I am about the baby.'

'Are you? I don't believe you. You made it clear you were only staying around because you felt some kind of responsibility towards your brother's child.' Her voice had a shrill edge to it.

147

He winced but he knew she was only lashing out. 'That's not true. I were hurt when I found out you'd deceived me but I stayed because I cared about you.'

She covered her face with her hands. 'Well, there's no baby now. No need to worry about me anymore.'

He pulled her hands away from her face. As he suspected, she wasn't crying though her features were contorted with anguish. 'Sally, even though there's no baby, I'm still here.' He pulled her into his arms and this time, she didn't resist him.

They stayed like that for a moment then she said, her voice muffled against his shoulder. 'One of the hardest things to bear is that my milk has come in. My breasts ache with wanting to feed him.' She pulled back and looked up at him. 'Did you know it were a little boy?'

'Yes, Betty told me.'

'Except for being a bit blue, he were perfect. I were going to call him Michael.'

Somehow the fact that she had had a name for the baby made the loss all the more poignant. He didn't know what else to say to her. To remind her at this stage that her life could return to normal didn't seem appropriate somehow even though he believed it himself. He could not utter the platitude though, however well meaning.

'This morning, Sister took me to register the birth,' Sally said now, her tone almost conversational but for a faint catch in her voice, 'and the death. Can you imagine how painful that were?'

'I can. You were very brave to do it,' he said. 'I didn't know you had to register a stillbirth.'

'Neither did I. It's not summat you think about.'

'Does that mean there will have to be a funeral?'

A flicker of pain passed over her face. 'Yes,' she whispered, 'but I won't have to go to it. The Home has an arrangement with the local hospital; they take care of everything.'

He took her limp hand in between his. 'Oh, Sally, what can I say?'

'There's nothing you can say.' From somewhere in the room, came the sound of laughter from one of the girls and her

148

visitors and Sally leaned forward. 'Have you any idea how difficult it is being here, seeing these other girls waiting for their babies? All hopeful, all optimistic? And hearing Margaret's baby cry? The way she jumps up to go to him?' When he said nothing, she said, 'I can tell you. It's a bloody agony! I can't wait to get away from here now.'

'When will you be able to leave?'

She gave an indifferent shrug. 'When my milk dries up, apparently.'

'Shall you go back to the Parrotts? Work for them again?' He knew instinctively, with the new season due to start at Easter, that would be the best thing for her. Betty had already told him they hoped she'd return to them.

'I haven't really thought about it. I suppose so,' she said listlessly.

'It would take your mind off things,' he pointed out. 'Besides, could you really return to your old life in Horwich? Back in the Mill? Somehow the Sally I've come to know wouldn't fit that picture. Not anymore.'

Something like a glimmer of hope came into her eyes. 'No, you're right. I couldn't go back to that. I like being independent … away from my family. And I do like working at the Shangri-La.' She hesitated then, looking down at her hand in his. 'Thank you for coming, Phil. You've always been there when I most needed you.'

'And I hope I always will be.'

* * *

Joyce and Dave were the last of the stragglers to come out of the side door of the cinema, he holding her hand and looking down at her while she fiddled one-handed with the buttons of her coat.

'Well, well, if it isn't the young lovers,' Jud Simcox's scathing voice broke into their intimacy. He, Bill Murphy and Jim Stephens were blocking their exit from the narrow side street.

149

'Does Nick know you're still meeting like this? It's not the first time, either, is it?'

'Have you been spying on us, Jud?' asked Dave. Although he was still holding her hand, his fingers in hers were tense.

'Not particularly but it's surprising what you can find out just by keeping your eyes and ears open,' Jud jeered.

She knew then they'd made a mistake. Their Saturday afternoon meetings had made them careless. They'd progressed to going to one or the other of the Bolton cinemas, simply for the pleasure of sitting close in the warmth. Tonight, they'd been so absorbed in one another, they hadn't taken note of who else was in the cinema as they usually did. And this was the result. What exactly did Jud have in mind? She was afraid, not for herself, but for Dave. She had no doubt he would defend her honour but he was outnumbered three to one.

'The question is, what's going to keep me from telling Joyce's brother?' Jud said now.

'Are you trying to blackmail us?' Dave had let go of her hand but she could feel his body taut at the side of hers and she guessed he was readying himself for some defensive move if necessary.

'Blackmail? That's against the law,' Jud replied.

'Since when did that bother you?' Dave snapped.

'Watch it, mate!' Jud took a step forward, as did his two mates.

She looked round, seeking an exit, but the only way out of this street was blocked by the three lads. Behind was the solid wall of another building.

'No, what I had in mind were share and share alike.'

Jud's suggestion was said so reasonably that she couldn't understand what he meant at first. Then, as realisation hit her, she shuddered. 'Never!' she cried. 'Why would I want to go out with you?' As soon as she'd spoken the words, she knew she shouldn't have said anything so inflammatory.

'You little bitch!' Jud made a grab for her but she side-stepped him, banging her shoulder against the door jamb of the exit.

150

'You'll touch her over my dead body!'

'That can be arranged,' Jud said and signalled to his two companions. They all rushed Dave together, bearing him swiftly to the ground where they started to pummel his face and body. She screamed at them to stop and tried to pull at the jacket of one or the other of them but her efforts were ineffectual. Although much of Dave's face was hidden by the bodies of the three lads, already she could see it was bloodied.

Casting around wildly for a possible weapon she could hit one of them with, she saw people were still passing the end of the street and looking in curiously at the fracas. 'Help me, please,' she yelled. 'They're killing him!' The first ones attracted by her pleas hesitated briefly then, seeing in the dim light from the side of the building that it was a scuffle between four Teddy boys, shrugged their shoulders and walked on. She yelled again and a couple halted briefly as if deciding whether to proceed but then they too went past. Sobbing now with fury, she pulled harder at Jud's jacket. Then she had an inspiration. She took off her stiletto shoe and, careless of who or where she hit, she lashed out, managing to give Jud's head a glancing blow. 'Leave him alone, you bastard!'

Jud threw his arm up in defence and seeing the anguish on her face, some kind of sanity came over him for he said to the others, 'That's enough. I think he's got the message.' As all three stood, Bill gave Dave a last vicious last kick. 'I said that's enough!'

The three of them strolled away and, heedless of her stockings, Joyce knelt down. Dave was a mess, both his eyes were swollen and rapidly purpling, his head where he had been kicked was bleeding and there was a pool of blood spreading outwards from the back of his head from where it had made contact with the rough surface of the cobbles. What was worse, he appeared lifeless. Not knowing what signs of life to look for, she turned to the rapidly disappearing lads and yelled, 'You bastards! You've killed him!'

This last cry alerted a couple of men passing the end of the street and Dave's three assailants had to push their way past them. Her two rescuers sprinted up the narrow street and one of them felt Dave's neck. 'It's all right, love, he's not dead, just unconscious. He looks to have a pretty nasty head wound though. He'll need to go to hospital.'

'I'll go and phone for an ambulance,' his companion said and shot off down to the main road.

'You all right, love? They didn't hit you?' the first man said. She shook her head, fear for Dave rendering her unable to speak. Now that Jud and his mates had gone, reaction was setting in. She felt sick and dizzy and she was glad when the man pushed her head between her knees and kept his hand on her shoulder. 'Take deep breaths, love. You've had a terrible shock.'

Within a few minutes, it seemed, she heard the clanging bell heralding either a police car or an ambulance. It turned out to be both and from then on events took on a nightmarish quality and she lost track of time. In the ambulance, she held Dave's hand, which hung limply down by his side, willing him to survive. The ambulance men had laid him on his stomach so as not to aggravate the head wound which was heavily padded with a dressing. She felt numbed by all that had happened. She had no idea what time she would get home or indeed how she would get there. It would all come out that she and Dave had continued to meet up and there would be another gigantic row. But she couldn't worry about that just then; time enough for that after the hospital had sorted Dave out. She leaned forward and whispered to him over and over again, 'Hold on, love. Keep going. I'm with you.'

* * *

Waiting for the Parrotts to come and collect her, Sally found she was strangely reluctant to leave Heywood House. She had been cocooned here for the past three weeks, safe from the reality of the outside world. Now she had to face it. And she didn't know if she was emotionally equipped to deal with it. Her grief was still too raw, too painful. She felt robbed, cheated and somehow angry. Illogically, she searched for someone to blame; at the same time, subconsciously, she knew it was her own body that had let her down.

There was a knock at the door of the new mother's dormitory and Mavis popped her head round the door. 'Is it all right for us to come in?'

She forced a smile to her face. 'Course it is. I've nearly finished packing anyway.'

Mavis was due to go into labour any day now and her bulky body waddled through the door, followed by Jean. 'We didn't want to interrupt but we wanted to see you away from the others in the Common Room.'

'You're not disturbing me. I've been alone with my thoughts for too long.' She clicked her suitcase shut and placed it on the floor. 'Come and sit on the bed while we talk.'

Mavis heaved herself on to the bed. 'I know you're going back to the boarding house for now but have you decided yet what you're going to do in the long term?'

'I shall probably stick it out for the season then decide. I like living in Blackpool. And I enjoy working in the guest house, seeing to the guests.'

'It's been great knowing you, Sally. I wish it'd been for longer,' Jean said.

'We'll keep in touch though, won't we? I should warn you, though, I'm not much of a letter writer.' She still hadn't contacted her family or Joyce and she felt guilty about that. At least she could write now she was no longer pregnant. Again, a pang of grief coursed through her.

'Course we will,' Mavis said. 'I'll let you know as soon as I've had the baby.'

Another knock came at the door and the new girl from Mavis's and Jean's dormitory poked her head round the door. 'Sally, the Chaplain's arrived and asked if he could have a word.'

She knew this was routine practice but she couldn't imagine what he would want to say to her. 'Tell him I'll be down in a minute.'

'We'd better go too,' Mavis said clambering off the bed.

'I need the lavvy anyway,' Jean said, wriggling from side to side and holding her belly.

'Now you've said that, I want to go too,' Mavis said, squirming at the thought. 'That's one thing we've all got in common.'

So, in the end it was a laughing goodbye with hugs and promises to stay in touch.

The Chaplain, Reverend Marchant, was in the Chapel, a small room adjacent to Matron's office which might have been a butler's pantry at some point. The Chapel was kept open day and night for anyone who wanted to go in there, perhaps to pray or to simply be quiet. A small table was set up as an altar with a candlestick standing on a snow white lace-edged tablecloth. There was a Holy Bible too, looking surprisingly well used. She had only ever been in here once before when the Chaplain had introduced himself.

Mr Marchant stood as Sally entered the room. 'Hello, Sally,' he said and bade her sit on one of the handful of chairs. He leaned forward with one arm on the table for support. 'I was sorry to hear about the baby, Sally. How do you feel now?'

She considered for a moment. 'Numb. Like I can't quite believe it.'

'That's a natural reaction. It will pass with time.'

'That's all anyone seems to say,' she burst out. 'In the meantime, no one can help me to deal with this pain.'

His kind, dependable face showed only care and compassion at her response. 'God can.'

She gave an exclamation of disgust. 'If there's a God, how come he let my baby boy die?'

'You're asking the question that has puzzled even theologians for nearly two thousand years,' he said quietly. 'And we won't know the answer until we come face to face with God at the end time.'

She was beginning to feel uncomfortable with all this talk of God. 'I'm not very religious, I'm afraid.'

He looked into her eyes with directness. 'Do you believe in God?'

She hesitated before answering. Like all children, she had had compulsory religious instruction at school and was familiar with most of the bible stories. 'I suppose so.'

'Loss and suffering are very much a part of living. As are birth and death,' he offered. 'And God does give us the strength to get through these sad times.'

She looked at him anew. For a man of the church, he had a definite physical and spiritual presence. 'I often find that if God has taken something from me, it's because He has something better planned for me,' he went on. 'I can quote you an example from my own life. My wife and I desperately wanted children yet it didn't seem to be happening. Finally, we adopted a dear little boy whom we loved from the very first moment.' On seeing her quizzical look, he laughed. 'No, it wasn't one of the babies from here. But it was a baby from another Mother and Baby Home. Once he entered our lives, we didn't give having children of our own another thought. But you know what? We've recently discovered my wife is pregnant.'

'What a lovely story!' she said.

'That's what I'm trying to say to you. That maybe God has something in mind for you that will be bigger, better. Now shall we pray for the future?'

After she had left the chapel, Sally found she was surprisingly comforted by the man's words. She'd never been one for going to church before but since attending the church here, she had experienced the same feeling of reassurance that this man of God had just given her. Maybe she would get through this dark period after all and make a new life for herself. Somehow.

CHAPTER 16

Joyce sat at the side of Dave's hospital bed, gazing down at his inert body. He was now in a medically induced coma until the swelling on his brain had gone down. His head, where he had been operated on, was swathed in bulky dressings and an assortment of tubes went into and out of his body. Now the bruises were fading, his face and the skin of his hands were almost as white as the sheet and pillow they lay on. The best you could say was that he was peaceful. The worst was that the doctors had warned there could be some brain damage.

Her own feeling was one of being drained, emotionally and physically, worn out by the battle she had endured simply to be at his bedside. It had started before she'd even reached home. She was still being interviewed by a policeman about what had happened when the door to the interview room burst open to admit a dumpy, dishevelled woman. She had pointed a finger at Joyce and yelled, 'What's she doing here?' It was Dave's mother, brought to the hospital by another policeman.

The constable with Joyce rose from his seat and stood between the older woman and her, while the policeman who'd come with Dave's mother, put his arm round her shoulder. 'Don't distress yourself at this stage, Mrs Yates. Let me take you to your son.'

As she was propelled out of the room, Mrs Yates shouted, over her shoulder. 'I don't want her anywhere near my son. It's her fault he's here anyway.'

In the silence of the interview room after she'd gone, the policeman said, 'Sorry about that. Someone must have told her you were here.' Joyce had already told him the background to her and Dave's story so he knew Mrs Yates was antagonistic to their being together. 'We're about finished here so if you're ready, I'll get someone to take you home.'

She'd given in because, with Mrs Yates there, there was little likelihood of her being allowed to see Dave when he came out of theatre. She'd vowed, in that moment, nothing or no-one would stop her from coming to visit him.

When she'd finally reached home, in the early hours of the morning, her mother and Nick were sitting up waiting for her. 'Now then, young lady, are you going to tell us what's been going on?' were her mother's first words. Joyce knew from the clipped way her mother spoke that she was angry as well as concerned.

'What were you told when the police called?' The policeman who had been detailed to pick up Mrs Yates, had also called at the house in Lancaster Avenue, to inform her worried parents what had happened.

'Only that you'd been involved in some sort of incident and had gone to the hospital with the person concerned,' Nick said.

She drew in a deep breath to give her the courage she needed. 'I'd been to the pictures in Bolton with … Dave Yates.'

'You little madam!' her mother cried. 'Sneaking behind our backs like that. What did you think you were playing at?'

'I'm sorry, Mam, we couldn't help ourselves. We love each other.'

'What happened, love?' Despite Nick's conciliatory tone, his lips were tight.

She told them then, halting here and there as she recalled the agony of seeing Dave bleeding and unconscious.

'But why did Jud and his mates attack Dave?' Nick asked.

Casting her eyes downwards, she'd said, 'Jud's been pestering me to go out with him for months now.'

'That bastard!' he'd raged. 'I won't have him sniffing round my kid sister. I shall be sorting him out once and for all.'

158

'You won't be able to,' she'd pointed out. 'They're going to arrest him … when they can find him.'

There had been more rows once her intention of visiting Dave in hospital had become clear. Once, she had actually run out of the house to catch the bus to Bolton before anyone could stop her. Relations in the Roberts' household were strained almost to breaking point but she stuck it out.

Then there had been Dave's mother. Her antagonism towards Joyce had not lessened but, in the face of her determination and Dave's precarious plight, they had reached an uneasy truce. As much as anything, it had been the Ward Sister who had smoothed the path between them. She had pointed out that arguments between the two of them at Dave's bedside were doing the patient no good at all. Faced with this, Mrs Yates had given in, though she had stipulated it was to be for half an hour only a couple of days a week. Then Mrs Yates would take over. This arrangement had worked well so far though it had only been just over a week. In that time though, she had managed to visit him three times.

'Oh, Dave,' she whispered now, squeezing the hand she was holding. 'Please, please get better.' She didn't know whether he could hear but the nurses said it didn't do any harm and might just get through to him. So she'd talked to him, of all the times they had gone out together, of their crazy plan to elope to Scotland. Well, that wouldn't happen now they'd been found out. She leaned forward, kissing his hand and resting her head on the bedspread. Lulled by the faint chatter of the other visitors and the warmth of the ward, her eyes closed and she dozed, worn out with the strain.

She was roused by Mrs Yates' voice. 'You shouldn't still be here.'

She let go of Dave's hand and stood awkwardly. 'I'm sorry, Mrs Yates, I must have fallen asleep.'

Dave's mother pulled up a chair on the opposite side of the bed and sat down. 'I'm not surprised. If you're owt like me, you're worn out.' To Joyce's surprise, her tone was kindly. 'Has there been any change? Any signs of him coming round?'

'Not while I've been here.'

Mrs Yates sighed. 'I keep willing him to wake up, telling him daft things about when he were a babby.' As Joyce made to move away, the other woman said, 'Oh, sit down again, lass.' Joyce stared at her in amazement. 'It looks as if we're in for a long wait,' she said, indicating Dave's prone body. 'Happen it's time we got to know each other. And if we're talking among ourselves, it might get through the fog what's clouding my lad's brain.'

She sat down again but remained silent, waiting for the older woman to take the lead. She did. 'You can start by telling me exactly what happened that night.'

'Haven't the police told you?'

'Yes, but I want to hear it from you.'

So Joyce told her everything. She listened, an intent look in her eyes, then said, 'That's all then? You haven't been two-timing our Dave with Jud Simcox?'

'No, I haven't!' She was appalled. 'Is that what he's saying?'

Mrs Yates's eyes flicked towards Dave then back to Joyce. 'It's what he claimed to the police. He also told them it were only a fight between him and Dave and that Dave cracked his head when he fell.'

'That's not true,' she burst out. 'The three of them charged him and brought him down.'

'Did you tell the police that?'

'Of course I did.'

'Then it'll be up to the courts to decide. Will you be called as a witness?' When she nodded, Mrs Yates continued, 'You'll have to convince them your version is the right one.'

Joyce, sickened by what Jud had been saying about her, said, 'Do you know when it will go to court? With me not being a relation, the police won't tell me owt.'

'He's already appeared before the Magistrates' Court but because of the seriousness of the injury, it's going to the Crown Court. In the meantime, he's on remand.'

She shuddered, glad there would be no possibility of running into him. 'Thank goodness for that.'

160

'For what it's worth, lass, I believe you.' Again Joyce stared at Dave's mother. 'You've been to see him as much as you can and that tells me you're loyal and that you really care about him.' She was stunned into silence by these words. Mrs Yates gave a small smile. 'I reckon we can sit these visiting times out together, if you're willing. If nowt else, it'll make time pass a bit quicker.'

* * *

It was one of those bright, clear days in mid-April where the wind picked up odd bits of litter and leaves left over from the autumn and swirled them up against lampposts and into the gutter. Phil was on his way to meet Sally for a walk. Three weeks had passed since he'd last seen her, slightly over that time since she had lost the baby and he wondered how she was feeling now. She'd sounded subdued, even reluctant, when he'd spoken to her to make the arrangements to meet. He couldn't help wondering if it was because she wanted nothing more to do with him, now their connection through Nick's baby had been severed. He hoped not. Her raw grief, which had shown through when he'd visited her, had been much on his mind and he found himself thinking of her often.

The first thing he noticed when she came to the door of the Shangri-la was that she was wearing more make-up than she had done throughout her pregnancy. He thought she was much prettier without it but maybe she was wearing it as a sort of armour against the world. Oh well, it wasn't his place to say anything. And the black pencil skirt was back, pulling a little tighter across her hips and belly. 'Hello, Sally,' he said.

'Phil, you're early.' Her voice was flat and weary-sounding, as if it was too much effort.

'If you're not ready, I can always walk round the block a few times,' he said, trying to lighten the mood.

She gave a ghost of a smile. 'No, I'm ready. I'll just get my coat.'

Moments later, they set off walking up Central Drive. 'Which direction do you fancy going in?' he asked.

'I don't mind. You choose.'

Phil interpreted that to mean she didn't really care. 'How about we catch a tram up North and walk back along the cliffs?'

'OK by me.' She gave an indifferent shrug. 'How's Pam, by the way? Doesn't she mind you meeting me?'

'She's fine and she wouldn't mind. It's not as if I'm two-timing her with you.' In fact, he'd kept quiet about meeting Sally. He couldn't have said why. It wasn't as if there was anything to hide. Truthfully, he hadn't seen much of Pam recently. Either she was tied up with her family or he hadn't been able to get time off.

They sat together on the tram as it rattled its way towards Fleetwood, both silent. It was as if a barrier had come between them and Phil had no idea how to break it down. He had something to tell her. That's why he'd arranged this meeting but he didn't know where to begin. He would have to pick his words carefully. 'Sally, have you heard from your family recently?'

She shook her head. 'No, I keep meaning to write but I don't have the heart just yet.'

'I've had a letter from my Mam. About Joyce and your brother.'

Her head swivelled towards him so quickly he heard her neck crick. 'Jud? What's he been doing?' He detected a note of panic in her voice. 'And where does Joyce come into it?'

'It seems he's been mithering Joyce to go out with him,' he began.

She put a hand to her mouth. 'Oh, no!'

'It seems she and Bragger – Dave – Yates have still been seeing each other on the quiet.' At her look of incredulity, he continued, 'Well, they'd been to the pictures in Bolton the other week when Jud and his two mates cornered them in a back alley.'

'Jim Stephens and Bill Murphy.'

'Mam didn't know their names. Apparently, all three rushed at Bragger and he cracked his head on the cobbles as he fell.'

Her face paled. 'Was he badly hurt?'

'Bad enough to have been operated on. He's still unconscious.'

'And Jud? What's happened to him?'

'He's in prison, on remand. The case goes to court very soon.' He hesitated before his next words.

'That's not all, Sally. He's claiming that Joyce has been going out with him as well as seeing Bragger.'

'That's daft,' she said. 'I've worked with Joyce, she wouldn't do that. How's she bearing up? Especially now it's out in the open about her still seeing Bragger.'

'She's been going to see him in hospital almost every day, despite the opposition.'

'How's Bragger's Mam taken that? Not kindly, I'm guessing.'

'There's been some kind of truce between them, by all accounts.'

'I suppose I'd better write to Mam,' then as if she thought about it, she said, 'no, I can't do that. She'll wonder how I've found out.'

'You can always say you've heard about it through Joyce. Which you have in a way.' He saw that the tram had now reached the North Shore. 'Let's get off here and we can talk some more.'

Telling her about Jud and Joyce seemed to have broken the dam of silence that had built up between them. At first they stuck to the ins and outs of what had happened between Jud, Joyce and Bragger and whether Jud would be sent to gaol. Then they turned to how things were at the Shangri-la since Sally's return. Although the summer season wouldn't officially start until Easter later this month, Blackpool was becoming busier and the boarding house had a few stalwart guests. So Sally was managing to keep busy which, she claimed, was helping her to get through the days.

'You seem to be coping well enough,' Phil said.

'That's what you think,' she snapped. 'I know I'm not. It's worse when I'm alone in my room.'

He heard the catch in her voice and he guessed she wasn't far from tears. 'I'm sorry, Sally. That were a pretty shallow thing to say. I know you're putting a brave face on things but no one

163

can really know how you're feeling.' He was floundering, he knew, but he was out of his depth here.

'Shall I tell you?' she said. 'At first I were numb, like I couldn't believe this were happening to me. One minute I were having a baby, the next minute he'd gone. He were all I was living for, everything I'd pinned my hopes on. I'd more or less decided to keep him, no matter what anyone said, or however difficult it were going to be.' She was crying openly now, her words interspersed with sobs.

An elderly couple walking a dog passed them in the opposite direction, glaring at Phil as if it was his fault Sally was crying. If only they knew, he thought. 'Let's sit down for a while.' He led her to one of the shelters located at intervals along the Promenade.

Once seated, she covered her face with her hands and sobbed. 'I don't know how I'm going to bear it, Phil. The baby's been my whole world for the last few months. Now there's nothing left of him except a massive emptiness. And do you know what one of the worst things is? People thinking it were all for the best. It probably is but I don't see it like that at the moment.'

Phil had thought that too but he didn't say anything. Instead, he pulled her into his arms and cradled her while she sobbed. After some moments, she calmed down and, from within the circle of his arms, looked up at him. Her mascara had run and smeared down her cheeks. Somehow, that spoke to him of her anguish more than the speech she'd made. He took a handkerchief from his trouser pocket and attempted to repair some of the damage.

She gave him a lopsided smile. 'I must look a mess.'

'Just a bit.'

She pulled herself away from his arms, sat up straight and took a pocket mirror from her handbag. With the aid of his handkerchief and a lot of spit, she succeeded in getting rid of most of the mascara from beneath her eyes and her cheeks. 'I've made a mess of your hankie again,' she said, as she handed the mascara-streaked handkerchief back to him. 'I seem to make a habit of that.'

'Doesn't matter,' he said, putting the blue RAF issue handkerchief back in his pocket, remembering the first time it had happened. He'd had to wash that himself as he would this one.

'Thanks, Phil,' she said now. 'I don't know where all that came from,' though whether she was referring to the make-up or her grief, he didn't know.

'You've probably been bottling it up,' was all he could offer.

'I think I must have been. I'm sorry for crying on your shoulder.' She pointed to a stain on his jacket where her Panstik make-up had smeared.

'I've got broad ones,' he said, jiggling both shoulders.

'And they've always been there for me.'

'A regular Sir Galahad, that's me,' he quipped.

'Seriously, Phil, I don't know what I'd have done without you these past few months,' she said. 'I don't deserve that.'

'That's nonsense. You were unlucky enough to fall pregnant. It happens.'

'Not just that. There's other things you don't know about me, nobody does, except ...' she broke off and he wondered what she had been going to say.

In the silence that followed, he pulled a packet of cigarettes from his jacket pocket and offered her one. 'Oh, sorry, I forgot you don't smoke,' he said as she shook her head.

'I used to,' she said 'but I couldn't face them when I was pregnant. I've never wanted one since. A legacy from losing the baby, I suppose.' Her eyes filled again but she shook her head to clear the tears. 'Look, there's a café across the road. I'd love a cup of tea and a sticky bun. My treat.'

* * *

165

It was early evening at the Shangri-la, tea for those few guests already staying there, Mr Wolfit among them, long over. Betty, Bob and Sally were relaxing after their own meal. All of them were tired after the rush to get things ready for Easter, just a few days away now. Sally was content to sit nursing a mug of tea in front of the sitting room fire, looking forward only to her bed that night, when Betty's voice broke into her thoughts. 'I'm sorry, Betty, did you say summat?'

'I asked if you'd seen anything of Phil over the weekend.'

'No, he said he might be on duty, covering for someone else, I think.'

'Why don't you keep your nose out, woman?' Bob said in mild exasperation. 'It's nothing to do with you what they get up to.'

'I was only asking out of politeness,' she flashed back. Sally smiled. There was never anything malicious in these bantering exchanges.

'She's trying to match-make between the two of you,' Bob said, grinning at Sally.

'Bob Parrott!' Betty had flushed pinkly at his words and Sally laughed to relieve the older woman's embarrassment. 'I simply said what a lovely young man Phil is and how nice it would be if he and Sally got together.'

Sally gave a snort. 'There's not much chance of that, Betty.'

'I don't know,' Betty mused, 'he's a well set-up lad with a steady career in front of him. That's not to be sniffed at.'

'Betty, for goodness' sake!' Bob said.

'What?' she asked, in feigned innocence. Betty was so transparent Sally had to laugh. The idea of her and Phil was unthinkable. And yet ...? No, best not go down that route. He was still Nick's brother, she must remember that.

'Don't forget the lad's got a girl-friend.'

To divert Betty's attention, Sally said, 'Have you heard anything further from the detective bloke?'

'You know that we've got Peter's birth certificate?'

'You showed me. I was surprised the Thompson's had been the one to register his birth,' Sally said. 'But I suppose it makes sense. After all, they had him almost from birth.'

'So we know Ada's husband's name was Albert and that he was a brickie by trade. And a letter to that address came back marked 'not known at this address." Betty ticked off the various facts on her fingers.

'Don't forget, love, 1932 was in the middle of the depression,' Bob reminded his wife. 'The building trade's one of the first to decline in any recession. Albert would maybe have moved where the work was.'

Betty glared at him. 'That's why the detective is checking the electoral rolls around Kendal.'

'Not having much luck though, is he?' reflected Bob on a gloomy note.

'If Peter's now 24, 25, won't he have done his National Service? He must be on someone's records somewhere for that,' Sally suggested.

Betty was never without a notepad in case she suddenly remembered something important and she reached in her overall pocket for it. 'Good idea.'

'There's always a possibility, too, that their former neighbours might know something.'

'Now there's a thought, lass,' Bob said. 'Mention that, Betty love, next time you write to the bloke.'

Betty scribbled something else on her notepad. 'I'll do better than that, I'll give him a ring in the morning.'

She was silent for a moment then said, 'Does it bother you, Sally, that we're talking about Peter this way?'

Sally looked at Betty, perplexed. 'What do you mean?'

'Well, with me thinking for years he was dead, then he wasn't. I mean, your own loss is so recent ...' Her voice tailed off in confusion.

'What you're trying to say is that there's no chance of my baby being found alive at some later date is there?'

'I suppose so, in a roundabout way.'

'Don't forget I insisted on seeing him.'

167

Betty glanced at Bob as if for courage. 'Truthfully, love, we haven't known what to say to you, even though we've gone through it ourselves.'

'It's all right, Betty.'

She leaned forward and patted Sally's arm. 'For what it's worth, love, I think you're handling all this admirably.'

'It doesn't feel like it to me, Betty. If anything, it hurts more than it did in the beginning.' She chewed her lip slightly then said, 'My arms are still longing to hold him. I feel he's literally been torn from my body.'

'That's because the shock's beginning to wear off,' Betty said. 'Remember how I was, Bob?'

'I certainly do. You treated me like it was my fault,' Bob said, then grinned at Sally. 'I couldn't do right for doing wrong.'

'In a way, we were in a similar position to you. We couldn't confide in anyone because no-one was supposed to know.'

A thought struck Sally. 'By the way, what did you tell Mrs Robinson next door? And no doubt Mr Wolfit asked you.'

'I stuck to the truth. That, unfortunately, you'd lost your baby.'

'And my mythical husband?'

Betty grinned. 'Still stuck in the Middle East, dealing with the aftermath of the Suez Crisis.'

'But that's all over, isn't it? With petrol rationing due to come off ration next month and ships going through the Canal again?'

'There's a lot of admin to get through,' said Betty, winking. 'Now then, Bob, time to get off your backside and give me a hand with the remainder of the pots.'

Sally jumped up. 'No, both of you, stay put. It'll give me something to do, save me from thinking too much.'

Later that night, in the solitude of her room, she wrote letters to her mother and to Joyce, skirting round the fact that she hadn't been in touch by saying she'd been busy, even though it was the winter months. She knew the real reason she hadn't written was because of her fear that Jud would seek her out again. Well, that wouldn't happen now. Seeing the two letters stamped and ready for posting gave her the feeling she'd surmounted yet another obstacle.

CHAPTER 17

When Joyce reached Dave's bedside on Easter Saturday, the tubes had been taken out, he was a better colour and, apart from his bandaged head and fading bruises, he simply looked asleep. She was whispering to him and stroking his hand when Mrs Yates arrived.

'Hello, love,' she said, slightly breathless. 'Oh, all the tubes have gone. That's a good sign.'

Joyce snatched her hand away. She was always careful about any physical contact with Dave whenever his mother was there. 'Let's hope so.' She rose and pulled another chair up for Mrs Yates and stood for a moment longer, looking down at him. 'Looks like he could wake up at any moment, doesn't he?'

Mrs Yates nodded and breathed heavily a few times, patting her chest. She sat and indicated that Joyce should do the same. 'You look tired. Are you still in trouble at home?'

'Unfortunately, yes. Mam and Dad have given up trying to stop me coming but their silence speaks for itself,' Joyce explained. 'Nick's OK about it now though. At least he never says owt.'

Mrs Yates undid the scarf at her neck and fanned her face with it. 'You know, Joyce, I've been thinking. Maybe we were a

171

bit hard on the two of you. I've come to realise what a good lass you are.'

She stared at Dave's mother. 'Thank you, Mrs Yates. I realise we should have been more open about how we felt. Perhaps then, none of this would have happened.'

'Did Dave tell you I had this crazy notion that he'd take Holy Orders?'

She gaped at Dave's mother. 'You mean become a priest? Dave?'

'Exactly. I was persuaded otherwise by my own priest.' Mrs Yates's cheeks were bright pink now and Joyce guessed it had cost her dear to admit to her own foolishness. 'He explained that to become a priest, it was first necessary to be called by God. That there'd never been any such indications with Dave.'

Joyce was giggling now. 'Somehow I can't imagine Dave as a priest.'

'I know, it's ludicrous, isn't it?' Mrs Yates joined Joyce's giggles.

'Mam, is that you?' came a croak from the bed and, with a flash of delighted understanding passing between them, their eyes turned to Dave.

'It is, son. How are you feeling now?'

'Got a thumping headache. Can hardly open my eyes.' Their talking, and perhaps their giggles, had obviously roused him for he tried to turn his head in Joyce's direction but couldn't. The movement was obviously too much for him and he closed his eyes again briefly. 'How did I get here?' he asked after a few seconds.

'You fell and cracked your head open,' Mrs Yates told him.

He attempted to smile but it came out more like a grimace. 'Feel like I've got a hangover. How long have I been here?'

'Almost a month.'

That seemed to rouse him more. 'Bloody hell! A month?'

Joyce slipped away to find someone to tell them Dave had recovered consciousness. It was only fair that Mrs Yates have these first few precious minutes with her son. She herself was giddy with excitement, couldn't wait to talk to him properly.

A crisp and efficient nurse came back with her to Dave's bedside, took his temperature and blood pressure but, with everything apparently normal, she left after the few minutes the procedure took, warning them not to tire Mr Yates too much.

When she'd gone, Joyce took the chair she'd sat in before. Dave, aware of the movement, tried to focus his eyes on her shape, blinked a couple of times, then said in a puzzled voice, 'Am I dreaming or is that Joyce, Nick's sister?'

The chatter of other visitors receded into the background as Joyce froze. The cold sensation round her heart told her he didn't remember that they had been in love. Taking a deep breath to control her sudden trembling, she said, 'Yes, it is.'

'But ... I don't understand ... why?'

With a warning glance in Joyce's direction, Mrs Yates said. 'Joyce were with you when it happened. It were she who got help.'

'But why weren't Nick around?' Dave was shaking his head in an attempt to clear it, wincing as he did so. 'I wish I could remember.'

Mrs Yates gentled her hand on his cheek. 'Don't try. You heard the nurse. We aren't to overtire you.'

'I do feel tired.' He was silent for perhaps a moment, during which time, Joyce and Mrs Yates exchanged knowing looks. 'Can't keep my eyes open.' His voice trailed off and he was asleep again.

He didn't wake up again before the end of visiting time and Joyce managed to contain her tears until then. Once outside in the long corridor that ran almost the length of the hospital, they came. 'He doesn't remember me, only as Nick's sister,' she sobbed.

Mrs Yates, though she was small compared to Joyce's slender height, didn't hesitate. She enveloped Joyce in a comforting hug, irrespective of other visitors leaving and having to weave past them. 'I know, love, I know. But the doctor did say any memory loss could be temporary. Hold on to that.'

'But what if he never remembers what we've been to each other?'

173

'That's a possibility, of course, but it's early days yet. You'll have to try and be patient.'

'It's as if the past year's never happened,' she whispered. That thought kept running through her mind as she sat on the bus back to Horwich. She was glad of Mrs Yates's silent presence at her side as she contemplated a possible future without Dave. She had to face up to the fact that Dave might never recover his memory. Her heart felt like it was breaking.

She met Nick on her way up the path from Mount Street to the Brazeley Estate. 'Been to see Bragger again?' he asked as they drew abreast. 'How is he? Any change?'

Not immediately trusting herself to speak, she nodded then drew a deep breath before saying, 'He's recovered consciousness.'

'Oh, good.'

'Not so good. He seems to have lost his short term memory.'

Nick threw down the cigarette he had been smoking and crushed it beneath his foot. 'Does that mean …?' He hesitated as if not sure what to say next.

'That he doesn't remember me? No, he doesn't. At least not as his girlfriend.' Her hands flew up to her face as she struggled not to cry again. 'Oh, Nick, I don't know what I'm going to do.'

Although they were never particularly demonstrative, he put his arm round her shoulder. 'I'm sorry, love. I know what he means to you but don't give up yet. It might only be temporary.'

She took her hands from her face. 'That's what Mrs Yates was told by the doctor.'

'There you are then.' He squeezed her shoulder then removed his hand. 'I've seen for myself how much you love him. If only Bragger had been straight about wanting to take you out in the first place, I wouldn't have been so against your seeing him.'

'That were me. Dave wanted to but I were afraid of what you might say or do, given his so-called reputation.'

He grinned at her. 'Bragger by name and by nature, eh?'

'You know he weren't really like that,' was her spirited response.

'He put on a pretty convincing act though.'

She looked at him quizzically. 'Do you mean that, provided Dave recovers his memory and wants to continue our ...' She suddenly didn't know what to call the relationship between her and Dave, '... You wouldn't object?'

'I suppose I do. But don't forget there might still be opposition from Mam. Dad's not really a problem, he blusters a lot but mostly, these days, he goes along with what Mam says.'

She managed a small smile. 'That's better, love,' Nick said. 'Are you planning on visiting him again tomorrow?'

'No, I've decided to give it a miss for a couple of evenings.'

'Then I'll go and see him tomorrow night.'

'Good idea. He were asking about you.' She watched her brother fondly walking down the hill, probably on his way to Kathy's house. Of all her family, she was closest to Nick. Perhaps one of the reasons for that was the physical similarity between them. They were both tall, dark-haired, dark-eyed and with an out-going personality. And he was right. Dave might well recover his memory.

* * *

At the Easter dance at Kirkham camp, Phil was sitting with Chipper, Fred, Pam and a couple of other girls she'd introduced him to but whose names he'd forgotten when he saw Sally. At first, he couldn't believe it was her. Surely not, was his first reaction. It was, after all, a mere month after losing her baby. But then he recognised the pink dress she'd worn for the Halloween Dance and, from what he could see as she twirled past in the arms of a good-looking erk, looking as lovely in it as she had then. She was laughing at the erk's stumbling efforts at dancing, her face vivacious again. What he wasn't prepared for the

175

unexpected rush of pleasure he felt when he first realised it was her.

He looked at Pam to see if she'd noticed anything but she'd turned away from him and was deep in conversation with one of the girls. Excusing himself to everyone, he stood and went to position himself on the perimeter of the dance floor. It wasn't long before Sally appeared in his vision again. He stood, his arms folded across his chest, as she drew abreast. Her face flushed when she saw him. He raised his hand to her and she gave him a quick smile of acknowledgement. At that moment, her partner took a wrong step, causing her to stumble. She might have fallen had not her partner, his own face now red with embarrassment, pulled her upright. Before Phil could think what he was doing, he stepped forward and, tapping the junior airman on the shoulder, said, 'I'll take over from here.'

With a quick glance at the two flashes on Phil's sleeve, the younger man relinquished his hold on Sally saying, 'Yes, Corp.'

She slid effortlessly into his arms, resting a light hand on his shoulder and putting her hand in his. 'Pulling rank, are you, Corporal?'

'One of the perks of the job,' he quipped back. He'd never seen her like this before, flirtatious and provocative, but then she'd always been pregnant in the time he'd known her. The thought was disturbing, especially when her feminine nearness was making his body respond in a physical way. He made a deliberate attempt to change the conversation. 'I was surprised to see you here.'

'Why?'

'I would have thought it would be way too soon.'

'If I'd thought about it too much, I'd have probably agreed with you,' she said quietly. 'Then Sandra phoned and asked if I wanted to come.'

'You're obviously enjoying yourself.'

'Why not? I've got to return to some kind of normality. It might as well be sooner rather than later.' Despite the flippancy of the remark, he sensed the underlying hurt in her heart. He was glad then, that this was a waltz and he could pull her closer.

Beneath his hand on her back, he could feel the warmth of her body and the perfume she was wearing, definitely not Evening in Paris, gave off a heady, intoxicating aroma.

The music ended and everyone began walking back to their original positions. He loosed his hold on her reluctantly and said, 'Dance with me later? If I can get to you through your horde of admirers.'

'What about Pam? I assume she's here?'

He didn't need reminding; his conscience was already troubling him. 'She's doing her share of dancing with other chaps.' She wasn't dancing at the moment though. She was watching him talking to Sally, looking isolated in the group of people at their table. He sighed. 'I'd better get back to her.'

Sally had followed his glance. 'By the look on her face, you better had.'

Back at the table, Pam said, 'How is Sally? She doesn't look like someone who's recently lost a baby.' Already, Sally was on the dance floor, quick-stepping past their group with yet another partner and laughing up at him.

'Perhaps throwing herself into life again is helping her come to terms with it,' he said, hoping he was right. He wasn't sure he liked the way she was behaving but knew he had no right to point a finger of condemnation.

Sometime later, when Pam had gone to the cloakroom with the other girls, he went in search of Sally with the intention of asking her to dance. He found her, with Sandra and the other two girls – he couldn't remember their names – surrounded by four National Servicemen, a couple of whom had had too much to drink. They formed an uproarious group with Sally herself laughing out loud at something someone had said. Phil was furious and had no hesitation in saying, 'Keep the noise down, you lot.'

'Says who?' asked one of the group but as he turned to face Phil, he said, 'Oh, sorry, Corp.'

Phil ignored him. 'Dance with me, Sally?'

Her head swivelled to the dance floor. 'But it's a bop.'

'So? I can bop.' She looked at him uncertainly and he grinned. 'At your party, remember.'

She reached for his hand. 'Daft barmpot that I am, I'd forgotten.'

They swung easily into the rhythm of the tune, her steps matching his and, as she swung away from him, he caught her hand on the return swing without hesitation. The band was playing a plodding version of Elvis Presley's 'Hound Dog' and they were laughing breathlessly at the end of it. 'I enjoyed that,' Sally said, her cheeks glowing and her chest heaving with the exertion. In the subdued lighting of the dance floor, her hair gleamed softly in the reflection from the glitter ball above their heads.

Just then, the MC announced that there would now be an interval for the band and the full lights came on, making everyone blink. Phil laughed. 'Time for a pee and a pint for the band. Maybe we can have another dance later?'

'OK.'

Phil took her back to the group she'd been with before, part of him wishing he didn't have to do that. He wasn't happy about the company she was keeping but, short of dragging her away, there was nothing he could do. And he didn't have the right especially when he was supposed to be with Pam.

Though he kept an eye on the dance floor, Phil didn't see Sally again until she and one of the lads she'd been dancing with came to the bar where he was queuing for last orders. The lad had his arm round her waist and she was laughing at something her companion had said, her face flushed with a combination of heat and possibly too much drink. Before he could even think what he was doing, he faced her and said, his voice tight with anger, 'What do you think you're playing at?'

She broke free from the erk's arm and, giving Phil an indignant look, said, 'What's it got to do with you?'

'I don't think what you're doing is appropriate for someone who's just …' Despite the white heat blazing within him, he managed to stop himself from telling everyone of Sally's loss.

'Steady on, Corp,' came the mild protest from her companion. Phil shot him a warning look and he backed away.

Sally's flush increased and her eyes flashed dangerously. 'It's nowt to do with you, Phil. You don't own me.'

'If I did, you wouldn't be behaving like a cheap little tart,' he flashed back, past caring now, despite everyone around staring at them.

'You bastard!' Her hand shot out as if to strike him but he caught her wrist and with it, pulled her close to him, wanting desperately, irrationally, crazily, to kiss her. They stood for some seconds as if frozen in time while he mastered the urge then let her wrist drop. It was only with a supreme effort that he walked away.

Back at the table, he found he was shaking and his jaw clenched tight. In an attempt to steady himself, he reached for his glass then realised it was empty. 'Shit! I forgot to get the drinks.'

Fred picked up his own empty glass, stared into it and said, 'I didn't really want another drink anyway.'

'Me neither,' Chipper chimed in. 'And the girls have still got some left.'

'Where's Pam, by the way?'

'Talking to some other girls she knows,' Fred said, nodding to where Pam was leaning down talking to, of all people, Sally's friend, Sandra and the other two girls. Sally wasn't with them; perhaps she'd gone to the cloakroom to cool down.

Phil nodded in the direction of the bar. 'Did you see all that?'

'Could hardly miss it, mate.' Chipper's nod indicated the proximity of the bar. 'We had a grandstand view.'

'It's not like you to lose it like that, Phil,' commented Fred. 'What brought your little fit of temper on?'

Much calmer now, Phil shook his head. 'I don't honestly know. I suppose I didn't like her flaunting herself like that. And with an erk too.'

'It looked pretty innocuous to me,' Fred said, raising an eyebrow. 'If you ask me, you're jealous.'

Fred's throwaway comment hit him like a blow to the stomach and he was forced to admit Fred was right. He was resentful that she was showing attention to everyone but him. But how could he when he was with Pam, who was even now coming back to their table? Had she seen the altercation with Sally? He was pretty certain she hadn't especially when she sat down at his side and reached for his hand. 'All right, sweetheart?'

Guilt consumed him. She was such a kind, loving person, how could he possibly be attracted to someone else? He needed to pull himself together. From that point on, he concentrated on her and her alone, holding her hand, talking to her, making sure she got on the coach back to Blackpool safely.

It was only once the billet had settled down for the night that he was able to think things through. He lay on his back, his hands pillowing the back of his head, while he tried to sift through the myriad of emotions going through his mind. He knew he had behaved badly to Sally but he'd wanted it to be him she danced with, flirted with, not some spotty erk. He should have taken into account that she was probably dealing with the loss of her baby by throwing herself into having a good time. Everyone dealt with grief in their own way. He wasn't usually so judgmental, so hasty. So why this time?

As he asked himself the question, the answer came with a dizzying clarity. Because he'd fallen in love with her. He shot upright on the bed and wrapped his arms round his blanketed knees. Now that he thought about it, it made perfect sense. The way her face lit up when she smiled had haunted him for months. This love had crept up on him born of her initial vulnerability and how she'd resolutely faced her pregnancy alone. But where did this revelation put him with Pam? He certainly didn't want to hurt her but what he felt for her paled into insignificance compared to the intensity of his feelings for Sally.

He threw himself back down on the bed and groaned. What a hell of a mess he'd got himself into!

180

CHAPTER 18

The trees in the gardens of the posh houses along Chorley New Road were showing the fresh greenness of May as Joyce travelled on the bus to Bolton. She hadn't been to see Dave for several days now. He had made good progress, they said, considering the seriousness of the injury but these things took time. The doctors had stressed that the issue should not be forced; Dave should be allowed to remember at his own pace. She hoped that, given time, he would recover his memory. At least that part of it where they'd been girlfriend and boyfriend.

When she reached the ward that Saturday afternoon, her heart gave a leap to see him in a chair at the side of his bed. He was reading the Bolton Evening News final edition and didn't see her approach so she was able to look at him for some seconds. He was still wearing pyjamas, with a blanket tucked around his knees. Then she noticed his bare feet, with slender bones and long toes, peeking out from under the edge of the blanket. The sight of them made him look so vulnerable and a rush of warmth and love flooded her.

As he turned the page, he looked up and saw her. 'Hello, Joyce. How long have you been standing there?'

'Only a minute.' She went to the other side of the bed and brought a chair round to sit opposite him. Somehow it seemed more intimate to be sitting like this, their knees almost touching, instead of at the side of his bed. 'I see they've got you out of bed.'

He folded the newspaper and tucked it down at the side of him. 'Yes, they've been gradually increasing the amount each day. Today, I'm allowed to sit out for visiting time.'

'And how are you feeling?'

'A bit light-headed and wobbly on my pins but not too bad.'

Joyce glanced around the ward. 'Is your Mam not here?'

'No, I asked her not to come today. She told me you were coming and I wanted to talk to you.' His face, she saw now, was set in serious lines and her heart sank.

She tried to be flippant. 'Oh-ho, that sounds serious.'

He ignored the remark. 'I know you came almost every day when I was unconscious because Mam told me. What I want to know is why?'

She wriggled on the chair, not knowing what to say. 'I was concerned about you,' she said eventually.

'But why would the sister of my best mate be so conscientious about visiting me? As far as I'm aware, I hardly know you.' She winced at his words.

'Not that you're not a sight to gladden any lad's heart,' he added, a flash of the old humour in those blue eyes. 'And how come you were the one to find me after the accident?' He leaned forward and took her hand and though she knew he didn't mean anything by the gesture, she thrilled to his touch. 'I know the doctors have said I shouldn't force myself to remember but the not knowing is driving me mad, Joyce. It's like there's something I know, even something I need to be doing, that I can't quite recall. I know whatever it is, it's important.'

She knew then that she had to tell him, whatever the consequences. Her mouth went dry and her throat closed up at the thought. She swallowed painfully then said, 'You and I have been going out together.'

He snatched his hand away and leaned against the back of the chair, the newspaper falling to the floor as he did so. 'You and me?' he whispered. 'For how long?'

'For the past year.'

'A year? Does Nick know?'

182

'He didn't at first. We met in secret for a long time. Then our families found out and we were forbidden to see each other.' She picked her words carefully.

He clapped the palm of his hand against his forehead. 'Bloody hell! I wish I could remember.'

He had paled a little, she saw. 'Are you all right?' she asked. 'Should I fetch a nurse?'

'No, I'm fine, honestly.' He took a deep breath. 'If we were forbidden to see each other, how come we were together the night of my accident?'

She gave a small smile. 'We still kept seeing each other though not as often and further afield.'

'Did we now?' Despite his pallor, there was a hint of humour around his mouth. 'I want you to tell me what happened that night.'

Again she chose her words with care. 'You know Jud Simcox and his mates were involved?'

'Yes, the police told me that much. Go on.'

'Well, Jud has been mithering me for months to go out with him.' She saw his hands clench and her heart lifted a little. 'We'd gone to the pictures in Bolton and Jud must have been in the audience.' She shivered as she forced herself to think about the events of that night. 'When we came out of a side door, he and his mates were waiting for us.' She hesitated then told him what had happened and how Jud had intimated to the police that she had been two-timing Dave with Jud.

This time the colour rushed to his face and she wondered if she had gone too far. 'The bastard! I might not remember about the two of us but I know enough about you to know you'd never do that. No wonder Nick's been so cagey when he's visited me.

'Speaking of Nick, he told me he's got engaged to Kathy Armstrong. That came as a surprise because I couldn't even remember that they'd been going out together.' To her surprise, he put his hand over hers and squeezed it. 'Thanks, Joyce. I do feel better for knowing at least some of what's missing.' Then he paused, his brow puckering, 'But I still feel as if there's something I should be doing.'

183

She knew it was their plan to elope to Scotland. She would never tell him now. She didn't want him to feel obligated to do something about it. 'Perhaps it will come to you later,' she consoled.

'I might not remember much but I know one thing for certain,' he said, his eyes twinkling. 'I always did fancy you.'

Those words were almost exactly the same as he'd said to her at the start of their relationship. She hoped that was a sign it would eventually come right between them.

* * *

Phil sat at his desk, papers piled up in front of him, waiting for his normally methodical mind to function. He'd been like this since he'd acknowledged his love for Sally. She was constantly in his thoughts even though he hadn't seen her for the last couple of weeks. What was he going to do? He was in love with one girl while supposedly going out with another. When he and Pam had been together, he'd seen the worry in her eyes as if she knew something was troubling him. Common sense told him he should forget Sally and devote himself to Pam. At the back of his mind were the enormous implications with Sally's family and his should she return his feelings. That alone gave him pause. But his heart was telling him otherwise. Round and round these thoughts went until he thought he'd go mad with them.

'Bloody skiving again, Corporal?' said a familiar voice at his side. Flight Sergeant Wilkinson strode into the room and stopped at Phil's desk.

'Just reckoning something up in my head, Sarge,' he replied, making a note on the sheet before him, anything, something he could erase later.

'There'll be hell on earth if there's no pay on Thursday,' Wilko warned, 'and it'd have to come out of your wages.'

184

'I'm almost there, Sarge.' Phil bent his head to the stack of papers before him. Bloody Wilko! He wasn't very tall yet he had the arrogant attitude of so many small men, that of a big man in a small man's body. He could be a nasty bugger too if he was crossed so everyone tended to steer as clear of him as they could.

Yet the man had his more human side. It had been he who'd told Phil about his brother Brian's death and had done so in a way that neither Phil nor anyone else would have given him credit for. He had already arranged for Phil to have compassionate leave and issued a rail warrant for his travel back to Horwich. And all with the minimum amount of fuss.

As if he'd been reading Phil's mind and wanted to erase such charitable thoughts, Wilko began clattering round in a filing cabinet. 'Don't know who you think you are, Roberts, with your know-it-all attitude. Why you're rated so highly, I'll never know.' He took a file out of the cabinet and banged the drawer with such force that the filing cabinet actually rocked.

'Yes, Sergeant.' Phil hid a smile. He couldn't care less what Wilko thought. He knew he was well thought of by his senior officers because he'd seen his file a couple of months ago. One of his jobs, while preparing the pay for the ranks was to go through the files to see if anyone had a court judgement against them. In doing so, he'd seen his own file and not been able to resist a peek. 'Capable and industrious in his approach to his work,' it had read, 'uses own initiative and needs little supervision.' The final comment had been a mere three letters, POM, which he knew meant potential officer material.

The phone on Wilko's desk shrilled and with a sigh he answered it. 'Sir!' he said. It was almost as if Wilko was physically standing to attention and Phil smiled. 'Yes, sir. At once, sir.' As he replaced the receiver, he gave Phil a look of disdain. 'That was the CO, Roberts. He wants to see you pronto.'

'Me?' Phil gaped at him. He didn't come into contact much with the CO, rarely saw him unless he passed through the offices or inspected the ranks on parade.

'If you're Corporal Philip Roberts, then yes, he wants to see you.' Phil looked at the more senior NCO warily. Was he about

185

to face a telling off by the big man? If so, he couldn't think of anything he'd done wrong. 'Get on with you! Doesn't do to be tardy with the CO,' Wilko prompted him.

A couple of minutes later, he was shown into the CO's office. He stood to attention and saluted smartly. 'Corporal Roberts, Sir.'

'Ah, Roberts. At ease, man.' Although the CO was tall, he was well-made and carried himself upright. He peered at Phil over his glasses as if assessing him. A file was open on the desk in front of him and Phil guessed it was his personnel file. 'You've been in the RAF now for two years. Is that right?'

'Just over two years, Sir. I came in as a National Serviceman.'

'And you've chosen to make the RAF your career. A wise choice. May I ask why you decided to do so?'

Phil wondered where this was leading. 'There was nowt – nothing – for me in Civvy Street, Sir; at least nothing I particularly wanted to do.'

'You didn't fancy an apprenticeship then?'

'I'm not practically minded, Sir.'

'Yet you've instituted a simplified filing system that has impressed everyone who has had to use it. And several more useful solutions to problems Admin have had, I'm given to understand.'

Phil was pleased with the compliment. 'I think I'm better suited to organising than anything else, Sir.'

'Can you tell me why?' The CO seemed genuinely interested.

Phil had to think for a moment. 'It's because I like the logicality and reasoning to see the job done more efficiently, Sir.'

The CO grinned which transformed his rather serious face. 'Think we could have done with a few more like you, Roberts, in the last war.'

'With respect, Sir, can I ask why you're asking me these sorts of questions?' Phil said diffidently.

'Your superiors think very highly of you, Roberts, and think you could go far in the Service.'

Phil was even more chuffed. 'Thank you, Sir.'

186

'What do you know of the career structure in the RAF?'

So that's where this was leading! They were thinking of promoting him. 'That Flight Sergeant is the highest you can go as a non-commissioned officer, Sir.'

'Well, as a first step, I can tell you that we are considering promoting you to Sergeant, Roberts.'

Although he was stunned by the news, he remained where he was, feet apart, hands behind his back. 'Thank you, Sir.'

'We'll send you on a course or two with a view to learning a little about man management skills, see how you go on with those,' the CO explained. 'That will probably happen later this year.'

Phil coughed to clear his suddenly dry throat. 'I shall look forward to the challenge, Sir.'

'Good man. I'm sure you'll do fine with your organisational skills. And Roberts?'

'Yes, Sir.'

'If you keep up the good work you've shown so far, there's no reason why you shouldn't make a Warrant Officer eventually.'

Phil was staggered by the suggestion. He knew about WOs, of course, that it was the rank between a non-commissioned and a commissioned officer and that it was not uncommon to rise from there to become a Flight Lieutenant. 'Thank you for the faith the Service has in me. I shall do my best to prove worthy.'

'Given your current record, I have no doubt that faith will be justified.' The CO closed his file and Phil guessed the interview was coming to an end. 'Do you have any questions?'

'I don't think so, Sir, but can I come back if I think of any?'

The CO stood and leaned over to shake Phil's hand. 'Of course. Just make an appointment.'

Phil took the proffered hand. 'Thank you again, Sir.'

The CO waved his hand airily. 'You may go, Roberts.

Back in the office, Wilko was still at the desk, apparently working through that pile of papers. 'What did the CO want, Roberts?'

Phil sat at his desk and drew his own paperwork towards him. 'I'm afraid I'm not at liberty to say, Sarge.'

Wilko harrumphed and returned his attention to his work while Phil tried to do the same. After the encouraging and satisfying news he'd been given, it was a major struggle.

CHAPTER 19

Sally woke with a start, conscious that the light coming through the now-repaired window of the attic bedroom – she'd moved back there now the boarding house was getting busier – was much brighter than it should have been. She reached for the alarm clock, saw it had gone half-past seven and groaned. Damn! She must have dozed off again after switching the alarm off. Betty would be furious and rightly so.

Within ten minutes, she'd washed, dressed and was making her way downstairs. Betty, carrying a tray through to the dining room, met her in the hallway, her face set in angry lines. 'Good of you to put in an appearance,' she said, holding the tray out to Sally. 'You can take this in to Mr and Mrs Johnson at the window table.'

Sally took the tray from Betty and said, 'I'm really sorry, Betty.'

Betty flapped her hand and turned to go back to the kitchen. 'We'll talk about it later when we've more time.'

That breakfast time descended into chaos and Sally knew it was her fault. She mixed up some orders and knocked over a jug of milk onto a clean tablecloth. The guests themselves, as if sensing she was near to tears, couldn't have been kinder. 'Never mind, love,' one elderly lady said, patting her hand as she tried to mop up the spilt milk. 'We all have days like that.'

The telling-off she'd been expecting took place as they were finishing off their own breakfast and relaxing with a second cup of tea. Bob had already gone through to open up the café so it was just Betty and her. 'That's the third time you've overslept in two weeks, Sally, and it's not good enough,' she began.

With a headache now pounding between her eyes, she said, more sharply than she'd intended, 'I've said I'm sorry.'

'This gallivanting has got to stop, love.'

'I'm free in the evenings, you said. That means I can go out if I want to.' She'd been going out almost every night, either dancing, or going into pubs with her friends from the Moncrieff.

'You're right, of course, but does it have to be every evening?' There was no mistaking the concern in Betty's voice. 'It's taking its toll on you. I'm sorry if I seem harsh but you look terrible. I just think it's too soon after your … experience. You should be taking more care of yourself.'

Sally gripped her cup tightly with both hands. 'I do my work, don't I?'

'Apart from missing out on three early morning teas, I've no complaint there, neither do the guests. On the contrary, you seem to put yourself out for them. But the fact remains, Sally, I need someone I can rely on and just recently I haven't been able to do that.' Betty reached out over the table and put a hand on Sally's arm. 'I think you're throwing yourself into this hectic social life in an attempt to forget your grief.'

Sally's defensive attitude now crumbled and tears stung at the back of her eyes. 'You're right, Betty, that's exactly what I'm doing,' she whispered.

'It's not working though, is it?' Betty said, gently removing her hand.

Sally shook her head. 'No, it's not. It's all still so fresh in my mind, especially when I'm alone in my room at night.'

'And what's happened to Phil? We haven't seen him around in a while either.'

She squirmed a little on her chair. 'We had an argument when I went to the last camp dance. He accused me of being a cheap tart.'

Betty looked at her over the rim of her own cup. 'Were you?'

'A bit,' she admitted, 'but he did humiliate me in front of everyone.'

'Perhaps one of you should apologise.'

'Well, it's not going to be me.'

But the more she thought about it afterwards, though, the more she realised he'd been right. She had been flaunting herself at the dance. She'd thrown herself into a hectic social life to try and forget the deeper, almost unspoken grief that still haunted her.

She was still debating whether to try contacting him when he phoned her that same evening. The first thing he said was, 'Are you still speaking to me?'

She experienced a feeling of warmth to hear his familiar voice again. 'Depends on what you want to say.'

'Is sorry enough?'

She smiled though there was no one to see her in the hallway. 'Not even nearly,' she quipped. 'Only saying it on your knees will do.'

'It's Wednesday tomorrow. Can I come round? We could go out for one of our walks.'

She didn't go out that evening and slept better as a consequence. She sailed through the morning's breakfast rush and the routine cleaning with a smile on her lips, admitting, reluctantly, that she'd hated falling out with Phil. He was the link, however tenuous, to her old life when her heart hadn't been marked by grief.

To her disappointment, it was raining by the afternoon, a miserable driving rain that came in off the sea on a raw wind. Instead of the planned walk, they paid the entrance fee to go into the Tower building. Apart from the circus and the ride to the top of the Tower, out of action because of the wind, most of the attractions were free.

There was still a little awkwardness between them and they didn't talk much to begin with. They wandered round the darkened Aquarium with its too-small viewing panels, and the

191

Zoo, where the animals paced restlessly round their cages. She felt sorry for them and said as much to Phil.

'Let's go to the Ballroom then. We can at least sit down and have a cuppa,' he said. Although the Ballroom was busy with so many people seeking shelter, they found a vacant table on the balcony overlooking the dance floor. Phil looked at his watch. 'Almost time for Reg Dixon.'

She thought he was serious at first till she looked at his face and saw the grin quirking his mouth. It was tradition that the oldies gathered in the Ballroom to watch the organist playing popular dance music on the famous Tower Ballroom organ. They sat in companionable silence for some moments, watching a gaggle of young children sliding on their knees across the dance floor. 'Seems a long time since I did that,' Sally said.

'Me too. Well, we had to do something to relieve the boredom while our parents waited for Reg Dixon.' Then, to her surprise, he got down on his knees and said, 'Will this do, Sally?'

'Get up, you barmpot!' Sally laughed. 'I didn't mean it literally.'

He rose from his knees and, dusting down his trousers, sat down opposite her. 'Seriously, Sally, I am truly sorry for the way I behaved at the dance. My mates had no hesitation in telling me what a complete ... idiot I were.'

Having an older brother, Sally could guess what he had been going to say and smiled. 'You were right though,' she said. 'I've been throwing myself into having a so-called 'good time' in an attempt to forget what happened.'

'Has it worked?'

She shook her head. 'It's failed dismally.'

He put his hand over hers where it lay on the table, squeezing her fingers. 'I'm sorry, Sally.'

'You've already said that.'

'I meant I'm sorry you're unhappy.'

'I've even wondered if I should go back to Horwich. Except I couldn't leave Betty and Bob in the lurch.'

'Is that really what you want?' he asked gently.

'That's just it, I don't know what I want,' she cried. 'I still feel like my life ended when I lost my baby.'

'How long is it now? Five or six weeks?' Phil said reasonably. 'It's still early days, love. Just give it time.'

She told him then about oversleeping and the telling-off she'd received from Betty. 'I deserved it though. Normally we take it in turns to do the morning teas but, being late up, both Betty and Bob had to get up to do it, especially as we're nearly full at the moment.'

'Best thing you could do would be to throw yourself into the job and see how you feel at the end of the season.'

'Thanks, Phil, I always feel better for having talked to you.' It was true, she reflected, his logical way of looking at things that were bothering her was invaluable.

He removed his hand and she felt its loss keenly. 'There's one thing I ought to mention,' he said diffidently. 'I've had another letter from my Mam.'

She had a feeling she wasn't going to like what she was about to hear. 'Is it about Jud?'

'Not this time,' Phil said. 'It's Nick. He and Kathy got engaged on her 21st birthday.'

She waited for some kind of reaction, a sinking feeling perhaps, a pang of jealousy. None came. 'Well, I'd been expecting summat like that, I suppose.'

'You're not bothered?'

'Not any more. Any remaining feeling for Nick died with our baby.'

His face brightened. 'That's good news.'

Just then, the faint strains of Reg Dixon's signature tune, 'Oh, I Do Like To Be Beside The Seaside,' were heard as the giant Wurlitzer organ began its rise to the dance floor. They gave each other a rueful look. 'Do you want to go? Or shall we stay?' Phil asked.

'Nowhere else to go,' she said. 'Might as well stay.'

He rose and laid a warm hand on her shoulder. 'I'll go and get us a cuppa now then.'

* * *

Phil sat in the Bellisima Coffee Bar, glancing out of the window from time to time to catch sight of Pam as she hurried to meet him after work. She had been puzzled by his request but he'd managed evade her curiosity by gabbling that he had to dash as someone urgently needed the phone box. He was dreading this coming meeting but knew it had to be faced. Since the afternoon at the Tower with Sally, when they'd laughed and talked together so companionably, he'd known he had to be honest with Pam. It wasn't fair on her otherwise. His feelings for Sally were too strong for him to ignore, whatever she might feel about him.

In the end, Pam took him by surprise, so deep was he in his thoughts that he hadn't seen her approach. She dropped a quick kiss on his cheek before sitting opposite him. 'Caught you out,' she said, laughing. 'You were miles away.'

He gave a rueful shrug of his shoulders. 'I seem to be doing a lot of that recently.'

'What did you want to talk to me about?' she said as she unbuttoned her coat. 'You were a bit cagey on the phone.'

'Let me get you a drink first. Cappuccino OK?'

In the ten minutes he had to wait while the waitress fussed about with the hissing espresso machine, he tried to pull his thoughts together. Even though he'd planned beforehand what he would say, the words had now disappeared. Instead, he was left with a dry mouth and sweating hands. This was not going to be easy and he hated hurting her.

Back at the table, a cappuccino in front of her, she looked at him expectantly. 'Well?'

'I had an interesting meeting with the CO the other day.' He swallowed and tried to clear his throat. 'They're thinking of promoting me to Sergeant.'

She reached across to take his hand. 'Oh, Phil, that is good news.'

194

'It means I'm going to have to go away from time to time on various courses.'

'But surely that's part of the standard procedure, isn't it? Why did you need to meet me to tell me that?'

He pulled his hand away and took a sip of his now cold tea. 'Once I'm promoted, I shall probably be posted somewhere else within a year.'

At the news, her face fell. 'Have you any idea where?'

He shook his head. 'It could be anywhere, even abroad to Cyprus or Germany.' Knowing how she'd hate the idea of moving away from her family, he'd thought this might be a way of letting her down easily.

When she sighed and said, 'Well, there's plenty of time, isn't there?' he knew he'd been wrong to think that. In the face of his sudden silence, she looked at him, a shrewd look in her eyes. 'That's not all, is it, Phil?'

'No, love, if I'm totally honest.'

'There's someone else. That's what you're really telling me,' she said in a small voice.

'Yes, there is. I'm sorry, Pam, really I am.'

Drawing in a deep breath, she said, 'It's Sally, isn't it?'

He looked at her in surprise. 'How did you know?'

'I saw you both at her birthday party, remember? I know you laughed it off but the suspicion was there. Then, someone told me about the argument you two had at the dance. You were very quiet after that, even though you never left my side.' Her hand, he saw, was shaking as she held the cup but he didn't think it was appropriate to cover it with his own. 'Does she feel the same about you?'

'I don't know. I haven't asked her. And I wanted to talk to you first.'

She put the cup down on the saucer so hard the froth came over the side. 'So, this business about being promoted and posted elsewhere was an excuse to get rid of me?'

'No, never that, but I did think you ought to know, given how you felt about moving away.'

195

'I could maybe have got used to the idea, but it was never going to happen, was it?'

'No, love, it wasn't.'

'Will you tell Sally … how you feel about her?'

'When the time is right but … there are complications that we'd have to overcome.'

'What complications?' she said sharply. 'Anything to do with the baby? Was the baby yours? A fling you had that you'd forgotten about till she approached you?'

'No!' he said. 'Nothing like that. I can't tell you without betraying a confidence.'

To his dismay, she started to cry. 'So, this is the end.'

Feeling wretched at having to hurt her, he nodded. 'You do see we can't carry on seeing each other when I feel the way I do about someone else?'

'Of course not. But that doesn't stop me feeling a bit used. I mean, we've been going out for a year now.'

'I never meant for you to feel that but that's why I thought you should know. It's only fair to you not to continue.'

'You know I love you, don't you?' The anguish in her voice was obvious to him.

'I'm sorry about that, Pam, but I never said I loved you, did I?'

'No,' she sobbed. 'But I thought … I see now I was wrong.'

'I'm very fond of you, Pam, you're such a lovely person, but it's not enough.' Although the coffee bar wasn't particularly busy, a couple of customers were whispering and looking at them. 'Look, love, let's get out of here.'

Outside, it had started raining, not the driving kind, but the persistent drizzle that seemed to typify Lancashire. They passed a few people hurrying home from work, looking as miserable as Phil felt. Pam was still crying, silent tears tracking down her face. Phil cursed himself. He felt such a heel doing this to her. It might come easy to some lads but it didn't to him. He pulled her into a doorway and put his arms round her, rocking her, soothing her. 'I'm so, so sorry, Pam.'

'I'll be … all right soon,' she gulped, already mastering her tears. 'It was a shock, that's all, but I see now … I took things too much for granted, didn't I?' She looked up at him, her eyes tear-filled still.

'And I suppose I let matters drift along between us without thinking,' he said, 'but I did enjoy your company.'

'I'm just not the one you see a future with.'

'No.' There seemed little point in saying anything else.

She pulled a handkerchief from her pocket, carefully dabbed her eyes. 'Well, there's no more to be said, is there?'

'I guess not.'

Drawing in a deep breath, she pulled away from him and buttoned her coat. 'Then it's goodbye, Phil.' As he moved towards her to give her a last hug, she put her hand against his chest. 'No, don't, please. Just let me walk away.'

And, with a straightening of her spine and a brisk step, she did just that, leaving Phil staring at her back with respect and admiration.

CHAPTER 20

When Sandra phoned Sally towards the end of May to ask if she wanted to go dancing with them to the Winter Gardens on Saturday night, she'd said no at first, until Betty had intervened. 'When I spoke to you about going out too much,' Betty had said after the phone call, 'I didn't mean you should become a recluse.'

Sally laughed. 'I've been out a few times.'

'And back early each time,' Betty said, raising a whimsical eyebrow. 'Seriously, love, it would do you good to go out with Sandra and the girls. You've worked exceptionally hard this last couple of weeks or so with us being so busy.'

Maybe Betty was right. It would do her good to go dancing with the girls. Deciding what to wear, she had to discard the rose pink dress, now a little on the big side. Betty had promised that she would show Sally how to take it in. Her own mother had been hopeless about anything like that. In the meantime, she puzzled over what to wear. She decided in the end on a sky blue blouse that accentuated the blue of her eyes and a midnight blue circular skirt she'd bought a few weeks ago. Even that was a bit loose but an elasticated waspie belt cured the problem and stopped the blouse from sliding out. When she was dressed, she looked in the full-length mirror in the old wardrobe in her room and saw that the outfit outlined her petite curvy figure in a more feminine way than the tight skirts and jumpers she'd worn previously. That phase in her life had belonged to Nick and it was over. She found she did not want to resurrect it.

In the beautifully embellished Empress Ballroom, she didn't lack for partners, none of them did. Late in the evening, she, Sandra, Ruth and Barbara were giggling at something that had occurred with one of their partners when she saw Phil. He was waltzing past with an attractive brunette, almost as tall as he was, and he was looking down at her face as she said something. Not expecting to see him, Sally was overcome with a surge of unexpected warmth, her legs began to tremble and her mouth became dry. As she tried to cope with these entirely new feelings, he saw her. In that instance, she saw the same emotions reflected on his face. But why wasn't he with Pam?

He'd danced past her by then but she knew he'd come to find her as soon as that particular dance had finished. Then he was at her elbow. 'Sally,' he said quietly. 'I didn't know you were going to be here.'

'I could say the same about you,' she challenged. 'Where's Pam?'

A shadow flitted across his face. 'I'm not seeing her anymore.'

Her heart did a somersault at his words. 'Oh, I'm sorry.'

'Dance with me?' he said, as the music started up again.

He looked different tonight but perhaps that was because she was looking at him through new eyes and seeing him as very attractive young man. For one thing, he was wearing a suit, a dark one with a faint sheen, a blue shirt so pale it was a milky white and a tie almost the same colour as her blouse. His fair hair, worn as always in the regulation short back and sides, was gleaming in the reflections from the rotating glitter ball over the dance floor. She had never thought him particularly good-looking but tonight the strong bones of his face had taken on a look of maturity and authority that belied his youth. Now, his mouth was quirked in a questioning smile and she realised he was waiting for an answer. 'Why not?' she said.

He didn't follow her on to the dance floor as most partners did; he took hold of her hand. This simple contact, which she'd known a dozen or so times previously, now sent shivers up her arm. She would have stumbled had he not had hold of her.

'Sally? Are you all right?' He was looking down at her, concern on his face.

'Just a bit dizzy, that's all,' she said. 'It's very warm in here.'

'If you'd prefer, we could sit this one out.'

'No, let's dance.' She suddenly wanted to feel his arms around her. But this was crazy! What on earth was wrong with her tonight? But she knew. She was beginning to be attracted to Phil.

He led her straight to the middle of the dance floor where, in the subdued light, younger couples were smooching, arms locked round each other, cheek resting against cheek. He put his arm round her back, her hand up to his chest and somehow it was more intimate that way. She gave up trying to understand what was happening and simply enjoyed the sensations surging through her body. The remainder of the dance seemed to pass as in a dream.

Neither spoke again until the music stopped and reluctantly they drew apart. 'Are you bothered about staying?' he said finally.

She was almost afraid to ask. 'What did you have in mind?'

'It's a lovely evening out there, quite warm, and it would be a shame to waste it. We could go for a walk.'

'All right then,' she replied, not wanting this reckless mood to end. 'But I won't be able to walk far in these shoes.'

Sandra gave her a knowing look when Sally and Phil walked back to tell her they were leaving. 'Don't do anything I wouldn't do,' she said with a grin.

'That gives me plenty of choice then,' Sally quipped, looking back over her shoulder.

'Will you need to tell Chipper and Fred?' she asked Phil as they made their way to the cloakroom.

'No, there's a whole gang of us here tonight. Someone's 21st, so they won't miss me.' He stopped and turned to her. 'You sure you don't mind leaving early?'

'Not at all. I didn't particularly want to be late getting back, with us being so busy now,' she said, collecting her coat from the cloakroom attendant. 'I've been doing what you suggested, concentrating on my work.'

'Is it paying off?' he said, helping her into her coat.

'Yes, I feel much more settled. What's more, I'm enjoying it. Something I never thought would be possible a couple of months ago,' she said. 'Thinking about what needs doing and planning ahead gives me such a lot of satisfaction.'

'So you're finding the more you put into it, the more you get out of it?'

'Exactly.' She took a deep breath. 'And I feel a kind of acceptance now about what happened ... with the baby.'

Within minutes, they'd left behind the ornate splendour of the Winter Gardens and stepped into the refreshingly cool night air. Although it was still fairly early in the season, there were quite a few people about. Most of the visitors would come later from the mill towns when they held their traditional Wakes Weeks holidays. Sally had found she liked Blackpool best when it was like this, not too busy. 'Where to, Phil?' she asked now.

He took hold of her hand and once again she thrilled to his touch. 'What about the North Pier? It's not too far away and it'll be quieter than the Promenade.' That wide esplanade was thronged with noisy groups of young people who'd come off the daily excursion trains and were parading up and down in the hope of attracting members of the opposite sex. Sally felt considerably older than them after all she'd been through. And, she suddenly realised, for all that Phil was younger than Nick, he always seemed more mature.

She pushed the vague thought of Nick from her mind. Tonight she was with his brother. Quite what was happening between them, she had no way of knowing. Nor was she going to question either of their motives for leaving the dance early. It was enough simply to be with him.

As they came up to the Promenade, one of the horse and carriages that traversed the Promenade passed them with two laughing couples inside. 'Do you know, in all the years I've been coming to Blackpool, I've never had a go in one of them?' she said wistfully.

202

'Neither have I,' he said, his face lighting up. 'Let's try and get one.' Five minutes later, an empty carriage bowled towards them and Phil hailed the driver. He agreed to take them down to South Shore and bring them back to the North Pier.

The carriage sagged a little as they climbed aboard, making it seem quite flimsy, but it righted itself as Phil tucked a rug over their legs and took hold of her hand under the blanket. Then they were off, the horse trotting effortlessly down the Promenade. Feeling the air rushing past their cheeks was exhilarating and Sally felt very grand to be looking down on the passers-by. The lights from the pubs, hotels and guest houses passed by in a kind of blur as her eyes watered in the onrush of air. The driver turned at South Shore and they were off again, this time with the Promenade on their left. The dark sea beyond showed only an occasional glimmer of light from some distant shore. The carriage stopped at the entrance to the North Pier and she and Phil argued mildly about who was going to pay. In the end, they compromised and laughingly paid half each. 'That were brilliant,' she breathed. 'I'm glad we did it.'

'It seemed the right thing to do tonight,' he said as they paid to go on to the Pier. It was quieter here with not many people about though, as they approached the theatre on the Pier, they could hear the laughter and applause coming from the show there. It was pleasant strolling along but Sally had to take care she didn't get her heel stuck in one of the cracks between the planks that made up the Pier. Below, the waves were lapping against the cast iron supports and the sound was soothing.

'It's so peaceful, isn't it?' she breathed. 'I'm glad you suggested it.'

Before reaching the theatre, there were some shelters looking out towards the sea. 'Let's sit down a while,' he said. 'It's more exposed here and I don't want you to get cold.'

She was glad of a sit-down. After dancing most of the night then walking, her feet were hurting. There was a cool breeze blowing off the sea, bringing a hint of salt to her lips, and she gave a slight shiver.

He was immediately concerned. 'You are cold, aren't you? Cuddle up closer to me and I'll try to keep you warm.' He put his arm round her, pulling her closer to him and she was glad of the solid feel of him. She hadn't before noticed how muscular he was.

It wasn't so much the coolness of the night air that was making her tremble; it was the almost tangible tension between them. In an attempt to break it, she pointed to the view before them. The street lights of the Promenade were casting rippling reflections on the sea, while overhead, in the comparative darkness of the Pier, stars twinkled in their millions. 'How romantic it all looks just now.'

'You can't see any of the shabbiness and the brassy stalls at this distance,' he said. 'Beautiful though the view is, it gives a false sense of glamour.'

'That's a very cynical thing to say, Phil,' she laughed.

'Living so close to Blackpool, seeing it in season and out, has made me that way,' he said. 'Despite all that, I have a fondness for the old place. I'm going to miss it when I go.'

She turned to him in consternation. 'Why? Where are you going?'

He looked uncomfortable as if he'd said too much. 'I can't say owt at the moment but it looks like I'm going to be moving on.'

The enormity of what he'd said made her heart sink and she spoke without thinking. 'Oh Phil, I can't bear the thought of you not being here.'

His arm tightened round her shoulders. 'Nothing's definite yet. I really shouldn't have said anything.'

'When will you know?'

'It might not come off at all.' He took his hand from hers and turned her face gently towards him, his fingers caressing her cheek. 'Will it really upset you if I get transferred?'

'You know it will,' she whispered.

Then his mouth was on hers and he was kissing her, a kiss at once tender and passionate. And, without thinking about the consequences, she was responding. The kiss went on for a long time until she broke away and said, 'What's happening here, Phil?'

'Don't let's think about it,' he said, his lips against her neck. The sensation sent delicious shivers down her spine. 'I just know that tonight I want to be with you.' He kissed her again and she gave herself up to the feelings he was arousing in her. She wanted to be with him too and for this night never to end, especially when he was kissing her like this. The consequences, whatever they were, could wait.

CHAPTER 21

Joyce and Dave sat in a functional, government-green painted room waiting to be called into Court. They were both anxious, neither having been in a courtroom before. The solicitor had explained what, as witnesses for the prosecution, they could expect and when. Dave would be summoned first and Joyce would have to wait alone until she was called. They'd heard via their solicitor that Jud was pleading not guilty which meant the case could drag on for longer.

'Calling David Yates.' The call echoed round the corridor outside and a Court official opened the door to the waiting room, beckoning Dave to him. 'Mr Yates, they're ready for you now.'

As he stood to follow, Dave turned to her and said, 'Just remember what the solicitor told us. Stick to the facts and don't let the defence barrister rattle you or trip you up.'

She pulled a face. 'That's what I'm afraid of.'

'You'll be fine,' he said, giving her a quick grin and followed the official.

After he'd gone, the time seemed to drag interminably. What made the waiting worse was that there was nothing to look at or read. Instead, to stop her wondering how Dave was getting on in the Court, she paced the distance between the walls. She was concerned that the proceedings would be too much for him so soon after leaving hospital. The doctors had said he was well enough to attend but, in her eyes, he still looked pale and the strain of today was showing in his eyes. His head had been shaved initially in the area of his wound but since coming out of hospital, he'd had the rest cut very short so the shaved area wouldn't look too obvious. The result had been to outline the fine bones of his face making it seem thinner than usual and, to her, more vulnerable.

Today was the first time she had seen him since he'd come out of hospital and their conversation was a little strained. Since that throwaway remark about fancying her, nothing further had been said. It was obvious that, apart from the accident, his memory was showing no sign of returning and she didn't know where she stood with him. Nor could she force the issue.

'Calling Joyce Roberts,' came the disembodied voice from the corridor and once more the Court official appeared in the doorway. 'Your turn now, Miss Roberts.' He gave her a warm smile.

She drew in a deep breath to try and stop her body from shaking and smoothed her skirt down. 'I'm ready.'

As they walked down the corridor, he asked if she was nervous. 'A little,' she confessed. 'I've never done anything like this before.'

'It'll be over before you know it,' he reassured her.

In the witness box, she was handed a bible on which to swear that she would tell the truth. She found the scene before her intimidating. The judge, suitably robed and wigged, was seated on a raised dais with royal coat of arms behind him. He had a round chubby face with a prominent double chin but he didn't look particularly stern. She had no idea if that was a good or a bad sign. In front of him and seated at a table were a couple of bewigged Court officials and an older woman whom she guessed was the stenographer. On either side were seated solicitors and barristers for the prosecution and defence. The jury, solid looking citizens all, were seated to one side.

In the public gallery, she could see Mrs Yates and a few seats further along, Nick, who gave her a surreptitious thumbs-up. Next to him was an older woman with frizzy blonde hair and a nondescript coat straining across an ample chest who she guessed was Jud's mother. Jud himself was in the dock, flanked on either side by Bill Murphy and Jim Stephens. All of them looked dishevelled and unkempt. At her first sight of them since the night it had all happened, she gave an involuntary shudder. She looked to Dave for reassurance. He gave a faint nod of the head as if to tell her that it would be all right.

She was asked to confirm her name, address and age and answered with a slight quaver in her voice. 'Miss Roberts, will you tell us exactly what happened on the night of 21st March when Mr Yates was injured?' This came from the kindly-faced man who was the barrister for the prosecution, Mr Taylor, whom she'd met earlier. She spoke hesitantly at first, until she was asked to speak up by the judge, then as her confidence grew, her voice steadied and she spoke clearly. Mr Taylor asked her a couple of times to clarify a particular point and when she had finished he said, 'Have you, at any time in the past, been out with George Simcox?'

For a second she was confused then realised he was talking about Jud. 'No, sir,' she said firmly.

'Has he ever asked you to go out with him?'

'Yes, sir, about three times.'

'And you refused each time?'

'Yes, sir.'

'Can you tell us why you didn't want to go out with him?'

'I was going out with Dave – Mr Yates – at the time and it would have been wrong. Besides, I don't like him in that way.'

'Are you and Mr Yates still boyfriend and girlfriend?'

The defence barrister leapt to his feet. 'Objection, your honour. This question has no relevance to this case.'

'Your honour, I believe that Miss Roberts's reply will indicate the seriousness of the injury inflicted upon Mr Yates,' Mr Taylor pleaded.

The judge looked over to Joyce as if weighing up her credibility then said, 'Objection overruled. You may proceed, Mr Taylor.'

'Miss Roberts, is Mr Yates still your boyfriend?'

She looked over to Dave but he was looking down at his hands in his lap. 'No, sir, he is not.'

'Can you tell me why not?'

'Because of the injury, he has no memory of our going out together over the past year.'

'Thank you, Miss Roberts.'

The defence barrister, a Mr Jones, then went through her account of the fight, asking her questions as he went along. To her satisfaction, he didn't trip her up once. That is until he said, 'Do you ever lie, Miss Roberts?'

'No, sir, I do not.'

'Yet you carried on a clandestine relationship with Mr Yates for almost a year. Surely that must have involved a great deal of lying and deceit.'

Fire rushed to her face and she had to grip the edge of the witness box. He had caught her out and she could say nothing to that.

Fortunately, he seemed pleased to have made his point for he said, 'No further questions, your honour.'

'You may step down, Miss Roberts,' the judge said. She was surprised to find her legs were still a bit wobbly and she was glad of the Court official's hand under her elbow as she stepped down from the witness box. As she sat next to Dave, he took her hand and gave it a squeeze. 'You did well, Joyce, I'm proud of you.'

The case for the defence followed with first Bill Murphy, then Jim Stephens and finally Jud. Their stories tallied. They had all, they said, acted in self-defence claiming that Dave had been the one to strike first. Joyce wanted to leap up and say that was a lie but Dave must have sensed her tension for he took hold of her hand again and shook his head. To her surprise, no mention was made of Jud's claim that she had been going out with him at the same time as Dave. The defence team must have decided that the claim wouldn't stick.

Next it was the turn of Mr Taylor to cross-examine the defendants. For his own reasons, he chose to concentrate on Jud. As the prosecution barrister had done with her, Mr Taylor lulled Jud with minor points of clarification, then he said, 'Am I right in thinking that you initially claimed you had been seeing Miss Roberts at the same time as she was seeing Mr Yates?'

Jud squirmed and flushed a fiery red. 'I said that on the spur of the moment. I weren't thinking straight.'

'Would I be right then in saying that claim was born of wishful thinking?'

For the first time, Jud looked directly at her. 'Yes, sir,' he said in a subdued voice.

'Are you aware that making such a claim besmirched the reputation of Miss Roberts?'

'I've already said I weren't thinking straight.' Again, he looked at her. 'I'm sorry for any aggravation I've caused Joyce – Miss Roberts.'

'No further questions, your honour,' Mr Taylor said.

'Do you have any further defence witnesses, Mr Jones?'

'No, your honour.'

'In that case, we shall adjourn the court for lunch and resume proceedings this afternoon.'

In the corridor outside, Dave said, 'Phew! I wouldn't like to go through that again.'

'Me neither. I still feel shaky,' Joyce said. 'And I'm dying for a cup of tea.'

Nick made his way over to them and clapped Dave on the back. 'Well done, Brag. You too, Joyce.'

'Isn't Kathy in Court today?' Joyce asked. Kathy was a trainee reporter with the Bolton Evening News and often covered court proceedings.

Her brother's face clouded over. 'She should have been but her father died last night at home.' Kathy's father had been terminally ill with lung cancer for some time and had not been expected to live so long.

'Oh, I am sorry. Tell her so, will you?' Joyce said. She and her future sister-in-law were close friends and Joyce had appreciated her warmth and sincerity last year when Brian, their younger brother, had died.

211

'Look, why don't we all go for a barm cake and a brew?' Nick suggested. 'If we go to the Market Hall, it'd be quicker than anywhere else. We don't want to be late back.'

Over their snack, they discussed the possible outcome of the case. Joyce feared that Jud would get off which would give him even more reason to swagger about.

'I don't think he will,' Dave said. 'He didn't do himself any favours by claiming what he did. Showed himself up as a liar.'

'But the same thing could apply to me. That Mr Jones was right, I did lie to everyone at home when I were seeing Dave,' Joyce pointed out.

Nick took a swig from the mug of tea before him. 'About that. I know things are uncertain at present with Bragger – sorry, Dave – losing his memory but I just wanted you both to know if you two do make a go of it with each other, that'd be ok with me.'

Joyce shot a glance at Dave who was looking uncomfortable and her heart sank. 'I can't speak for Mam and Dad, of course,' Nick went on. 'Best thing you could do, Dave, would be to come up to our house and ask them.'

'I'm still hoping I'll start to remember,' Dave said. 'I'm having occasional flashbacks, especially when I were reliving it all this morning.'

'Oh, that is good news!' Joyce said.

Dave looked directly at her. 'Nothing would give me greater pleasure than to remember everything but I can't force it, Joyce.'

'No, I know that.'

Nick checked his watch. 'Bugger! Is that the time. We'd better scoot or we'll be late.' He gulped the remainder of his tea.

After lunch, Mr Taylor addressed the jury and related the events of the night of the accident and Joyce was impressed at how well he put his case together from so many disparate facts. He made it seem so obvious, in her mind, that the jury would have no option but to find the three of them guilty.

But then she was equally amazed when the defence barrister, Mr Jones, summed up the defence's version of events and again, the facts seemed perfectly logical. She was glad she wasn't on the jury.

Finally, the judge presented his summation of the facts as he saw them. First of all, he said, with the defendants and the principal prosecution witness being Teddy boys, the jury should put on one side any preconceptions they might have concerning Teddy boys. The crux of the matter, he said, was that the jury should decide if the three defendants had acted in self-defence as they claimed or whether the three of them had rushed Mr Yates, causing him to fall to the ground and thus sustain a serious injury. They should take particular note of the severe head injury Mr Yates had incurred and his subsequent loss of memory. Then he adjourned the court so that the jury might deliberate on their verdict.

'That were amazing,' Nick said, as they stood around in the corridor. 'They all made it seem so plausible.'

'I'm glad it weren't just me who thought that,' Joyce said. 'I found myself swaying from one side to the other and I was there.'

'I know what you mean,' agreed Dave. 'No way could I be a barrister or a lawyer.'

Although the corridor was crowded, Joyce caught sight of Jud's mother, her face contorted with anger. 'Don't look now but Jud's Mam is glaring at us. If looks could kill, I'd be dead by now.' She found it hard to reconcile that this dumpy woman was Sally's Mam too. She'd been thrilled to finally hear from Sally though she'd wondered about the long months of silence. What had happened in between that she couldn't write?

After about an hour, an official bade everyone back into the Courtroom as the jury had reached a verdict. When everyone had settled down, the judge said, 'Members of the jury, have you reached a verdict?'

A podgy man wearing an old-fashioned double breasted suit, probably demob issue, rose and said, 'We have, your honour.'

'How do you find the defendants?'

'Guilty, your honour.'

There was a wail of 'Oh, no!' which Joyce guessed came from Jud's mother. Jud himself paled and gripped the rail of the dock with his hands.

Nick cheered while Dave grabbed hold of Joyce, smacking a kiss on her unprepared lips. Then, as he realised what he had done, he said, 'Sorry, Joyce.'

'Don't be.' She laughed, giddy with relief. With a bit of luck, Jud would be behind bars for a while.

As if reading her mind, the judge banged his gavel down. 'Silence in Court, please. Sentence will be passed when the psychiatric reports have been reviewed but it will, in all probability, result in a custodial sentence.'

Those words were music to their ears.

CHAPTER 22

Sally hadn't been able to stop thinking about Phil since that magical evening on North Pier. They had spent what seemed like hours kissing and hadn't wanted to say goodnight. It was only because he had to get back to camp that they had reluctantly parted. Even then, their goodbye had been a lingering one with Phil promising to get in touch when he got back from a course he was due to go on. He'd be away for two weeks.

Now the time was up and she was waiting anxiously to hear from him. They desperately needed to talk. Her head was telling her that having a relationship with Nick's brother wasn't a good idea but it seemed as if her heart and body had a different opinion.

'Away with the fairies again, is she?' Bob's voice broke into her wayward thoughts.

Sally tried to pull herself together and saw that both Betty and Bob were looking at her with amused expressions. 'Did you say summat?'

Betty picked up the large teapot she used at mealtimes. 'I asked if you'd like another cup of tea.'

She held her cup out towards Betty. 'Sorry, Betty. Please.'

'If you ask me, the lass is in love,' Bob said, picking up his Daily Mirror.

'Well, no one's asking you, Bob Parrott, so you can keep your opinions to yourself,' Betty said, more sharply than Bob's remark had warranted. 'And hadn't you better get back to the café?'

'No need. Peggy's in there and doing a grand job.' With both the boarding house and the café being so busy, Bob had had to take on an assistant who came in part-time.

Sally was stunned and shocked by Bob's words, no doubt meant in jest. She hadn't thought of herself as being in love with Phil but now, for the first time, she acknowledged the truth of her love for him. It had crept up on her, as their friendship had grown, sometimes wavering under external circumstances but always providing that constant thread drawing them together again and again. Now she couldn't imagine life without him. But how did he feel about her? If that night on the North Pier was anything to go by, he reciprocated those feelings. Would he shy away from the idea because of any possible problem with their families? That did seem an unsurmountable obstacle.

She was brought back to the present by Bob saying, in a pretend huff, 'Pardon me, I'm sure.' He made a show of shaking the newspaper to straighten it but not before giving Sally a wink.

Betty laughed. 'Take no notice of him, love. Seriously though,' she said, looking at Sally with intent, 'is everything okay? Only you have been a bit distracted this last couple of weeks or so. Not like when you were out till all hours, I hasten to add.'

'I have got summat on my mind,' Sally admitted. A serious understatement, she added silently, longing to be alone to ponder on the newness of this feeling that now seemed so obvious she wondered why she had been blind to it for so long.

'Anything I can help with?'

Sally decided it might indeed help if she were to tell Betty what was troubling her. 'It's about Phil.'

Betty allowed herself a smug smile. 'I thought it might be.'

'I know it's been a secret hope of yours that we might get together,' Sally said diffidently. 'Well, we have, sort of.'

Betty gaped at her. 'When? Where? How?'

'A couple of weeks ago when I went with Sandra and the girls to the Winter Gardens. He were there, one thing led to another and, well, we ended up together.'

216

'And you're worried that he hasn't been in touch?'

'Not really. He's away on a course and he's due back any time,' Sally explained.

'What about his girlfriend? What was her name?'

'Pam. That's all over apparently.'

'Then what's the problem with the two of you taking it further?'

Sally looked at Bob but he seemed to be immersed in his newspaper. Not that it mattered. She didn't mind him hearing. 'It's not straightforward. You know the lad I was involved with before?'

'The father of your baby? Mick, was he called?'

'Nick. Well, Phil happens to be his brother.'

Betty chewed on her bottom lip. 'I can see that might make it complicated. Does Phil know who you are?'

'Yes, he knows now. Someone told him when he went home for Christmas.'

'How did he take it?'

'Not well at first,' she admitted, 'though he came round to the idea in the end. To be honest, things were more relaxed between us once he knew.'

'And you're worried about what his family might think were they to find out?'

'My own family too, come to that. Particularly my brother,' Sally said, grimacing. 'He can be very … possessive.'

'I gathered that, from what you've said. Well, you won't need to worry about him for some time, will you?' Betty pointed out.

The only reply she'd received from her mother was when she'd written to inform her that Jud and his mates had been found guilty and sentenced. Mam's letter had been full of self-pity, more or less begging Sally to come home as she didn't know how she was going to manage without Jud's wages. Sally hadn't been moved by her mother's begging. Her two sisters were working in the mill now; anyway her mother had been pleading financial hardship all her life, even when her father was alive,

217

mainly because she wasn't a good manager. Still, she'd sent her Mam a postal order for ten shillings.

Sally had received another letter, from Joyce this time. The tone of Joyce's had been apologetic though Sally didn't blame her or Bragger for any of Jud's misfortune. On the contrary, she felt sorry for them, because the injury had wiped out any memory of their previous relationship. Joyce had no idea how things were going to work out between them.

Returning her thoughts to what Betty had said, Sally now said, 'That's true. A lot can happen while he's in prison.' She stood and began gathering the remains of their lunch in preparation for washing up.

'One thing I would advise, love, is not to let either family interfere. It's your lives, not theirs. And, as you know, I'm speaking from experience. Our families nearly ruined our lives, didn't they Bob?'

Bob lowered his newspaper. 'Were you talking to me?'

'Oh, go back to your paper.' When he did so, she turned to Sally. 'Silly old sod!' But there was true affection underlying the words.

'I heard that,' came from behind the paper.

'Perhaps you were meant to,' parried Betty.

The front door bell interrupted the banter. The outside door was kept locked to discourage guests from returning before tea time. 'Will you go, love?' Betty said to Sally. 'It's probably someone wanting accommodation.'

She put the pots she had been holding down on the drainer. 'Course I will.' She smoothed down her skirt and ran her fingers through her hair, knowing she probably looked a little dishevelled after a busy morning's chores.

The smartly-dressed young man standing in the doorway didn't resemble a prospective holidaymaker and she could tell he was nervous by the way he swallowed before speaking. 'Do Mr and Mrs Parrott live here?'

For a few seconds, she wondered if he was some legal person, perhaps a solicitor or a tax inspector but then he seemed a bit young for that. 'They do, yes.'

He fingered his tie hinting at some nervousness. 'Is it possible to see either of them? Or both?'

'Who shall I say is asking?'

'Sorry, I should have said. My name is Peter Thompson.'

For a few seconds she puzzled over why the name seemed familiar. Then she realised. This was the long lost son, pre-empting any action the Parrotts intended to take. Now that she looked more closely, she could see the resemblance, albeit a younger version, to Bob, the stocky build, the wisp of hair at the front that always refused to lay flat, the warm brown eyes.

'Would you mind waiting in the hall a moment?' she said. 'I'll go and tell them you're here.'

Betty and Bob both looked up expectantly when she re-entered the kitchen. 'Who was it, love?' Betty asked.

She chewed her lip, not knowing how to tell them. 'A visitor. For you.'

A puzzled look passed between them. 'You aren't expecting anyone, are you love?' Betty said to Bob.

He shook his head. 'Did he say who he was?'

'You'd better prepare yourselves. It's Peter Thompson.'

Bob shook his head in confusion. 'Peter Thompson? We don't know …,' he started to say, then dropped the paper on to the table. 'Good God, Betty, it's our boy.'

Betty, who had clapped a hand to her mouth as Sally spoke the name, whispered through shaking fingers, 'I know who he is. You'd better bring him through, Sally. Then will you make us some tea?'

While she busied herself with the kettle and tea things, Peter Thompson faced Betty and Bob. It would have been hard to say who was more nervous. All three were white-faced. He coughed as if to clear his throat of dryness and faced Betty. 'I came because I wanted to know why you gave me away, why you had me adopted.'

'They took you from me, told me you'd died,' Betty whispered, unable to take her eyes off her son.

Peter Thompson's eyes widened. 'But why?'

'Bob and I were too young to get married and I was sent away to have my baby.'

Peter turned to Bob. 'So you're my real father?'

'Definitely, lad. If we could have kept you, we would have done.' Bob moved closer to Betty as if to protect her from any hurtful remarks. 'Now, I've a question of my own. How did you find us?'

'My ... mother died recently from cancer and I found a letter from some former neighbours. She must have been intending to reply but she was too poorly by then. I couldn't understand why you wanted to get in touch until I discovered another letter, much older, which explained everything.'

'So no-one told you? You never knew?'

Peter shook his head. 'No, it was a complete shock to me. My father died during the War so there was no-one I could talk to.'

'The second letter,' Betty said, 'was it from a Bertha Hutton?'

'Yes, how did you know?'

'She was my grandmother ... the one who told me you'd died,' here Betty's voice faltered.

Sally placed the tray of tea-things in front of Betty and squeezed her shoulder. Much as she would have loved to stay and hear the full story, she left them to it. This was private family business and they had much to talk about. Besides, she had enough to think about herself. Or rather, she could return to thinking about Phil and the shock of finding she was in love with him.

* * *

As Phil walked along Central Drive, butterflies danced about in his stomach and his mouth was so dry, he had to keep swallowing to relieve it. The reason for his nervousness was, not having seen or spoken to Sally since that wonderful night on North Pier, he wasn't sure what to expect. Had she regretted what had passed between them that night? Had that romantic and passionate time meant as much to her as it had to him? Perhaps she hoped they could put it all behind them and return to the friendship they'd had previously. The trouble was, he wanted more than that now.

Unusually, the front door to the boarding house was unlocked so he walked straight into the hallway which served as a reception area and rang the bell to summon someone. While he waited, he recalled how he had first kissed Sally here on the night of her 21st birthday party. She'd responded then too before she remembered who he was and pulled away.

It was Sally herself who answered the summons and, at first glance, he thought she looked a little distracted. Then, as she realised who the visitor was, her face was transformed into radiance. 'Phil!' she gasped.

'Hello, Sally. Sorry I couldn't let you know I was coming but I only found out at the last minute that I could get off camp.'

'It doesn't matter. When did you get back?'

'This afternoon.'

'What were the course like?'

'Exhausting, mentally and physically.'

'You shouldn't have come.'

'I came because I wanted to see you.'

'I'm glad.'

'Can you get out for an hour or so?'

'I'll just check with Betty but it shouldn't be a problem.' She turned to go through to the kitchen then half turned to face him. 'I'd normally invite you in but they've got a visitor.'

'Not to worry. I'll wait here.'

She was gone about ten minutes and returned wearing a light jacket he hadn't seen before, a blue that almost exactly matched her eyes. Although she had on one of her trademark tight skirts, she was wearing ballerina-style shoes on her feet. The nearly natural blonde curls, shining with health, only served to enhance a new softer look.

Outside the door, he asked her whether she wanted to go for a drink or a walk. She pondered for a moment then said, 'A walk, I think. It's too nice an evening to be inside. We could always call for a drink later.'

He couldn't resist the urge for physical contact any longer. He took hold of her hand. 'You don't mind, do you?'

'No, it feels sort of natural,' she replied, giving his hand a slight squeeze.

As they cut through towards the Promenade, she told him about the Parrott's long lost son turning up at the house this afternoon. She still didn't know all the details because, apart from preparing the guests' teas, she had left Betty and Bob to get to know him. It had been somewhat strained to begin with, she said, but now the three of them seemed more at ease with each other and when she had gone into the kitchen to tell them she was going out, Bob and Peter were laughing uproariously at something Betty had said.

Once on the Promenade, they ignored the assorted stalls of the Golden Mile, still doing good business, and crossed over to the seafront side of the Promenade. Here it was quiet with mostly young couples like themselves seeking privacy or middle-aged and elderly folk either walking their dogs or simply enjoying the pleasant evening air. With the tide far out, the normally stiff breeze had calmed to a soothing ruffle. It had rained earlier in the day and there was still a freshness to the evening.

When neither had spoken for a while, he thought he'd better break the silence. 'Sally, about that night …'

She spoke at the same time. 'I wanted to ask …'

They both laughed and once more subsided into silence. Finally, he exploded into speech. 'I wanted to say how much it meant to me. The memory of it were one of the things that kept me going while I were away.'

'Me too,' she whispered.

'I don't want this to end, Sally.' He turned to face her, his heart thudding. 'But how do you feel about that?'

'I want that too,' she replied softly, looking up into his eyes.

He turned to kiss her, oblivious to an elderly couple who went past tutting and muttering about the youth of today. 'They've obviously forgotten what it's like to be young and in love,' he said, laughing as they walked on.

She stopped and stared at him. 'What did you just say? About being in love, I mean?'

Her face was now set in serious lines and he was instantly worried. Hell, had he said too much too soon? He looked deep into her eyes and said simply, 'I love you, Sally. I'm sorry if it's too soon but it's true.'

Her face changed again and a smile curved her mouth. 'That's all right, then, because I love you too.'

'You do?' he grabbed her and twirled her round in a spin while she laughed. 'Bloody hell, Sally, that's marvellous!' He put her down and she clutched at his arms dizzily. 'But when, how, did you realise?'

'Just today. It were summat Bob said about me being distracted for the last couple of weeks,' she said. 'What about you?'

'The night of the dance when I behaved like a pratt. Like you, it were summat one of the lads said that made me realise.' Ignoring the looks passers-by were giving them, they sealed their love with a lingering kiss.

They had started walking again when Sally turned to him, a worried look on her face. 'I hope you don't mind me asking but … what happened with Pam?'

'It wouldn't have been fair to continue seeing her, knowing how I felt about you.'

'How did she take it?'

'She were upset,' he admitted, 'and I felt bad about hurting her.'

'Poor Pam! I feel sorry for her.'

They tucked themselves into a convenient shelter near South Shore. There, in between prolonged kissing, they talked, as lovers do, of their feelings and how amazing it was that they should find each other, especially given their family circumstances.

'Just think, Phil, I could have been your sister-in-law,' she said at one point, breathless from his kisses.

'I'm bloody glad you're not,' he said with feeling. 'Nick's loss is my gain.'

At the mention of Nick, her face became serious again. 'It's not going to be easy though, is it? What do you think Nick will say about us getting together?'

'Knowing Nick, he'll wish us well. No, it's Mam who might kick up a fuss,' he said. 'When she wrote to me after it were all over, she weren't being kind.'

Her eyes clouded over. 'And there's our Jud. I can't think he'll be very pleased.'

'When the time comes, we'll face them all together,' he reassured her. 'Don't forget the meeting with Jud will be delayed for a while yet. Let's not think about the future at this stage.' He kissed her again, feeling the passion rising within him at her loving and enthusiastic response.

CHAPTER 23

The glass-ridged roof of the weaving shed of the Beehive Mill, on the boundary between Horwich and Bolton, made it cold in the depths of winter and hot in the summer especially when the sun was beating down as it had been this June day. Joyce's blouse and overall were sticking to her back and she could feel sweat trickling between her breasts. She was glad when the hooter went to signal the end of the day and one by one the looms fell silent. Along with her fellow workers, she trudged through the dyeing and bleaching shed, trying not to breathe in the noxious fumes, and out into the mill yard. She gulped in the precious fresh air, letting it fill her lungs, instead of the cottony, oily atmosphere of the weaving shed. She thought enviously of Sally living and working in the salty breezy air of Blackpool.

Seeing the sprawling site of De Havilland Propellers further down the road, she was reminded of Dave, who worked there. She hadn't seen him since the court case a couple of weeks ago and they'd made no plans to meet. Her heart ached with the uncertainty of the situation and she could see no way out of it. The only hope she was clinging to was that his memory would eventually return. So intense were her thoughts that she didn't see who was waiting for her across the road until he spoke to her. 'Joyce?'

She shook her head slightly as if to clear it, thinking she'd conjured Dave up, then realised his presence was solid enough.

'Dave! This is a surprise. What are you doing here?' She hoped she had succeeded in keeping her voice light.

'Waiting for you. I managed to get out of work a few minutes early so's I could catch you.'

'You're back at work then?' She moved to one side to let a gaggle of cheerful weavers, arms linked through each other's, pass.

'This is my second week.'

'How are you finding it?'

'I'm tired by the end of the day but I'm determined to get back to normal as soon as possible.' He fumbled with his tie, betraying an uncharacteristic nervousness. 'Which brings me to my reason for being here.' She waited with a thudding heart for him to continue. 'I still haven't got my memory back but I keep having elusive flashbacks to the time when we were together. It's always just out of reach but I know it were important to me. What I want to know is, will you come out with me and see how we go?'

They were the words she had been waiting for but had almost given up hope of hearing. 'Oh, yes, Dave.'

'I'm hoping if we go out a time or two, it will jolt my memory into action again. It's got to be in the open though,' he warned. 'Nick's already given us his OK but I want to ask your Mam and Dad face to face.'

'Then come up to our house with me now,' she said.

He grinned. 'I were hoping you'd say that. I've already told my Mam I'd be late in for my tea.'

'That sure of yourself, were you?' she laughed, her heart lighter than it had been since Dave's accident.

As they started walking up Alexandra Road towards the bus stop, they chatted about inconsequential things. For her, it was enough that the ease that had been so characteristic when they'd been together before seemed to have returned. The awkwardness that had been noticeable after Dave had been injured seemed to have disappeared.

Walking up the hill towards Lancaster Avenue, she asked if he knew what he was going to say. He grimaced. 'Not a clue. I'll admit to being nervous though. I hope your Nick's there to ease the situation.'

'He might not be home yet,' she warned. 'Sometimes he stays longer to finish a job off.'

He fell silent then until they were walking up the alley between their house and the one next door. Towards the end, he stopped and turned to her. 'Can I have a kiss to see me through this?'

In answer, she put her hands on his shoulders and kissed him, putting the agony and uncertainty of the past few weeks into it.

Finally breaking apart, he staggered a little. 'Now I know this is the right thing to do.'

She laughed, her heart lighter than it had been since that fateful night in March. 'Best get it over with then.'

Her mother was in the kitchen peeling some potatoes and she looked up as Joyce came in through the open door, Dave hidden by the door itself. 'Hello, love. Had a good day?' Mam asked.

'Not really. It were scorching in the weaving shed,' she said, then hesitated. 'Mam, I've brought someone home with me.'

At that, Dave stepped into the kitchen behind Joyce. Mam frowned, then as if remembering how seriously injured he'd been, her innate kindness came to the fore. 'Hello, lad, how are you feeling now? Back at work, are you?'

'Just about, Mrs Roberts, thank you.' He gulped as if to swallow a knot of nervousness. 'Is Mr Roberts home? If he is, can I have a word with you both?'

Mary Roberts wiped her hands on a towel and shouted, 'Danny, you're wanted.' She indicated the table. 'You still look a bit washed out. You'd best sit down. We don't want you passing out.'

The three of them were seated when Danny, carrying a Bolton Evening News in one hand, ambled through, muttering under his breath, 'Can't a man be left in peace after a hard day's work?' He stopped when he saw Dave. 'Bloody hell! What's he doing here?'

Dave rose and faced him. 'I'm sorry to disturb you, Mr Roberts, especially at tea time but I needed to ask you both something.' With a quick glance down at Joyce, who gave him a reassuring smile, he said, 'Is it all right if I take Joyce out?'

'Not bloody likely,' Danny snorted.

'Wait a minute, Danny,' Mary said. 'What does your Mam say, Dave?'

'Since she met Joyce at the hospital, she's dropped her objections,' he said.

Footsteps echoed in the alleyway, and a grease-smeared Nick appeared in the doorway. 'Hello, mate. How are you doing?'

'OK, thanks. Back at work now.'

'Dave's come to ask if we might go out together,' Joyce told her brother.

'About time too,' Nick grumbled good-naturedly. 'You should have done that last year.'

'What do you think, Nick?' Mary asked.

'I don't see how we can keep them apart, Mam. Joyce has shown us how she feels by being at Dave's bedside all those weeks.'

'Don't I have a say in this?' demanded Danny.

'There's no point in keeping them apart, Dad,' Nick reasoned. 'This is 1957 not 1857. They've long since stopped locking up rebellious daughters.' Joyce flashed him an appreciative smile. 'And the way I see it, it's better all being out in the open rather than having to sneak behind the bike shed.'

Joyce wriggled on her chair. Nick's remark was an uncomfortable reminder of the number of times she and Dave had done just that at St Mary's School on Chorley New Road. Now she realised how much easier life would be if they could be open about their relationship.

'Since you all seem to have made your minds up, I might as well save my breath,' Danny said and took his newspaper back to the front room.

Mother and son exchanged a knowing look then Mary said, 'Well, it looks like you've got your answer, lad. But if there's any funny stuff or our Joyce gets hurt then you'll know about it.'

'I'll take care of her, Mrs Roberts, I promise.'

Two grubby figures, Derek and Lucy, hurtled through the door. Joyce was struck how much Lucy had changed from the timid child of last year to the tomboy who was now Derek's shadow. 'We're starving, Mam. Is tea nearly ready?' Derek asked.

For a second, he sounded so much like Brian, and Joyce's heart sank, expecting her mother's eyes to cloud over. Instead, she laughed and said, 'I'd better get cracking then. Do you want to stay for tea, Dave?'

'No thanks, Mrs Roberts. I'd better get back. Mam's expecting me.'

Together, they walked to the end to the alley. 'Fancy going to the pictures tomorrow, Joyce?'

'Only if you're sure.'

'I'm sure. Meet me at the Picture House, seven o'clock?' At her assent, he began to walk down the path then turned to face her, that familiar cheeky grin on his face. 'Any chance of another kiss? Just to remind me?'

CHAPTER 24

Sally stood on the doorstep of the Edwardian detached house and hesitated before ringing the doorbell. Something in her past and on her conscience had brought her here. She had kept this secret so deep within her for so long but now she needed to know whether she should tell Phil. So she had come to Preston on her day off to talk to the only person who might be able to help her decide, the chaplain at Heywood House. Not at the Home itself; she didn't think she could go there again. Too many memories. No, she had come, by arrangement, to his home, the vicarage of the church of which he was vicar.

Even as she dithered on the doorstep, it was flung open to reveal a pleasant-looking woman in her late thirties clutching the hand of a little boy of about three. Both were dressed as if going out. A warm smile lit up the woman's face as she saw Sally on the doorstep. 'Hello, are you Sally? My husband said he was expecting you.'

'Yes, I'm Sally. I'm sorry if I've come at an inconvenient time,' she said, experiencing a pang of pain to see that the other woman was obviously pregnant.

'Not at all. We were just on our way to the park, weren't we, Neil?' she said, to include the child who by now had withdrawn to the folds of his mother's skirt. 'Would you mind going through to Luke's study on your own? It's down the hall, second door on the left.'

In the hall, an old-fashioned coat rack was piled high with coats and a Victorian hat and umbrella stand was littered with an assortment of keys and letters opened and unopened. She walked the length of the hall and knocked on the door Mr Marchant's wife had indicated.

'Come in,' came a voice from the interior and she entered the smallish room diffidently. It was as cluttered as the rest of the house appeared to be, with books on shelves lining the walls and in stacks on the floor. There was barely an inch of desk to be seen with pile upon pile of papers. Reverend Marchant stood to greet her. 'Sally, good to see you. Do sit down.' He removed several newspapers from the comfortable looking armchair at the side of the desk. 'How are you keeping? You look well.'

She sat down, her fingers clenched round the handles of her handbag. 'I'm all right, thank you, although I still feel as if part of me is missing.' In fact, coming to the area today had brought it all back in a way she hadn't expected.

'It's only been what … three months?' He leaned back in his chair, his fingers steepled under his chin. 'You know Mavis and Jean both had their babies?'

She gave a watery smile. 'Yes, I had a letter from Mavis telling me. She's gone back home now, hasn't she?'

'She has. She was understandably devastated at having to give her baby up especially as she hopes to marry the father one day.'

'The people I work for had the same thing happen to them,' she said.

He leaned forward. 'That's interesting. How did it affect them in the long term?'

She told him about the Parrotts not having had any further children, then recounted how they and Peter had found each other again recently and the heartache and joy it had brought to Betty and Bob. They seemed to accept that they could never be a family again, that the best they could hope for was to be friends with their son. He'd rung several times since his visit and promised to come and see them as soon as possible, bringing his fiancée whom he hoped to marry next year.

'That's a lovely story, Sally, but that's not what brought you all this way,' he said, a shrewd look in his eyes. 'Do you have something to wish to discuss with me?'

She put her bag on the floor beside her chair, her hands clammy where she had been gripping it. 'Mr Marchant, I've got a problem.'

'Then I hope I can help,' he said. 'But before we start, let me reassure you that whatever we discuss here will not go any further.'

'Well, I've met someone. That is, I've known him for some time but we've only recently realised we love each other.'

'That's wonderful news, Sally, especially after what you've gone through. There's a 'but' though, isn't there?'

'For one thing, he's the brother of the lad who fathered my child,' she said.

He arched an eyebrow. 'I can see that might be a complication.'

'I think – hope – we can get around that particular stumbling block but there's summat else.' She hesitated, wondering if she dared go on, if he would be shocked by what she had to confide. 'Summat I've never told anyone else.'

'And you're wondering if you should tell this young man. Are you sure you want to tell me?'

She wished she'd kept hold of her handbag; she needed something to cling to. 'I trust you, Mr Marchant. You're the only person I can tell. Apart from Phil, that is. The thing is … I had sex when I was 14.' She stopped, drew in a deep breath and continued with a rush. 'With my brother.'

Mr Marchant didn't seem surprised. But she supposed that in his position, he heard all sorts of things. 'Tell me how it happened.'

'We're quite close in age, barely a year between us, so we'd always got on well together. One day, we were mucking about in the bedroom I shared with him and my sisters, something we'd often done before. He were tickling me and it seemed like a bit of harmless fun at the time. Then he started putting his hand up my skirt.' She stopped again before continuing in a faltering

233

voice. 'The horror of what he were trying to do hit me and I tried to wriggle away from him.'

'So you did try to stop him,' he pointed out.

'Yes, I did. But it was no use. Jud's not very tall but he's strong and he managed ... to do it.'

'If you tried to stop him at any stage, Sally, it was rape because it was against your will,' came his gentle voice. 'What happened after? I take it you were a virgin up to that point?'

She nodded. 'I think it dawned on him then, what he'd done because he just lay there as if he were stunned,' she whispered. 'Then he grabbed hold of my arms and threatened me with a beating if I mentioned it to anybody. I wouldn't have told anyone anyway, I were too ashamed. I felt it were my fault, that perhaps I'd led him on.'

'You have nothing to reproach yourself for. As your older brother, he should have been the one to take responsibility for the situation not put the onus on you,' he pointed out. 'You'll feel better for having spoken about it.'

And, she discovered, she did. There was a lightness of spirit that had been missing before. If only she could decide whether to tell Phil. She said as much to Mr Marchant.

'I'm afraid I can't help you with that decision, Sally. Only you can decide that. What you need to think about is whether telling him would simply make you feel better about yourself. Or whether it would be wiser to keep quiet.' He gave her a speculative look. 'If he's a decent young man, he'll understand.'

'I don't know if I dare take the risk of him finding out. You see, Horwich is the sort of place where everyone knows everyone else and usually their business,' she explained. 'And Jud's recently been sent to prison for assaulting the boyfriend of Nick and Phil's younger sister so there's no love lost between the families.'

He shook his head. 'I'm sorry to say this, Sally, but your brother sounds a most unsavoury character.'

'Do you suppose what happened between us has perverted him in some way?'

'It's possible that the guilt has twisted him to some extent,' he pointed out, 'but you need to forgive yourself for what happened. Will you try to do that?'

'I'll try,' she said softly.

'Do you mind if I pray for you?' he asked. Although she felt uncomfortable about it, she agreed, but when he prayed, he used none of the thee's and thou's she associated with religious ceremonies. Instead, his sincere and simple words touched and warmed her heart.

A hint of that warmth stayed with her until Wednesday afternoon when she was seeing Phil. Once she'd helped Betty clear away after their lunch, she began to feel nervous as the time approached for Phil to arrive. She'd spent much time in deliberation, swaying first one way then the other, wondering if she should confess to him or not. Then, last night, she had decided she must. She wanted no secrets between them. But what if Phil turned against her because of it? The thought, now that she loved him as he loved her, was unbearable.

She was hovering in the dining room, pretending to make final adjustments to the tables already set for tea, when Phil rang the front door bell. With her heart thudding and her mouth dry, she opened the door. 'Hello, Phil.'

With not a word, he stepped into the hall, grabbed hold of her and gave her a kiss more enthusiastic than passionate. 'Mm, that's better,' he murmured against her lips. 'I know it's only been a couple of days but I've missed you.'

She sensed an excited air about him that made her groan inwardly. She knew she had to quash his exuberance, probably even hurt him deeply. 'I'm sorry, Phil, especially when you've just arrived but we need to talk.' Her mouth was so dry now she could barely get the words out. 'Come through to the Residents' Lounge. We'll be quiet there.'

He put a hand to his forehead in an exaggerated dramatic gesture. 'You haven't changed your mind about us, have you?'

She gave a small smile though she didn't feel like smiling. 'No, but you might when you hear what I have to say.'

Instantly, his face set in serious lines. 'Oh, dear, that sounds ominous.'

To her, it sounded like a death knell to their blossoming relationship but she knew she had to do it, whatever it cost her. She dare not risk her brother's anger. He had a nasty vindictive streak and she wouldn't put it past him to tell Phil when he found out about them, even though it would reflect badly on him. So, not looking at him – she couldn't – while he sat beside her on the sofa of the impersonal Residents' Lounge, she told him about Jud, using almost exactly the same words as she'd said to Mr Marchant. He didn't say anything as she stumbled over her words but his face set in grim lines and he seemed to withdraw from her, in spirit, if not in actuality.

When she faltered to a halt, he said nothing, merely looking at her, his features frozen. Then, finally, he said, ' Were it just that time? Has it happened since?'

'No! I took care never to be alone with him after that.'

'That bastard! I could kill him.'

'You must never let on you know,' she pleaded. 'You know what he's done to Bragger Yates. I don't want owt similar to happen to you.'

He stood then, pulling his uniform jacket down where it had ridden up and putting his cap on. 'I'm going now, Sally. I need to think about this rather than make a hasty decision.'

'Please don't condemn me, Phil. I really did try to stop him.'

'I believe you. It's just that …,' his voice broke a little and he coughed to clear it before continuing, '… I want to be alone for a while.' He strode to the door, leaving her on the sofa, totally drained. At the entrance to the Lounge, he turned. 'You know, I had some important news of my own I wanted to share with you but it doesn't seem to have the same relevance as your news.' With that, he was gone.

She buried her face in one of the cushions to hide the scream of anguish that had risen to the back of her throat. The gamble she'd taken had been lost.

Phil had been walking for what seemed like hours with no clear destination in mind. His legs carried him forward seemingly without any input from his brain. He simply knew he had to get away from the holiday crowds thronging Blackpool on this sunny June day. So it was that he was in Lytham almost before he knew it. Kirkham camp was only a few miles further on. Except that he didn't want to go there. Not yet anyway. A few things needed to be sorted out in his head first.

He sat down on a vacant bench on Lytham village green, with its landmark windmill to his left, overlooking the Ribble Estuary. A myriad of thoughts whirled round in his mind with no particular cohesion but dominated by the mental picture of Sally and her brother. When she'd first told him, that picture had sickened him. The fresh air had revived him and now his predominant feeling was one of anger. That slimy bastard, Jud Simcox! What kind of man was he to do that to his own sister? It didn't even seem as if he'd apologised to her. Instead, he'd threatened her. He'd never liked Jud. There'd always been a sly devious side to him. He was glad Jud was where he deserved to be, behind bars.

For some reason, at that point, came the thought of the cramped bedrooms in the house in Winter Street. His parents had slept in the front bedroom, young Lucy, when she'd arrived, on a truckle bed, while in the only other bedroom, he and Nick had shared a double bed, Brian and Derek had slept top to toe in a single bed – with many squabbles – while Joyce had a single bed to herself separated from the boys by an old blanket slung over a washing line. Such an arrangement was common in overcrowded housing, more so in the past than recently, when large families had been the norm. He recalled reading somewhere that in the 19th century many illegitimate children were born as a result of liaisons between brothers and sisters, or worse, between fathers and daughters. That such a thing was possible between himself and Joyce or Nick and Joyce was repugnant yet he could see the dangers of such enforced intimacy.

But how did what had happened, seven years ago now, affect his relationship with Sally? This last two weeks had only served to strengthen his feelings for her. They had been spending as much time together as their respective responsibilities would allow and had treasured every moment. If her unrestrained response to his kisses were anything to go by, she felt the same. Not only was there the promise of passion between them but they fitted together comfortably in an easy companionship, the result, he assumed, of all the months when they had simply been friends. So had what she'd revealed changed anything? Of course not, the love that was becoming stronger with each passing day could survive something that had happened years ago. It was the future, their future, which was important. So what was he doing sitting on an uncomfortable wooden bench when he could have been with Sally?

He looked at his watch, amazed that so much time had elapsed since he'd left her. All the same, he decided to catch a bus back to Blackpool so as not to waste any more time. By the time he got back to the Shangri-la, she was actually clearing the tables after tea. With guests in the building, the front door was open and he was able to walk into the reception area in the hall. From there, he could see her through the open doorway to the dining room, gathering up dishes and placing them on a tray. He appreciated the pert little bottom encased in its ubiquitous tight skirt, the well-shaped legs tapering into the neat ballet style shoes she now favoured. She turned to face the door and the tray wobbled dangerously as she saw him. 'Phil?' she said, a questioning look on her face. 'You came back.'

He took the tray from her. 'Yes, and I'm staying.'

Her relief was obvious in the way a smile lit up her face. 'I'll be a while yet.'

'That's all right, I can wait. In fact,' he said, 'I'll give you a hand if you like.'

What with helping with the washing up then Betty inviting him to eat with them, it was some time before the two of them were free to talk. After walking so far this afternoon, he didn't feel like more walking this evening, so they went for a drink. The pub Phil took her to had that shabby appearance so many public buildings and houses had worn in the immediate years after the war. Despite its dark brown woodwork and nicotine-stained walls and ceiling, it had a homely, welcoming atmosphere.

Once tucked away in a corner with their drinks, he said, 'I'm sorry about this afternoon, leaving you like that. I needed some time to digest the news.'

'How do you feel about it now?' she asked.

'That it's not important. It's so long ago and you were very young.'

'Can you forgive me?'

'There's nothing to forgive on your part,' he said. 'It's that brother of yours who's the guilty party.' At the look of concern that came on her face, he reassured her. 'Don't worry; I won't say anything to him. Though if he starts any funny stuff when he comes out of prison, I can't promise I won't retaliate.'

She gave him a sideways glance. 'That's assuming we'll still be together.'

He placed his other hand over their clasped hands. 'There's no doubt in my mind. Is there any in yours?'

'Not at all,' she said. 'I've never been so sure of anything. This is like a dream come true.'

'But I'd better give you my news. I'm being posted to another camp.'

Her face fell, then she recovered a little and said, 'Oh, where to? When?'

'I'm not quite sure yet. But,' he cleared his throat by swallowing, 'it's because I'm being promoted to Sergeant.'

'Phil, that's wonderful. But aren't you a bit young for such a role?'

'They obviously think I can do it, that's what the training course was for. There'll be others in due course.' He could see conflicting emotions chasing across her face, joy at this opportunity to advance his career, concern it was going to take him away from her. He hastened to reassure her. 'When I go, I want you to come with me.'

'How can I? I won't be allowed.'

'You would be if we were married.' She gazed at him, suddenly speechless, so he hurried on. 'Sally, I love you and I want to spend the rest of my life with you. Will you marry me?'

'What about Nick? And what happened with the baby?'

'That's in the past too. I know you won't forget your baby, but what led up to its conception is over. So, what's your answer?'

'Oh, yes, please, Phil,' she breathed. 'And I'll go with you wherever you're posted.' Then she stopped as if remembering something. 'But I can't leave Betty and Bob before the end of the season. It wouldn't be fair.' Suddenly she blushed and he laughed. 'Sorry, I didn't mean to sound presumptuous. I know the wedding won't be for a while yet.'

'I were rather hoping we could get married soon after I'm 21.'

'So soon?' she gasped. 'That's only next month.'

'I don't want anything fancy we've to save years for. Are you bothered about having a grand wedding?'

'No, the important thing is that it's for the two of us. But,' she said, 'what are we going to do about our respective families. We've yet to face them with the news. Bringing them together might start another war.'

He grinned at her then. 'I had in mind for us to get married first, then tell them.' When she looked dubious, he carried on. 'Don't you see, love, it would be the best way? They wouldn't have any choice but to accept it.'

'And if they don't?'

'Then they'll just have to lump it. This is about the two of us, remember? No one else. Not Nick, not Jud and certainly not your mother or my Mam and Dad.' He raised his glass to her. 'So drink up and let's get out of here. I badly need to kiss you to seal the deal.'

CHAPTER 25

Today was her wedding day.

Was it really only nine months since she'd stepped off the train in Blackpool and met Phil? She recalled how desolate she'd been, the emptiness she'd felt that day. How different were her feelings today! Now she was on the verge of a new life with the man she loved and, perhaps more importantly, who loved her deeply, passionately. They had not made love yet. With the wedding day so close, they had both decided to wait. It had been difficult to restrain themselves though. Their bodies were clamouring for the fulfilment of their love. The thought of the night to come sent a shiver of anticipation through her.

There would be a proper honeymoon too for Betty and Bob had lent them the cottage in the Lake District for a few days. Sally had demurred at first. She didn't feel she could leave them without help, as it was now the height of the mill towns Wakes holiday season, not to mention a large influx of Scots from the industrial towns and cities of Scotland. But Betty had arranged for Janet, the student who'd worked for them last year and was currently on vacation from college, to cover for Sally. At some point during that time, she and Phil were to go to Horwich and face their families but she refused to think about it today.

'Ready, Sally?' Sandra's voice broke into her thoughts. As her bridesmaid, she was helping Sally to prepare. 'You look lovely, by the way.'

She looked at her reflection in the mirror critically. Her hyacinth blue dress, a present from Betty and Bob, brought out the blue of her eyes and highlighted the natural blonde of her hair. Made of some silky material, it accentuated her breasts and flowed over her hips. Over the top, she wore a matching lace bolero. She drew in a deep breath to calm her fluttering stomach. 'Yes, I'm ready.'

The two of them went downstairs where Bob, who was to give her away, was waiting for them. She and Phil were getting married at a church just off Palatine Road so that they could all walk there. There was no money for such luxuries as wedding cars. Fortunately the weather was fine and dry if not exactly sunny. As they left the Shangri-La, some of their current guests had come back to see her off. They gave her a clap and she felt herself blush with the attention. Mrs Robinson, their neighbour, was there too, clapping as enthusiastically as anyone. Betty had been the one to confess to her that there was no husband in the Army. Mrs Robinson had snorted and said she'd had her doubts anyway. From a ladder propped against another building further down Central Drive, a window cleaner called, 'I'm not a chimney sweep, love, but good luck.'

The church was dim and cool after the brightness of the day and as she and Bob stood in the entrance, Sandra behind them, she couldn't, for the moment, see Phil. Music had been another expense they'd chosen to forego. Yet, somehow, the lack of it added to the solemnity of the occasion as she and Bob walked slowly down the aisle. Phil turned to face her, a beaming smile on his face, as if it was lit from within. With that look she knew with a certainty that this was the right thing to do. Phil was the other half of herself, the man she needed to make her feel complete, no matter what opposition they faced in the future.

The actual service was simply a jumble of words and she remembered little of it. What mattered was the look of adoration on Phil's face when he made his vows. She looked deep into his eyes as she made hers and hoped the same look was on her own face. Then, after the formality of signing the register, they were walking down the aisle together, man and wife, her hand in the crook of his arm. He looked resplendent in his uniform and she was reminded again, briefly, of the first time she had seen him on Central Station.

Outside the church, a small crowd had gathered and they clapped when she and Phil stood on the steps while Fred, also wearing uniform, took a picture of them with a Kodak Brownie camera he'd bought especially for the wedding. There weren't many guests either. Chipper, as best man, was there, Fred of course, as well as Ruth and Barbara, who both gave her a kiss and a comic rolling pin done up in a fancy bow. Then, coming towards her, was old Mr Wolfit, who shyly presented her with a lucky cardboard horseshoe and wished them both lots of happiness. She was so touched, she kissed him on the cheek.

He rubbed his cheek and said, 'I won't wash my face for a week now.'

She leaned forward and gave him a kiss on the other cheek. 'Might as well make it worth your while then.' He'd been another person to whom Betty had had to admit the truth about Sally's mythical husband.

As they stood waiting for Fred to wind on the Brownie, Phil turned to her and whispered, 'You look gorgeous, Sally. I'm so proud to call you my wife.'

'No regrets then?' she teased.

'None whatsoever, Mrs Roberts,' he said as they dodged a shower of confetti.

The rest of the day passed in as much of a haze as the wedding service. Because of the constraints of the boarding house, all the guests were to go back to the Shangri-la for a buffet lunch, been prepared previously, with Janet and Mrs Robinson putting the final touches to it. Once there, they followed the traditional reception format as much as possible with a touching speech from Bob, standing in as her father, and a hilarious and somewhat suggestive one from Chipper as best man. After a quick change of clothes, they caught the train north to the Lake District, glad to draw breath after the excitement of the day. They shared a compartment with a middle-aged couple so could do no more than exchange loving glances and hold hands. It was only much later that she discovered several bits of confetti in her hair.

The cottage in Kendal the Parrotts had inherited was a shrine to times gone by and it's quaint old-fashioned charm made them smile. Having been left empty since early in the year, the house was cold despite the weather outside being reasonably warm. Phil proved to be an old hand at lighting a fire while Sally filled a couple of stone hot water bottles she'd found under the sink and tucked them in the ancient brass bed in the main bedroom. Looking at the patchwork quilt, threadbare in places, covering the bed, she experienced some nerves about the night to come. What if making love proved to be a disaster? She didn't know how much experience Phil had had but she guessed not much. Not that she had much herself. There had been that one time with Jud which, she found, no longer bothered her. Then there had been that one night with Nick, now a distant memory.

'Sally? Are you all right, love?' Phil's voice came from the bottom of the stairs.

She came out onto the tiny landing between the two bedrooms. 'I've been putting hot water bottles in the bed.'

He gave her a wry look. 'I don't think we'll be needing those.'

'It was only to air the bed. It hasn't been slept in since Betty and Bob were here,' she said as she descended the stairs.

He waited for her at the bottom and when she reached the last two steps, he held his arms out and said, 'Jump!'

She hesitated for only a few seconds then launched herself towards him. He staggered a little with the impact but held her firmly. While he had her trapped, he kissed her hungrily. 'Are you sure the bed needs airing?' he sighed against her lips.

She pushed her hands against his chest, laughing. 'I'm quite sure.'

He reluctantly dropped his arms. 'I can see you're going to be a bossy wife. Well, if you're going to be practical, so am I. What about me going for some fish and chips?'

They ate their fish and chips on the thick rag rug in front of the merrily blazing fire, mugs of tea stationed at the ready on the hearth. 'Mm, they were good,' murmured Sally, licking her fingers to rid them of the smell of vinegar.

Phil grabbed her hand and put her fingers, one by one, in his own mouth. The gesture was both tender and intimate, the feel of his tongue on her fingers strangely exciting.

He obviously thought so too for he groaned and said, 'Oh, Sally, love, I don't think I can wait any longer.'

She made as if to rise. 'Shall we risk the bed then?'

He pulled her down to lie beneath him, looking deep into her eyes. 'Sod the bed. What's wrong with right here? Right now?'

'Why not?' she whispered, putting a hand up to his face and, with her hand behind his head, drew him down to kiss her.

Interspersing his actions with kisses, he undressed her slowly until she was completely naked underneath his gaze. He ran his fingers lightly down from her face to her breasts, first one then the other, her nipples rising to his delicate touch. He took first one, then the other into his mouth, sucking, licking, nipping with his lips. His fingers trailed down to her stomach then finally to her inner thighs, stroking them gently and parting them before putting his fingers inside her, delicately exploring.

She gasped with the exquisiteness of his light but sure touch, arching her hips a little under the pressure of his fingers. 'Time to take your clothes off,' she whispered urgently.

There was none of the delicacy he'd shown in undressing her. Aided by her, he ripped at his clothes as if desperate to rid himself of them. When he was naked, she stroked his muscular chest, his slim waist and hips and let her hand slide down to the brush of dark fair hair cushioning his erect penis. She took it in her hand, revelling in its velvet silkiness.

He took hold of her hand. 'No more, Sally, please, or I'll come.' Gazing down into her eyes, he entered her almost uncertainly at first then with more sure and steady movements. She matched him thrust for thrust, her hands pulling his buttocks towards her, the sensations soaring within her and reaching a crescendo of pleasure just as he came within her.

They lay there, side by side, in the glowing firelight, their bodies bathed in sweat, reluctant to part. He covered her face in kisses. 'What can I say, love? That was wonderful,' he whispered.

'We didn't use any protection though,' she reminded him. They had already discussed the possibility of children but had decided to wait until Phil was more established in his promotion.

'I know we said we didn't want children for a while but does it really matter now? We'll cope with whatever life throws at us as long as we're together.' He kissed her again and whispered, 'I do love you, Sally.'

The mugs of tea, long since cold, stayed forgotten on the hearth.

CHAPTER 26

'Are you ready for this?' Phil asked as he and Sally walked through the alley between his parents' house and the one next door. His own heart was thudding, the butterflies in his stomach were doing somersaults and his mouth felt so dry, he wondered how he would get the necessary words out. They had chosen to come to Horwich on the Saturday of their brief honeymoon so that their families might be at home but both of them were already longing to get back to Blackpool and their cosy room at the Shangri-la. While they'd been in the Lake District, Betty and Bob had swapped Sally's single bed for a spare double, which meant Phil could stay with her whenever he was free to do so. He had to report back to the camp by tomorrow evening and they had no idea when they'd next be able to spend the night together.

'As I ever will be,' she replied. Although her voice quavered, her mouth was set in a determined line, her back straight, her head held high. This wasn't going to be easy for her, after last year, but he knew she would take whatever was said.

'A kiss before I open this door?' he whispered. They kissed and for long seconds, clung tightly to each other.

Drawing a deep breath, he opened the kitchen door. Joyce was in the kitchen warming the teapot before brewing some tea. 'Hiya, Joyce,' he said, deliberately keeping his hand on the door to shield Sally.

His sister beamed at him. 'Phil! I didn't know you were coming home. Mam never said.'

'She doesn't know. We've only come for the day.'

She gave him a knowing look. 'We?'

'Yes, I've brought someone with me.'

'A girl? Phil, you're a dark horse.' She came closer as Phil pulled Sally further into the kitchen.

A look of shock flitted across Joyce's face as she took in the identity of his girl, followed quickly with one of genuine delight. 'Sally!' He noticed that she kept her voice down while she gave Sally a hug. 'You know, it did cross my mind to wonder if you two would meet up with the camp being so close to Blackpool. But how long have you been going out together?' she asked, looking from one to the other.

He exchanged an amused look with Sally who gave him a quick grin. 'Quite some time,' he hedged.

Joyce gave Sally an accusing look. 'You never said when you wrote.'

'We decided to keep it quiet in view of the circumstances,' Sally replied. Her voice was stronger now.

'Are Mam and Dad here?' Phil asked though he didn't doubt that they wouldn't be.

'In the front room. I was just about to make a brew,' Joyce said.

'Best leave it for a while, love. I'd like to get this over with.' He made for the door through into the hall, Sally behind him, then stopped. 'Is Nick here, by the way?'

Joyce shook her head. 'No, he's still at the garage.' She glanced at the old-fashioned clock on the wall. 'He should be home soon though.' She hesitated. 'Happen I should go in first, sort of warn them.'

At his nod of agreement, she went into the front room.

'Did I hear voices, love?' he heard his Mam's voice.

'You did, Mam. It's our Phil, come for the day and ... he's brought a girl with him.'

'You didn't tell me he had a girlfriend.' His Dad's voice rumbled as Phil stepped into the room, by now holding Sally's hand tightly.

'Mam didn't know, Dad. No one did,' Phil said. As far as he knew, Mam and Dad had only met Sally once, when Nick had brought her to meet them before they were due to be married. It had, Sally said, been an awkward meeting and she'd been glad when it was over. They had decided not to tell their families they were married but to use that as a trump card so Sally's wedding ring was tucked inside her purse. 'Mam, Dad, you know Sally, don't you?'

His Dad lumbered up from the armchair to greet Sally, looking uncouth as he usually did, his shirt creased and wearing crumpled trousers. 'Can't say as I do but you're welcome, lass.'

Mam, it seemed, had been struck dumb by the shock of it but at Dad's words, she said crossly, 'Sit down, you daft barmpot. That's Sally Simcox as was going to marry our Nick.'

Dad peered up at Sally, puzzled at first, then said, 'Bugger me, so it is.'

'So she's wormed her way into the Roberts family after all,' Mam said.

'That's not true, Mrs Roberts!' Sally said hotly. 'When I first met Phil, I didn't know who he was. And Phil only found out at Christmas.'

'This has crept up on us over several months, Mam, almost without us realising what was happening,' he said. 'We both fought against it for a while.'

'Serious, is it?' Mam asked.

He exchanged a knowing smile with Sally. 'You could say that, Mam.'

'Then I'll say the same to you as I said to your brother. You're a bloody fool.'

Phil released Sally's hand, putting an arm round her shoulders instead. 'I would ask you to be civil about my wife, Mam.'

The colour faded from his mother's face while his Dad's mouth fell open. 'Wife?' he said, shaking his head in disbelief.

'Yes, Dad, she's my wife. We were married on Tuesday.' He turned to Joyce who had also been shocked into silence by the news. 'Go and make that tea, love. It looks like Mam and Dad need it. So do we.'

Joyce departed but not without giving Sally a kiss on the cheek and saying, 'So you're to be my sister-in-law after all.'

'Now I've got my breath back, I'll say this,' his mother said to Phil. 'You're an even bigger fool than I thought you were.'

He tightened his grip on Sally's shoulders. 'If you're going to insult Sally, Mam, then we're leaving and won't be coming back. Ever.'

Mam subsided back into her chair. 'It wasn't meant as an insult to her,' she nodded in Sally's direction, emphasis on the word 'her'. 'I was meaning you're very young to be married. You've only just turned 21.'

'Come on, Mam, you know I've always been older than my years.'

'That's true. You've always had an old head on your shoulders,' she conceded. Then, as if something occurred to her. 'She's not pregnant, is she?'

He felt Sally's body tense under his hand. 'I'm not something the cat dragged in, Mrs Roberts, if you've got owt to say, say it to me,' she snapped. 'And no, I'm not pregnant.'

There was a snort, which could have been the beginning of a laugh from Dad's chair, until it was silenced by a withering look from Mam. 'Have you nowt to say about this, Danny Roberts?' she asked.

He looked surprised to be consulted but to give him credit, he didn't hesitate, 'Well, it seems to me that if they've wed, we've little option but to accept the lass. Otherwise, we might well end up losing Phil.'

Phil looked at his father in amazement. The voice of reason at last. 'Thanks, Dad.'

At that point, a begrimed and overalled Nick burst into the room, disbelief on his handsome face. 'Bloody hell, Phil! Our Joyce has just told me the news. Or was she having me on?'

Phil grinned at his brother, who was looking from him to Sally. 'No, she's not. Me and Sally are married.'

'Well, this is a turn up for the books,' he said, shaking his head as if to clear it. 'What do you think, Mam? Dad?'

'That he's far too young to be married,' Mam sniffed.

Phil stiffened but to his amazement, Nick spoke up for Sally. 'Mam, whatever you might think, Sally's a good girl and deserves this chance of happiness with Phil. He'll be a much better husband to her than I would have been.'

'And I've already said my piece,' piped up his father. 'We've no choice but to accept the lass. With a bit of grace, Mary,' he said, with a stern look at his wife.

'I suppose I'm a bit upset that he got married without telling us,' she conceded. Then, for the first time, she looked straight at Sally. 'I'm prepared to give it a go if you are, lass.'

Sally gave her new mother-in-law the radiant smile that Phil loved. 'That's all I can ask for, Mrs Roberts. I'll be a good wife to Phil, I promise.'

Mam coughed as if to clear her throat. 'Now, where's our Joyce got to with that tea? She's taking her time.'

Phil heaved a sigh of relief. It looked like the worst was over. At least until they told Sally's mother.

* * *

Fortified by a couple of meat pies from Cases' pie shop in Winter Hey Lane, Sally and Phil made their way to the Crown, to reach Sally's family home in Mary Street West. If anything, Sally was dreading this more than the visit to the Roberts' house. There, at least, the reception to their news had been, if not exactly congratulatory, had at least been restrained. Whereas with her mother, Sally knew she'd have a hysterical fit of one kind or another. Much like Phil, Sally had always thought of herself as the odd one out at home. Jud was their mother's favourite and she felt Mam had resented her for coming along ten months after Jud and taking her attention away from her first-born. Her two sisters were several years younger and hadn't experienced as many problems as Sally had. Their father had ruled them all, including their mother, with the threat of his leather belt. She shivered slightly as she recalled some of the beatings she had received at his hands.

'Are you cold, love?' Phil asked, though the day was not cold, merely cloudy with an occasional shower.

'No, I was just remembering how strict my father was.' During those few days in the Lake District, she had been able to confide in Phil in a way she had never been able to do before. She felt there was nothing now that he didn't know about her. 'I should warn you that the house will be in a mess. With her precious Jud being in prison, she's probably made less of an effort than usual. Eileen and Mary'll have been doing their best but I know from past experience, it's a thankless task.'

'Don't worry about it. We'll soon be out of here and back home.' The loving look he bestowed on her held the promise of long hours lying in each other's arms. They were determined to make the most of them. She was longing for the time when he would be posted and they'd hopefully be allocated married quarters. If not, she would rent a room nearby and get a job to fill in the hours till he could come to her. She couldn't imagine not working, having her own little bit of independence.

She stopped outside the house, aware how shabby and rundown it looked after the Roberts' more modern house. The windows were grimy and the net curtains were more grey than white. Only a token effort had been made with the doorstep, unlike the neighbours' pristine donkey-stoned doorsteps. 'This is it,' she said, her heart sinking. 'I'm sorry, it's not much to look at.' As soon as she opened the peeling front door into the hall, she was overwhelmed by stale cooking smells and old cigarette smoke. 'Oh, Phil, it's worse than I remembered,' she said, under her breath.

He put both arms round her and kissed the top of her head. She loved the way she felt protected when he did that. 'It doesn't matter, love. We'll soon be on our way.'

She led the way through to the kitchen, her heart racing, her legs so shaky they would barely support her. 'Eileen, is that you?' came her mother's voice from the kitchen.

Sally opened the door to be met by a fog of cigarette smoke, which caught in her throat and made her eyes smart. 'No, Mam, it's Sally.'

From her armchair by the fire, her mother swivelled her head. 'So, you've come home then,' she said, no hint of emotion in her voice.

Sally gritted her teeth and grimaced at Phil who was right beside her, giving her a reassuring look. 'I've only come for the day.' Now she was fully in the room, she could see that the kitchen was the usual frowsty mess. Her mother was wearing a grease- and tea-stained jumper over a baggy skirt that had long since lost any hint of pleats. Her legs were bare, mottled from being too close to the fire, and on her feet were a pair of sandals that should have been thrown out long since. Between her tobacco-stained fingers was the ubiquitous cigarette with an inch of ash on the tip. She waved a blubbery arm in Phil's direction. 'Who's this, then?'

'Someone I want you to meet, Mam. His name's Phil Roberts. He's in the RAF, based at Kirkham.' She sat in the chair opposite her mother, while Phil pulled up one of the kitchen chairs and sat down close to Sally.

'Are you doing your National Service, then?' At least Mam addressed Phil directly, not like Mrs Roberts, who'd initially behaved as if Sally wasn't there.

'No, Mrs Simcox. I'm a regular, signed on for a full 12 years,' he replied.

'More fool you, then,' she sniffed and stubbed out her cigarette in the overfull ashtray resting on the arm of the chair, not particularly taking care with it.

Sally grabbed it before it slid on to the floor, where it had probably landed before if the remains of ash on the worn grubby rag rug were anything to go by. 'Still smoking as much I see,' she said, putting the ashtray on the hearth where her mother would have to exert herself to reach it.

'I have to have some pleasure in my life,' Mam complained. 'There's little enough to look forward to.'

Sally ignored this remark. It had been too often repeated to have any relevance. 'Mam, it smells disgusting in here. Why haven't you at least got the back door open? It's warm outside.'

'I feel the cold these days, that why,' she said in a whiny voice.

Sally couldn't stop the next remark coming out. 'If you moved about a bit more, did a bit of housework now and then, you wouldn't feel the cold. You sit in that chair for far too long.'

'I do what I can but I get so tired.' Again, this was an old argument and Sally didn't rise to it.

'Where's our Eileen and Mary?'

'Mary's gone off into Bolton with her mates and Eileen's gone up the Lane for a few errands for me. She shouldn't be long now.' Mam pulled a packet of cigarettes from down the side of the chair and lit another from a spill on the hearth. Then she turned to Phil and said, 'Where are you from then, lad?'

'From Horwich, Mrs Simcox.'

'What did you say your name was?'

'Phil Roberts.'

Sally waited, almost not breathing, for her mother to make the connection. 'Now why is that name familiar?' She puzzled for a few seconds then said, 'Wait a minute, are you related to that Nick Roberts who got our Sally in the family way?'

'I'm his brother, Mrs Simcox.'

Mam's normally ruddy face went an even deeper shade as she turned to Sally. 'That sodding family! They've already caused me enough grief without you going out with him. Don't you know it was his sister, Joyce Roberts, who got Jud put in prison? Egging him on to begin with then reckoning as he'd been mithering her.'

Phil rose, his own face set in angry lines. 'I'd rather you didn't talk about my sister like that, Mrs Simcox.'

'Don't you come all hoity-toity with me, young man,' she jeered. 'I haven't forgotten that you come from Winter Street and that your father went to gaol. No better than you should be, the lot of you.'

'At least our house in Winter Street was clean,' he retaliated, 'no matter how little money was coming in.' Sally winced but couldn't blame Phil. He was only sticking up for his family.

'If you don't like it, you can bugger off, the pair of you.'

'We will when we've given you our news,' Sally said, motioning Phil to sit down again.

'In the club again, are you?' Mam gloated.

'No, I'm not, Mam, but even if I was, it wouldn't matter because Phil and I are married,' she said quietly.

'Married!' Mam hefted herself out of her chair, her face by now almost purple. Sally was afraid she would have a stroke. 'What the hell do you mean, tying yourself to that family, you who's been so well brought-up.'

Sally rose to her feet to face her mother. 'You've got to be joking, Mam. Dragged up more like, especially since Dad died. Before that, he beat us all so often, we were frightened of our own shadows. No wonder our Jud's such a mess.'

'You leave Jud out of it,' Mam screamed. 'It's not his fault he's in prison. It's that Roberts girl who put him there.'

'It's always been about your precious Jud, hasn't it? He's the only one you really care about.' Sally was now so angry she was shaking. 'Shall I tell you something about your beloved son?'

Phil stood again and put a restraining hand on Sally's arm. 'Careful, love.'

She shrugged his hand off. 'I don't care anymore, Phil. Mam needs to know.' She turned once more to face her mother. 'When I was 14, Jud forced me to have sex with him.'

Mam fell back into her chair, her face losing all its colour. 'No, no,' she whispered. 'He can't have done. He wouldn't. You must have led him on.'

'Oh, it started innocently enough. We were mucking about then …,' she hesitated then continued, '…he wouldn't stop. That makes it rape, Mam. I could get him into all sorts of bother if I wanted to.'

'You wouldn't, would you?' Mam pleaded. Then she pulled herself together and her voice rose. 'You wicked girl! It's all lies, I tell you. Lies! Lies!'

Sally was sickened with the injustice of it all. It would never be any different, she knew that now.

'I've had enough of this,' Phil said, rising again and putting his arm round Sally's shoulders. 'We only came because we thought you ought to know that we're married.'

'The pair of you can get out now and don't bother coming back,' Mam shouted.

'Don't worry, we're going,' Sally said. 'I don't care if I never see you again. Tell Eileen and Mary I'll write to them.'

'I'll burn any letters. And I'll make sure they know the truth about what a lying conniving bitch their sister is.'

'I refuse to let Sally hear any more of this, you old harridan,' Phil said, towering over her mother. 'It's you that's the wicked one, not Sally.' And he led her, shaking, into the hall, her mother still screaming insults at the pair of them.

Outside the front door, he held her while she sobbed. 'Oh, Phil, that were awful. Worse than I expected. I should never have told her about Jud. She'll tell him, I know she will.'

'So what if she does? What can he do? He'll be too afraid of you telling the police. He's got a criminal conviction now. If this came out, it'd be even worse for him,' he soothed. 'Don't you see that getting it into the open, it's lost its power over you?'

He was right. At long last, she was free of the shadow of shame that had hung over her for seven years.

'Besides,' he continued, 'if Jud causes any trouble in the future, he'll have me to reckon with. And you need never come back again unless you want to.'

'I don't want to. Mam'll never be any different, I know that now.' They set off walking back towards the Crown, an arm wrapped around each other's waist. 'It's Eileen and Mary I feel sorry for. They're good girls at heart.'

'Couldn't you write to them?'

'You heard what she said. She'd throw any letters on the fire unopened.' She stopped as a thought occurred to her. 'I could ask Joyce to pass them on to Eileen. She works at the Beehive too. She's about the same age as Joyce and they probably know each other.'

'I'm sure Joyce wouldn't mind.' They'd nearly reached Lee Lane when Phil stopped and said quietly, 'Sally, I have to ask you this. How do you feel about Nick now you've seen him again.'

She looked up at him with love in her eyes, noting the concern on his own face. She guessed the question had been bothering him since they'd left the Roberts' house. 'Nothing, nothing at all.' She turned to face him and slipped her arms round his waist. 'Running away to Blackpool and meeting you were the best thing I ever did.'

'That's all I wanted to hear,' he said, as he looked deep into her eyes. He kissed her, heedless of the woman pushing a pram who happened to be passing and who threw them an indulgent glance. 'Now let's go home.'

THE END

If you have enjoyed Bittersweet Flight, you may like to read its predecessor, A Suitable Young Man. Available at
http://www.amazon.co.uk/dp/B00OXUYOUA

Made in the USA
Charleston, SC
19 May 2016